T0318221

Understanding Your 7 Emotions

Understanding Your 7 Emotions explains how emotions help us to respond to the world around us and are fundamental to our existence.

The book provides a detailed understanding of the main human emotions – fear, sadness, anger, disgust, guilt, shame and happiness – showing how to live with them and how to resolve problems with them. Each of the seven chapters also includes an 'emotional trap' to highlight what happens when we get stuck responding in unhelpful ways and explains how to get out of the trap. Grounded in emotion science and cognitive behavioural therapy, the book provides a powerful alternative to mental health diagnosis. Examples and exercises are provided throughout to help apply the ideas in everyday life and achieve health and happiness.

This easy-to-read guide will help anyone who is interested in emotions or is struggling with common mental health problems to better understand how emotions work and improve their own and others' mental health and emotional wellbeing. It will also be an invaluable resource to those working in the caring professions.

Lawrence Howells is a clinical psychologist and associate professor specialising in cognitive behavioural therapy and emotion science. He works clinically with adolescents and adults using these approaches, and he is the author of *Cognitive Behavioural Therapy for Adolescents and Young Adults*.

Understanding Your 7 Emotions

CBT for Everyday Emotions and Common Mental Health Problems

Lawrence Howells

Routledge
Taylor & Francis Group

LONDON AND NEW YORK

Cover image: © Getty Images

First published 2022
by Routledge
4 Park Square, Milton Park, Abingdon, Oxon OX14 4RN

and by Routledge
605 Third Avenue, New York, NY 10158

Routledge is an imprint of the Taylor & Francis Group, an informa business

© 2022 Lawrence Howells

The right of Lawrence Howells to be identified as author of this work has been asserted by him in accordance with sections 77 and 78 of the Copyright, Designs and Patents Act 1988.

All rights reserved. No part of this book may be reprinted or reproduced or utilised in any form or by any electronic, mechanical, or other means, now known or hereafter invented, including photocopying and recording, or in any information storage or retrieval system, without permission in writing from the publishers.

Trademark notice: Product or corporate names may be trademarks or registered trademarks, and are used only for identification and explanation without intent to infringe.

British Library Cataloguing-in-Publication Data
A catalogue record for this book is available from the British Library

Library of Congress Cataloging-in-Publication Data
A catalog record for this book has been requested

ISBN: 978-0-367-68564-5 (hbk)
ISBN: 978-0-367-68563-8 (pbk)
ISBN: 978-1-003-13811-2 (ebk)

DOI: 10.4324/9781003138112

Typeset in Times New Roman
by Apex CoVantage, LLC

Lucy, for love, support and proof-reading

Contents

Foreword

Dear Reader,

My name is Lawrence, and I am a clinical psychologist. A clinical psychologist is someone who applies the ideas of academic psychology to the 'clinical' population – to people who are struggling. To become a clinical psychologist, I had to do two degrees and undertake lots of study. I spent over 10 years studying psychology and its application to individuals who are finding things difficult. Yet almost all of what you'll read in this book I have sought out myself. Nobody taught it to me, it was not the subject of any modules in either of my degrees, and nobody really ever referred to it.

That is because emotions – bizarrely – are not a part of what we study as psychologists. We study cognition (thoughts), memory, child development (but without a strong focus on emotional development), and animal behaviour. We study different types of therapy (cognitive behavioural therapy, cognitive analytic therapy, systemic therapy), and we study disorders. We learn the symptoms of depression, of anxiety, of schizophrenia; we learn about the treatments for these problems. But nowhere in all of this do we learn about emotions.

This became a real issue for me. I was working in a new youth mental health service, designed for people between the ages of 14 and 25. Young people were coming to me with difficulties, and I struggled to tell the difference between what was 'normal' and what was 'abnormal'. How could I tell what was 'normal' if I did not know how emotions worked, what they were for, what went on when they were working in healthy, helpful ways? Even when young people came with experiences that seemed quite 'abnormal', how could I help them move back towards 'normal' if I didn't know what that was?

So I started to find out. I read up on research into human emotion. I found that lots of psychologists are interested in emotion and have explored emotion in a variety of ways. They have looked at emotions across cultures; they have explored the impact of emotions on our bodies, on the way in which we think, on our performance of different tasks. I was fascinated to learn how emotions worked and what their function was and to link this to what I had learnt about treatment for different problems. I was surprised to find a strong link between emotion science and therapy – cognitive behavioural therapy (CBT) in particular. In fact, bringing these two bodies of knowledge together explained lots of mysteries that I had wondered about for some time.

So this book represents an important work for me. It is the culmination of many years of work, both academic work and work with my clients in therapy. It has answered some of the questions I struggled with during the course of my earlier career, some of which I was too embarrassed to ask. For example:

- What is the function of anger?
- Why is extreme sadness associated with helplessness and hopelessness?
- How can we tell if we are responding to emotions in a healthy way?
- What should I do if I feel shame?
- What, exactly, is a mental health problem?

This last question I struggled with for a long time. I tried to read about it, tried to figure it out and tried to adopt the received wisdom by doing, saying and thinking the same as those around me, but nothing worked. I could never, in my own mind, really figure out what was fundamentally different about the people I was working with and the way that I seemed to think, feel and behave. This led me to the conclusion I will invite you to consider in this book: that there is nothing fundamentally different about the emotions we all experience and the ways in which we experience them. Whether we're thriving or struggling with our emotions, we work in the same way. The differences come from how we respond to our emotions: emotional difficulties are the result of problematic ways of responding to emotions. If we can understand and accept emotions, tolerate and use helpful ways of responding to emotions, and understand how to get out of emotional traps, then we have all the information we need to lead fulfilled and healthy lives. That is what this book provides. If it sounds weird, then read on, because the following chapters explain it all in more detail.

I'm sure you have questions about the seven emotions at this point. Perhaps make a note of them because, hopefully, they will be answered during the course of this book. If they're not, let me know and I'll do my best to answer them (and hang on to them for the second edition!). I am a professional and an academic, so this book is designed to be academically rigorous while still easy to read. There is evidence to back up what I say and if you are interested, there are endnotes to highlight what this evidence is and references at the ends of the chapters. Of course, you can just read the text and ignore these bits too! I have enjoyed putting this book together. I have enjoyed the years of exploring the ideas outlined in the book, discussing them with clients in therapy, exploring them with colleagues in supervision and training and teaching students about them. I use it all on a daily basis for myself and in my work. I have also enjoyed writing the book and making sure that the ideas are clear in my head, so that I can share them properly with you. I hope you enjoy reading the book and that it provides some answers and ideas in response to whatever led you to pick it up.

Lawrence

Introduction

You may be reading this book because you feel that your emotions are difficult to manage, problematic or troublesome. You may feel that your emotions are more or less intense than those of the people around you. You may have difficulty with one particular emotion – like fear or sadness, perhaps. You may be interested in your emotions and want to know how you can be happier. You may have received (or given yourself) a diagnosis of some kind that labels the difficulties you have with emotions. Maybe you are reading this book to better understand somebody else's emotions – your child or somebody else you know.

Whatever your starting point, this chapter will introduce you to the idea that emotions are part of our fundamental human experience. We all have seven basic emotions that we experience in similar ways. They have an impact on how we feel, on how we think, on our bodies, on our facial expressions and on what we feel like doing. Each of these seven emotions has a particular function that can help us in our lives.

From here, the chapter moves on to explore different ways to understand difficulties with emotions. It outlines some significant problems with mental health diagnosis, with viewing ourselves as 'ill' and trying to use an illness model to achieve health. It goes on to show how emotional difficulties can be understood as problems responding to emotions rather than problems with emotions themselves. These problems are called 'emotional traps' and are based on cognitive behavioural therapy (CBT). This chapter outlines the three principles that this book uses to help you from here: understanding and accepting emotions, tolerating emotions and using helpful responses and getting out of emotional traps.

This introduction forms the foundation for the rest of the book. Whether you are reading this to learn how to better respond to your seven emotions, to get out of a particular emotional trap, or to help understand somebody else's emotions, the foundations are in here.

DOI: 10.4324/9781003138112-1

That is what makes this book unique: it uses emotion science to help you move towards a happier, more fulfilled life.

Seven emotions

The *Stanford Encyclopedia of Philosophy* states that "No aspect of our mental life is more important to the quality and meaning of our existence than the emotions. They are what make life worth living and sometimes worth ending."[1] As you are reading this book, you will probably share this idea that emotions are important parts of our lives. Exercise 0.1 asks what you know about emotions. The questions in this exercise are answered in the next section, so you can see how much of this you already know.

Exercise 0.1   What do you know about emotions?

What causes emotions?
What are the different elements of emotions?
What are emotions for?

Even though there are hundreds of words in the English language to describe emotions, most theories of emotion have identified a few main emotions from which others are assembled. Early theories proposed different numbers of basic emotions. Aristotle proposed a group of 14 different core or irreducible emotions: anger, calmness, enmity, friendship, fear, confidence, shame, shamelessness, kindness, unkindness, pity, indignation, emulation and envy.[2] Robert Plutchik identified eight primary emotions: anger, anticipation, joy, trust, fear, surprise, sadness and disgust.[3] He arranged these in a wheel, like a colour palette in which primary emotions could be combined like primary colours to produce others. He cites, as examples, anger and disgust combining to produce hatred, or joy and acceptance to produce love. Paul Ekman suggested that there were seven basic emotions, and that people from different cultures could recognise these on each other's faces.[4]

This book covers our seven main emotions: fear, sadness, anger, disgust, guilt, shame and happiness.[5] Each has its own chapter, and together they are designed to cover the main emotional experiences we all have during the course of our lives, as well as the main problems we might have with our emotions.

Causes of emotion

Each emotion has a different cause; there is some kind of prompt or change that results in an emotion. It might be something obvious, like the approach of somebody or something; it might be something that somebody says or does, a way that somebody looks at us; it could be something that we do or say; or it could be a thought, idea or memory that pops into our heads. Whatever it is, there is always something that causes or prompts how we feel. Sometimes we might know what this something is, and it can be easier to understand and respond to our emotions when we are clear about what's caused them. It is for this reason that many of the exercises in this book ask you to think about a time when you felt a particular emotion intensely. At other times, we might notice an emotion without knowing its cause, and so we have to think a bit more about why we might feel that way.

Sometimes, we'll feel more than one emotion at once or a series of emotions in turn. At other times, we might find that lots of different situations make us feel a similar way. One of the important parts of understanding an emotion is to be able to link it to the cause, and each chapter in this book has a section on the causes of the seven emotions to help you with this.

Five elements of emotions

Emotions are made up of five different elements. The most obvious is the feeling, the conscious experience of the emotion. But there are other elements, like changes in the body and the face, different thoughts and ways of thinking, and different behaviours or urges to act. How many of these did you get in Exercise 1? Did you write down any others? These elements are covered in more detail next.

Feeling: conscious experience

The feeling is often the most noticeable element of the emotion. Each emotion is linked with an awareness of what it feels like. There are hundreds of words that we can use to describe each of these feelings, ranging from the most basic, like 'sad' or 'angry', or even just 'rubbish', to more colourful phrases like 'on cloud nine', 'making my blood boil', or 'over the moon'. The experience of emotion as a feeling is separate from the other elements of emotion.

Bodily responses

Another of the most obvious elements of our experience of emotion is our bodies. Our bodies can go through a whole variety of changes when we experience emotion, and these changes are mainly due to shifts in the balance of one part of our nervous system: the autonomic nervous system. Different emotions are characterised by different levels of activation of the two states of the autonomic nervous system: sympathetic and parasympathetic.

The sympathetic state is like the accelerator pedal in a car: it involves the activation of many different parts of the body at the same time (in sympathy). This state is triggered by the release of adrenalin and cortisol. Our bodies are prepared for quick, physical activity; our muscles are tense and receiving maximum blood flow from our heart and high levels of oxygen from our lungs. Some of the most important changes – ones that many of us know less about – are to our senses and our attention. All of our senses are heightened; things seem brighter, louder and sharper. Our attention, which we can think of like a spotlight, is narrow and focused in on the threat. Other, less immediately important things – like digestion, immunity and libido – are reduced. The emotions of anger and fear are characterised by intense activation of the sympathetic system, which is often labelled 'fight or flight'.

The parasympathetic state is like a car's brake: it slows the body down to save energy and to allow the slow, gradual processes of digestion, absorption and expulsion. Our heart rate is slowed, our muscles are heavy and the energy of the body is directed inward. Our attentional focus is much softer and wider than with the sympathetic activation. We can call this 'rest and digest' or 'feed and breed'. Sadness is one emotion dominated by parasympathetic activation.

Facial expressions

Each emotion has a characteristic facial expression.[6] The most basic of these appear to be recognised across cultures, but many are more subtle and harder to distinguish.

In many ways, facial expressions link with the bodily response to the emotion. For example, in fear, our eyes widen to allow us to see better in situations of threat. In disgust, we close our noses to reduce bad smells, and we might stick out our tongues to get rid of horrible-tasting things.

Thoughts/interpretation

One of the most important elements of our emotional lives is the way in which we interpret situations. Sometimes we can easily notice how we are interpreting situations, as the thoughts are running through our minds. At other times, our interpretation might be hidden or harder to detect. Either way, the meaning we place behind what has happened is an important element of emotion. An example can illustrate the importance of interpretation in emotion.

Imagine that you send a text message to your friend, and they don't reply. You could interpret this situation in a number of different ways:

1. "Their phone has run out of battery," which could lead you to feel neutral, or maybe a little annoyed
2. "They're bored of me," which might make you feel sad or ashamed
3. "I've offended them," which might leave you feeling guilty
4. "Something terrible has happened," which might make you scared

Each interpretation of this same situation is associated with a different emotional response.

> **How we interpret situations
> has a dramatic impact on our emotions**

Behaviours

Each emotion is associated with a behavioural urge: a desire to act or not to act. These behavioural urges could be running away, shouting, crying, hugging, withdrawing or laughing. We can override these impulses or replace them with different behaviours – for example, biting our tongue instead of shouting, or closing our eyes instead of running away. This behavioural impulse links to the function of the emotion, the reason we have the emotion.

Putting it all together

Various theories of emotion place different emphasis on the elements outlined here: feelings, bodily sensations, facial expressions, thoughts and
behaviours.[7] Some have prioritised body sensations, others the thoughts
and interpretation; lots have investigated facial expressions. In this book,
we will take the approach that the emotional experience arises out of the
interaction between all of these different elements.[8] Each chapter in this
book goes through these five elements in detail in relation to each of the
seven emotions.

**Emotions arise out of changes in feelings,
bodily responses, facial expressions,
thoughts/interpretations and behaviours**

Function of emotions

The idea that emotions serve a useful function was included in Charles
Darwin's theories about evolution and natural selection. His central idea
was that emotions and how we express them had evolved, like other characteristics, because they helped the survival of the species. Emotions were
thought to coordinate different systems to produce a coherent response
to different situations, to protect and ensure longer-term survival.[9] The
majority of theories of emotion since this time have accepted this idea.

Exercise 0.2 asks you to think about the emotions you might have felt
in relation to things or people that are important to you.[10] Think about
each emotion and the reasons you might have felt it in this situation.
What do you think the emotion might have prompted you to do, and how
might you have responded when feeling this way?

Exercise 0.2   The functions of your emotions

For this exercise, you will need a blank piece of paper.

Think about someone important to you and write their name in
the middle of one side of your piece of paper.

Now turn over your paper and write down the emotions that you
have felt in relation to this person. They may be feelings you have
now, feelings you have if you look into the future, or feelings you
have had in the past. Try to think of all of the feelings and write
something about why you think you may have felt that way.

The most obvious function of emotions is the protection from threat. In the presence of a threat, the five elements outlined earlier in the chapter are organised together to help us respond. But all creatures have to do more than just protect themselves from threat. Cowering in a corner, avoiding everything threatening, is not a great strategy for longer-term survival. They have to look for food, shelter, company and a mate. So emotions also provide motivation to explore, to play and to interact with others.

These are examples of the functions of emotions at the individual level, but emotions also function at a group level. Some of the emotions you felt in Exercise 0.2 might not have made you do anything helpful for yourself but instead for the other person – looked after them or done something nice for them. So emotions also function at a group level, to hold families and communities together.

Each emotion helps us to respond to a different kind of situation, and functions to benefit the individual and/or wider society

Refer again to Exercise 0.2 and look at the two sides of your paper. On the back, you have written the emotions that you might have felt; some of these are likely to have been difficult or unpleasant emotions. If you wanted to rid yourself of the unpleasant emotions you experienced – of fear, sadness or anger – what would have to happen? The problem you face is that you would have to get rid of everything on both sides of your paper: the important person in your life and all of your emotions that relate to them, whether pleasant or unpleasant.

This highlights an important idea in this book: emotions are a part of life. We cannot choose to have emotions or not to have them; we cannot get rid of them. We also cannot hang on to them, as they move along and change depending on the situation. We have a feeling right now, we probably felt differently earlier and we'll probably feel differently later. If we try to force our emotions, try to feel happy all the time, try to never feel scared or to get rid of anger, it will lead us into problems. These problems will be explained in later chapters of this book.

Emotions are not a choice; they are part of all our lives

Emotions and the brain

There is a great deal of interesting research investigating emotions and problems with emotions by mapping these experiences onto different parts of the brain. In this book, we will use a simple theory to illustrate

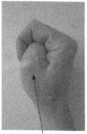

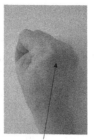

Reptilian Brain   Mammalian Brain   Rational Brain   'Flipped Lid'

this. The brain can be separated into three different parts that correspond roughly to the phases of evolution through which human brains have progressed.[11] The original idea has been made even more user-friendly by being mapped onto the hand, an idea known as the 'Hand Brain'.[12]

Take your hand, spread out your fingers and thumb. Then fold your thumb in and curl your fingers over the top. This is the 'hand brain' and the image above shows the different parts, described next.

Reptilian brain

The reptilian brain is represented by the wrist and the base of the thumb. It sits at the bottom of our skulls, just above our spines. It is the oldest part of the brain in evolutionary terms, around 300 million years old. The reptilian brain controls basic survival, like defending ourselves and our territory, hunting, foraging for food and mating. This collection of activities is sometimes known as the 'four Fs': fleeing, fighting, feeding and fornicating.

Mammalian brain

The mammalian brain is represented by the thumb tucked into the fist. This mammalian brain is younger than the reptilian brain but still very old – around 200 million years in evolutionary terms. The main difference between mammals and reptiles is that mammals are social creatures that are born in a helpless state and require parental care to grow and develop. The mammalian brain is therefore responsible for playfulness and parental instinct.

Rational brain

The final major phase of the evolution of the human brain was the development of the 'rational brain'. This part of the brain is around 80% of the mass of the human brain and is represented by the back of the hand and all the fingers. It developed much more recently in evolutionary terms, with *Homo sapiens* first appearing around 200,000 years ago. It is unique to humans and contains abilities not seen in other mammal species, like language, planning, abstraction and perception. It is called the 'rational brain' as it contains the functions that enable rational thought, although it is not always entirely rational.

"Flipped lid"

The three different parts of the hand brain often work well together and in harmony. However, there are times when there is conflict or when one part of the brain overrides another.

The clearest example of this is when the fight-or-flight response is activated. We are in threat mode and the reptilian brain is in charge, knocking the rational brain offline. This is called 'flipping the lid', illustrated by the fingers of the rational brain flipping up to reveal the reptilian brain. This concept is what happens with extreme fear (Chapter 1) and anger (Chapter 3). Alternatively, the rational brain can find itself sucked in and restricted, so that its rationality is compromised, as highlighted in sadness (Chapter 2). Each chapter refers back to this model to think about how the brain responds to different emotions.

Emotional difficulties and mental health diagnosis

Many people who have difficulties with their emotions will receive some kind of mental health diagnosis. The rates of mental health diagnosis have been increasing for some time, as has public awareness, but there are facts about diagnosis in mental health that many people do not know. There are major gaps in the science to support mental health diagnosis and there are significant problems with the way diagnosis is used in mental health. This section provides an overview of mental health diagnosis, its benefits and its problems.[13] It is designed to help you think about what this means and to give information that was probably not provided when the diagnosis was given. It does not suggest that there is nothing wrong, or that the distress is not real or that the impact on life is not significant.

It is an encouragement to think about mental health diagnosis in a different way.

Many of us use diagnosis without really thinking about what a diagnosis is or how it works. Exercise 0.3 is a good way to highlight the questions we may have never asked ourselves about diagnosis.

Exercise 0.3 What is diagnosis?

What is a diagnosis? How does it work?

If you have a diagnosis (or you have given yourself one), what does it mean to you? Do you see yourself differently? In what ways?

If you have a diagnosis, does it make you do anything differently?

If you have a diagnosis, do you tell other people about it? How do you explain it, and why do you tell them?

If somebody else tells you about a diagnosis, what do you think about them? Does it change how you see them?

A diagnosis is medical term that describes an illness. A collection of observable symptoms is grouped together and linked with some underlying cause. Treatment targets this underlying cause, which relieves the symptoms and makes us 'well' again.

We can take an example from physical health. If I go to the doctor with:

- High fever
- Sore throat
- Swollen glands in my neck
- Swollen, spotty tonsils

The doctor might suspect that I have bacterial tonsillitis. This diagnosis can be confirmed with a throat swab tested for streptococcal bacteria and then treated with antibiotics. The symptoms indicate the possible underlying cause, a test can confirm it and then the treatment targets the cause to relieve the symptoms.

Diagnosis links a group of symptoms to an underlying cause
Treatment targets the cause and relieves the symptoms

In mental health, diagnosis doesn't work in this way. This is because there are no identified underlying causes for mental health diagnoses. Mental health diagnoses are collections of experiences that have been grouped together and called an illness, but they are not linked with any underlying cause.[14] This is a fact that experts in mental health accept but that often astonishes other people.

So, if I go to the doctor and say:

- I am miserable most of the time
- I don't have much energy
- I've had difficulties concentrating
- I haven't been hungry
- I've had lots of negative thoughts about myself

My doctor might give me a diagnosis of depression. But there are no x-rays, no blood tests, no brain scans, and no genetic tests that can tell me apart from people without a diagnosis of depression. There is no evidence that my brain is working in a different way than the brains of people who aren't diagnosed with depression. Despite suggestions that mental health difficulties are caused by chemical imbalances in the brain, there is no evidence that the chemicals in my brain are different. There is absolutely nothing to distinguish me from anybody else, apart from what I said about my own experience.[15] This produces a circular argument, where I feel miserable because I 'have depression' and I know that I 'have depression' because I am miserable.

No underlying causes have been identified for any mental health diagnosis

You may be thinking at this point about medication – surely if there are medications called 'antidepressants' or 'mood stabilisers', there must be a chemical imbalance in the brain that is corrected by medication?

For medication to be licensed, there must be evidence that it is safe and that it works. There have been many trials of medications, and many have shown some effectiveness. However, research also finds that medication does not appear to be specific, so that medicines commonly called 'antidepressants' are recommended to treat not only depression but also various other conditions, like obsessive-compulsive disorder, social anxiety disorder and panic disorder.[16] It also seems that so-called antidepressants are not directly targeting the experiences classified as depression but instead work in other ways – for example, reducing anxiety, at least initially.[17] There are similar findings in relation to medicines used in other mental health diagnoses.[18]

What this means is that while medicines are called 'antidepressants' or 'antipsychotics', they do not appear to work by readjusting whatever has caused the issue in the first place but rather through some other mechanism. This is likely to be a much more general effect, like by improving sleep, reducing tension or through the placebo effect.[19]

**Medication in mental health
does not correct an underlying problem**

Is diagnosis useful?

Mental health diagnoses do not link to any underlying cause, so they are not diagnoses in the same way as many physical health diagnoses are. This means that diagnosis in mental health is just one way of understanding the distress and disruption that people can experience with their emotions. Many experts in the field concede this point but argue that mental health diagnosis remains useful.[20] They highlight that diagnosis has had a positive impact on our ability to research, fund, treat and understand problems with mental health. The usefulness of diagnosis is often overstated, however, and there are a number of significant problems with it.

Firstly, while there are up to 541 different diagnostic categories,[21] these categories do not work particularly well. Many people who are struggling with mental health will not meet criteria for any specific diagnosis. Those who do meet criteria for a specific diagnosis are more likely to meet the criteria for more than one diagnosis than they are for one alone.[22] Secondly, where people do meet criteria for a diagnosis, they might find that different clinicians give them different diagnoses or that their diagnosis changes over time.[23] Thirdly, the diagnosis that a person is given does not give reliable information about quality of life, need for treatment or longer-term outcome.[24] In addition, there are a number of extremely unhelpful outcomes associated with diagnosis, discussed next.

Diagnosis and identity

Most people given a diagnosis of depression, to use a common example, have experienced something painful before receiving this diagnosis, like the loss of a loved one or of a job.[25] Many people given any kind of mental health diagnosis have also experienced difficult things in early life.[26]

There is a strong link between the events of people's lives and how they are. But a diagnosis is defined as a disorder 'that occurs within the individual';[27] i.e., that there is something wrong with the person rather than with what has happened to them. It focuses on people in isolation and on what makes them different from others. This can have a significant impact on the way that people with a diagnosis see themselves and how they are seen by others. Exercise 0.4 asks you to consider two different people and how you see them.

Exercise 0.4   Imaginary conversations

Bill is a colleague whom you see from time to time, and you occasionally stop to have a short conversation. You see him at work one day and realise that you haven't seen him for a few weeks. You ask him how he is and comment on your lack of contact. He tells you that his wife died three months ago, and he has been struggling since. He talks about feeling lost without her to care for, not having so much companionship and feeling sad and down. What are your next questions – how is the conversation likely to progress?

Linda is a friend of a friend whom you bump into on your way shopping. She tells you that she was laid off from her job and has been struggling as a result, with not much going on and not much to do. She says she went to see her GP, who told her she is depressed. What are your next questions – how is this conversation likely to go?

People with diagnoses of mental health problems face stigma and discrimination that is often described as worse than the conditions themselves. They can be excluded from certain careers, can face more barriers in others, and can face disadvantages in personal relationships, education, health and social care.[28] Stigma and discrimination is linked with a whole range of diagnoses ranging from anxiety disorders and depression to schizophrenia and personality disorders.

When people are given a diagnosis, they don't only experience negative attitudes from others but also apply these beliefs to themselves – something called self-stigmatisation. People who have been given a diagnosis have a more negative self-image, are more socially withdrawn than others and see themselves as having lower self-worth.[29] Accepting a mental health diagnosis also reduces the sense of control people feel over their lives and their belief in their ability to bring about change.[30]

Exercise 0.4 asked you to consider two people in similar circumstances: one gave a diagnosis, and the other did not. What were the differences in terms of how you could imagine the conversation going? What did you focus on and what were you interested in for each of them? We might expect that for Linda (who provided a diagnosis), you were drawn to focus on her as an individual, to think about her in isolation and also maybe to see her in a more negative light and less able to do things for herself. For Bill (who did not provide a diagnosis), you may have been more likely see him in his context, to think more about his situation and the interactions he had with those around him and to feel more empathy.

Diagnosis and health

Mental health has been receiving considerable attention in recent years: weeks of the year dedicated to mental health, campaigns focused on children and in the workplace. Almost all raise awareness about different mental health diagnoses, which means that what they are in fact doing is raising awareness about mental illness. But illness and health are not the same thing; being in good health is different to not being ill.

Take the example of a rally car. The mechanics responsible for the car focus on how to improve its performance: how to get an extra second off the lap time, how to improve its handling in the corners, how to improve its braking. This is a different approach from the one a mechanic in your local garage would take with your car that has a fault, who might be focused on the battery, the starter motor or the alternator. There is overlap between the two, but they are not the same thing. A mechanic diagnosing faults in cars to keep them on the road has a different focus than one who is tuning cars to get the best performance out of them. It's the same for us: focusing on mental illness is of limited benefit to encouraging good mental health.

An absence of illness is not health

To put the point a different way, we can use a curve to represent the whole population of people. Most people fall somewhere in the middle

% of population

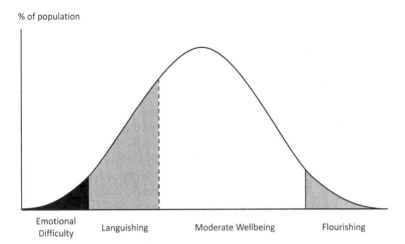

Emotional
Difficulty   Languishing   Moderate Wellbeing   Flourishing

of the curve, with moderate wellbeing. People in this area are generally functioning okay but have times when things are difficult, and there are aspects of their lives they would like improved. Some people are flourishing towards the right, where things are going very well, and they are mostly happy and content. On the far left of the curve, in black, are those people who are having significant emotional difficulty. Diagnosis is only relevant to these people on the far left, those deemed to be 'ill'. A diagnosis is not designed to help the majority of the population to the right. It focuses on what is going on when people are 'ill' and is not much good to help think about how to be well or healthy.

Most of us, when we are struggling with our emotions, have a clear idea about what we want to be different. We usually phrase this in a positive way: "I would like to feel happier" or "I would like to get along better with my friends". A diagnosis does not help us to move towards the right of the graph; it does not even help us to avoid finding ourselves in the black part of the graph. In fact, using diagnosis as if it were a model of health can lead to real confusion when thinking about what health is and what emotions are and identifying 'normal' human experience. If we are unsure how emotions are 'supposed' to work or how most people experience things, it can be very difficult to be clear about when and why it is not right, or what we are aiming for when we are making change.

Using emotion science to help

Hopefully this discussion about mental health diagnosis has made you think. It may have shocked you, as most of us have the sense that a diagnosis in mental health is the same as a diagnosis in physical health, and few professionals will explain that this isn't the case. If you have been given a mental health diagnosis yourself, hopefully you haven't read this section as if you are being told there is nothing wrong with you. There is a great deal of distress and difficulty experienced throughout society, and many people are struggling in a whole variety of ways. The point is that understanding these struggles and difficulties by using a model of illness that is not supported by evidence may not be the best way to help.

That is why this book takes a different approach. Rather than starting with illness and diagnosis, it starts with the science of emotion. We know that we all have seven basic emotions, which are important and normally useful, protecting us from harm and holding our communities together. When they become unhelpful and we have emotional difficulties, this is not because we are 'ill' or there is something fundamentally different about us; it is because we have problems *responding* to emotions. These problems lead into 'emotional traps' that get in the way and disrupt our lives. Mental health problems are not caused by differences in the brain or differences in emotions between people but by differences in how we respond. Changing our response to emotions can help us gradually move towards healthy emotional experience and happy, fulfilled lives.

Mental health problems are not illnesses of the mind or body but the result of problems in responding to emotions

Three abilities from emotion science form the structure of the rest of this book: understanding and accepting emotions, tolerating emotions and using helpful responses and getting out of emotional traps. Each of these is supported by and linked with the others, as shown in the diagram. The seven chapters of this book use this structure to help you with the seven emotions.

Understand and accept emotions

Some difficulties with emotions can be traced back to unhelpful beliefs about emotions. For example, if we had a belief that "emotions are a sign of weakness", this would encourage us to suppress our emotions and try to live in spite of them. This would lead to problems tolerating them and into emotional traps. One of the problems with mental health diagnosis is that it can encourage unhelpful beliefs about emotion, like "normal people don't feel like this" or "if I'm sad, I must be depressed". Trying to push an emotion away, expecting treatment to get rid of it or hoping somebody else can fix it all lead to difficulties and into emotional traps.

Each of the following chapters in this book has lots of information about the seven emotions: things that cause them, changes in the five elements that follow and the reasons why all of this might usually be helpful. It's all based on emotion science and will help you put your experiences together and consider your understanding of emotion.

Tolerate emotions and use helpful responses

Tolerating emotions and using helpful responses are two related processes, the impact of which are illustrated in the diagram overleaf. The grey box in the middle is the 'window of emotional tolerance'. In this window, we function well, the different parts of the brain work together, we can tolerate our emotions and we respond in helpful ways. Outside this window of tolerance, things do not work so well. When we are too emotionally heightened – out of the top of our window of tolerance – the reptilian brain is in charge; our thoughts are quick, threat-based and disorganised; and we feel overwhelmed and in chaos. When we are emotionally shut down – out of the bottom of our window of tolerance – our thoughts are slow, we feel heavy and we have a sense of numbness, lifelessness and disconnection.[31]

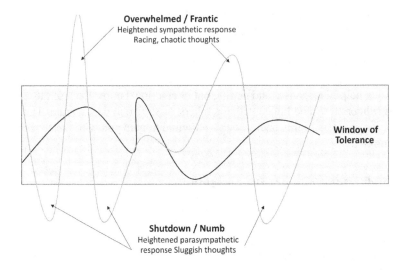

In the diagram, the black line shows healthy responses to emotion: a range of emotions are experienced, and the responses to them adjust their intensity and duration to stay in the window of tolerance. The grey line in the diagram represents problems tolerating and responding to emotions: extreme experiences of emotions and responses to these emotional experiences move straight through the window of tolerance and out the other side. Emotions feel intense, overwhelming and out of control and can become things to be wary or even afraid of. This happens because of a lack of tolerance of emotions and a lack of helpful emotional responses.[32]

The window of tolerance is not fixed or static; it can expand. If we can practice tolerating emotions without always immediately acting upon them, over time we can learn to tolerate more. The seven chapters of this book apply these ideas to the seven different emotions. Using different ways of responding will help you to adjust your emotional experience, build tolerance and have more experiences of emotions as helpful things that improve your life and your connections with those around you.

Get out of emotional traps

The final part of the process is getting out of emotional traps. Emotional traps are cycles or patterns of responding to emotions that keep us stuck with repeated experiences of emotion and unhelpful responses. They can make us feel distressed and interfere significantly in our lives. For example, we might experience high levels of fear and do lots of avoidance that disrupts our lives (this might be given a diagnosis of an anxiety disorder). We might experience high levels of sadness and withdrawal that gets in the way of normal life (this could be labelled depression). Emotional traps are patterns of responding to emotions that, rather than helping us, get in the way and disrupt our lives. Importantly, it is the pattern of response to the emotion rather than the emotion itself that produces the problem. There are different emotional traps outlined in this book that cover common emotional and mental health difficulties. These traps correspond to many of the ways in which cognitive behavioural therapy (CBT) understands common mental health problems. It shows how to get out of the emotional trap and reduce the distressing and unhelpful impact of this trap on life. The techniques outlined to get out of the traps are based on common CBT techniques that have been shown to work for different situations.

> **Emotional problems arise when we get stuck**
> **responding in unhelpful ways to emotions**
> **The problem is our response and not the emotion itself**

Conclusion

Seven main emotions coordinate our minds and bodies to help us respond to situations in which we find ourselves. Problems with these emotions are not defined as illnesses of the mind or brain – as in mental health diagnosis – but as problems in responding to emotions. This book will help you to understand and accept your emotions, tolerate and use helpful responses and get out of emotional traps. This will help you to move towards a more fulfilling and happy life.

Notes

1 This is the first statement in the encyclopedia entry (Scarantino & de Sousa, 2018).
2 Aristotle's ideas can be found in translation (1984).
3 Plutchik (1984)
4 Ekman and Keltner (1997), although more recent research suggests it might only be four emotions that we can reliably detect on other people's faces (Jack et al., 2014).

5 As this section highlights, there are problems with defining the number of
   emotions we experience, as there is overlap between them and disagreement from a theoretical perspective on how exactly an emotion is defined
   (e.g., Izard, 2009, see also note 10). This book takes a pragmatic position,
   sticking with the main emotions upon which most agree and those that are
   likely to be most helpful to focus on with a view to reducing problematic
   emotion experience and moving towards a healthy and fulfilling life.
6 See for example Ekman's (e.g., Ekman & Keltner, 1997).
7 One of the earliest theories of emotion has become known as the James–
   Lange theory. It was proposed by two theorists independently of each other
   (see Cannon, 1927), and both suggested that the conscious experience of
   emotion was driven by the physiological changes in the body. An environ-
   mental stimulus was thought to cause a physiological response, which was
   interpreted as an emotion. Walter Cannon and his doctoral student, Philip
   Bard, found that emotions were still experienced even when the sympathetic
   nervous system had been completely removed and that emotions were not
   experienced when physiological responses were artificially manipulated
   (Cannon, 1927). They proposed an alternative model in which physiological and emotional responses are simultaneously produced through separate
   pathways (Cannon–Bard theory of emotions). The Schacter–Singer two-
   factor theory of emotion (Schachter & Singer, 1962) suggested that a cognitive appraisal is assigned to the initial trigger and the resulting physiological
   state to determine the emotion. Lazarus (1991) also produced a theory of
   emotion in which the cognitive appraisal was central to the experience.
8 Much of the science referenced in this book derives from research into 'dis-
   crete emotion theory' (e.g., Izard, 2009), which states that there are specific
   core emotions that are biologically determined and similar across cultures.
   Other theories, like Barrett's (2017) 'theory of constructed emotion', suggest
   that our emotional experience has far more to do with the way in which we
   construct our emotional experience than with biological predetermination.
   This book doesn't take a position on the degree to which the origins of emotion are biologically predetermined or socially constructed. Rather, it takes a
   pragmatic position that there are emotional experiences to which we can all
   relate that link with the five elements of emotion outlined earlier.
9 Darwin (1872).
10 This exercise is adapted from one that one of my colleagues has used to great
   effect. Many thanks to Dr Andre Bolster, a senior clinical psychologist working in Norfolk.
11 This idea comes from Paul MacLean (1990), a neuroscientist and theorist
   who brought the concepts of neuroscience and the study of the brain together
   with theories of evolution. The idea was called the 'triune brain', and it has
   been highly influential not only in neuroscience but also in social science.
   Since it was published, the idea has been criticised for a variety of issues,
   most of which relate to its oversimplicity. Whilst the model does simplify a
   complex science, it nevertheless provides a useful way of thinking and talking about the brain for those of us outside the field of neuroscience. Indeed,
   one author notes that the concept of the triune brain is still by far the best
   concept we have for linking neuroscience with social science (Cory, 2002).
12 Siegel (2015).

13 For a more detailed examination of these issues, please see these articles and books: Schnittker (2017), Davies (2013) and Szasz (2013).

14 Thomas Szasz, a fellow of the American Psychiatric Association, wrote many books on this subject, including *The Myth of Mental Illness* in 1961. A detailed and compelling examination of how the *Diagnostic and Statistical Manual* was written is provided in *Cracked* by James Davies, 2013.

15 Van Os et al. (2003) and Johnstone (2014).

16 This example relates to a group of medicines called selective serotonin reuptake inhibitors, or SSRIs. These are recommended for lots of different diagnoses – see, for example, the NICE Guidelines at www.nice.org.uk.

17 A recent trial of one particular SSRI antidepressant (sertraline) by family doctors, which represents one of only a few 'real life' trials, found that it actually had no short-term impact on the experiences classified as depression but rather reduced those classified as anxiety. Over 12 weeks, there was a positive impact on quality of life, but its impact on experiences classified as 'depression' was again small. The authors concluded that whilst there was evidence of the benefit of sertraline over and above placebo, it does not appear to operate by targeting experiences classified as depression. This suggests that labelling these products as 'antidepressants' may be misleading (Lewis et al., 2019)

18 There is also a longstanding debate regarding antipsychotic medications, with some authors arguing that they do more harm than good (e.g., Whitaker, 2004). Other authors have claimed that there is insufficient evidence to assess this claim (e.g., Sohler et al., 2016).

19 There is a detailed review of a number of studies showing this effect in Kirsch (2014).

20 A recent investigation was undertaken in relation to the development of the *International Classification of Diseases*, Volume 11, in which those receiving diagnoses were interviewed about the process, and the usefulness of the process was highlighted and a collaborative approach recommended. Importantly, whilst the views of those receiving diagnoses were sought, individuals were not offered any alternative to a diagnostic model (Perkins et al., 2018).

21 The *DSM-V* contains 541 diagnoses, compared to the 128 in the *DSM-I* (Blashfield et al., 2014).

22 Regular surveys of mental health in England collect information on 'Common Mental Disorders' using an assessment of 14 clusters of symptoms (for example, sleep problems, depression, and worry). What this survey typically finds is that most people who experience problematic levels of these symptoms do not meet criteria for any particular diagnosis. In addition, when people do meet criteria for a diagnosis, they usually meet criteria for more than one (McManus et al., 2016).

23 Studies have examined the degree to which the same diagnosis is given in different situations; for example, by different clinicians, a concept known as reliability. Studies tend to find that reliability is variable across different diagnoses and with differing levels of information. For common diagnoses, some controlled studies have found high levels of reliability across clinicians (Ruskin et al., 1998), but for less common diagnoses it is significantly lower, much closer to chance levels (Matuszak & Piasecki, 2012). In addition, the

information collected in routine clinical practice, being less than that usually collected in structured diagnostic interviews, often results in extremely low levels of reliability (Saunders et al., 2015).

24 Diagnoses have not been found to be particularly good predictors of relevant constructs, such as need for services, quality of life or treatment outcome (Johnstone et al., 1992).
25 Kessler (1997).
26 Matheson et al., 2013; Weich et al. (2002).
27 APA (2013).
28 A history of mental health diagnosis can be an exclusion for various professions, including the armed forces and emergency services. A recent review in *The Lancet* brings together studies of stigma and discrimination from across the world (Thornicroft et al., 2016).
29 High levels of self-stigmatisation have been associated with low scores on measures of self-esteem, and this is after controlling for other factors such as diagnosis, level of depression and demographic variables (e.g., Corrigan et al., 2006). Other studies have linked this self-stigmatisation to behaviours such as social withdrawal (Link et al., 2001), which is likely to compound the effects on self-esteem. From a different perspective, those with higher levels of self-stigma tend to tell stories about themselves and their lives with lower social worth (Lysaker et al., 2008).
30 e.g., Corrigan et al., 2006.
31 These ideas come from the work of Daniel Siegel (2015).
32 Emotion dysregulation has been operationalised by referring to six related dimensions (Gratz & Roemer, 2004): 1. lack of awareness of emotional responses; 2. lack of clarity of emotional responses; 3. non-acceptance of emotional responses; 4. limited access to emotion regulation strategies perceived as effective; 5. difficulties controlling impulses when experiencing 'negative' emotions; and 6. difficulties engaging in goal-directed behaviours when experiencing 'negative' emotions.

References

APA, 2013. *Diagnostic and statistical manual of mental disorders* (5th edn). Washington, DC: Author.
Aristotle, R., 1984. *The complete works of Aristotle: The revised Oxford translation*, Jonathan Barnes (ed.). Princeton, NJ: Princeton University Press.
Barrett, L.F., 2017. The theory of constructed emotion: An active inference account of interoception and categorization. *Social Cognitive and Affective Neuroscience*, 12(1), pp. 1–23.
Blashfield, R.K., Keeley, J.W., Flanagan, E.H. and Miles, S.R., 2014. The cycle of classification: DSM-I through DSM-5. *Annual Review of Clinical Psychology*, 10, pp. 25–51.
Cannon, W.B., 1927. The James-Lange theory of emotions: A critical examination and an alternative theory. *The American Journal of Psychology*, 39, pp. 106–124.

Corrigan, P.W., Watson, A.C. and Barr, L., 2006. The self-stigma of mental illness: Implications for self-esteem and self-efficacy. *Journal of Social and Clinical Psychology*, 25, pp. 875–883.

Cory, G.A., 2002. *Reappraising MacLean's triune brain concept. The evolutionary neuroethology of Paul MacLean. Convergences and frontiers*. Westport, CT, London: Prager, pp. 9–27.

Darwin, C., 1872. *The expression of emotions in man and animals*. London: John Murray.

Davies, J., 2013. *Cracked: Why psychiatry is doing more harm than good*. London: Icon Books Ltd.

Ekman, P. and Keltner, D., 1997. Universal facial expressions of emotion. In U. Segerstrale and P. Molnar (eds.), *Nonverbal communication: Where nature meets culture*. Oxon: Routledge, pp. 27–46.

Gratz, K.L. and Roemer, L., 2004. Multidimensional assessment of emotion regulation and dysregulation: Development, factor structure, and initial validation of the difficulties in emotion regulation scale. *Journal of Psychopathology and Behavioral Assessment*, 26(1), pp. 41–54.

Izard, C.E., 2009. Emotion theory and research: Highlights, unanswered questions, and emerging issues. *Annual Review of Psychology*, 60, pp. 1–25.

Jack, R.E., Garrod, O.G. and Schyns, P.G., 2014. Dynamic facial expressions of emotion transmit an evolving hierarchy of signals over time. *Current Biology*, 24(2), pp. 187–192.

Johnstone, E.C., Frith, C.D., Crow, T.J., Owens, D.G.C., Done, D.J., Baldwin, E.J. and Charlette, A., 1992. The Northwick Park 'functional' psychosis study: Diagnosis and outcome. *Psychological Medicine*, 22(2), pp. 331–346.

Johnstone, L., 2014. *A straight-talking guide to psychiatric diagnosis*. Monmouth: PCCS Books.

Kessler, R., 1997. The effects of stressful life events on depression. *Annual Review of Psychology*, 48(1), pp. 191–214.

Kirsch, I., 2014. Antidepressants and the placebo effect. *Zeitschrift für Psychologie*, 222(3), p. 128.

Lazarus, R.S., 1991. Cognition and motivation in emotion. *American Psychologist*, 46(4), p. 352.

Lewis, G., Duffy, L., Ades, A., Amos, R., Araya, R., Brabyn, S., Button, K.S., Churchill, R., Derrick, C., Dowrick, C. and Gilbody, S., 2019. The clinical effectiveness of sertraline in primary care and the role of depression severity and duration (PANDA): A pragmatic, double-blind, placebo-controlled randomised trial. *The Lancet Psychiatry*, 6(11), pp. 903–914.

Link, B.G., Struening, E.L., Neese-Todd, S., Asmussen, S. and Phelan, J.C., 2001. Stigma as a barrier to recovery: The consequences of stigma for the self-esteem of people with mental illnesses. *Psychiatric Services*, 52(12), pp. 1621–1626.

Lysaker, P.H., Buck, K.D., Taylor, A.C. and Roe, D., 2008. Associations of metacognition and internalized stigma with quantitative assessments of self-experience in narratives of schizophrenia. *Psychiatry Research*, 157(1), pp. 31–38.

MacLean, P.D., 1990. *The triune brain in evolution: Role in paleocerebral functions*. New York, NY: Plenum Press.

Matheson, S.L., Shepherd, A.M., Pinchbeck, R.M., Laurens, K.R. and Carr, V.J., 2013. Childhood adversity in schizophrenia: A systematic meta-analysis. *Psychological Medicine*, 43(2), p. 225.

Matuszak, J. and Piasecki, M., 2012. Inter-rater reliability in psychiatric diagnosis: Collateral data improves the reliability of diagnoses. *Psychiatric Times*, 29(10), pp. 12–13.

McManus, S., Bebbington, P.E., Jenkins, R. and Brugha, T., 2016. *Mental health and wellbeing in England: The adult psychiatric morbidity survey 2014*. London: NHS Digital.

Perkins, A., Ridler, J., Browes, D., Peryer, G., Notley, C. and Hackmann, C., 2018. Experiencing mental health diagnosis: A systematic review of service user, clinician, and carer perspectives across clinical settings. *The Lancet Psychiatry*, 5(9), pp. 747–764.

Plutchik, R., 1984. Emotions: A general psychoevolutionary theory. In K.R. Scherer and P. Ekman (eds.), *Approaches to emotion*. Hillsdale, NJ: Lawrence Erlbaum Associates, Inc., pp. 197–219.

Ruskin, P.E., Reed, S., Kumar, R., Kling, M.A., Siegel, E., Rosen, M. and Hauser, P., 1998. Reliability and acceptability of psychiatric diagnosis via telecommunication and audiovisual technology. *Psychiatric Services*, 49(8), pp. 1086–1088.

Saunders, K.E.A., Bilderbeck, A.C., Price, J. and Goodwin, G.M., 2015. Distinguishing bipolar disorder from borderline personality disorder: A study of current clinical practice. *European Psychiatry*, 30(8), pp. 965–974.

Scarantino, A. and de Sousa, R., 2018. Emotion. In Edward N. Zalta (ed.), *The Stanford encyclopedia of philosophy* (Winter 2018 Edition). Available at: https://plato-stanford-edu.uea.idm.oclc.org/archives/win2018/entries/emotion/.

Schachter, S. and Singer, J., 1962. Cognitive, social, and physiological determinants of emotional state. *Psychological Review*, 69, pp. 379–399.

Schnittker, J., 2017. *The diagnostic system: Why the classification of psychiatric disorders is necessary, difficult, and never settled*. New York, NY: Columbia University Press.

Siegel, D.J., 2015. *The developing mind: How relationships and the brain interact to shape who we are*. London: Guilford Press.

Sohler, N., Adams, B.G., Barnes, D.M., Cohen, G.H., Prins, S.J. and Schwartz, S., 2016. Weighing the evidence for harm from long-term treatment with antipsychotic medications: A systematic review. *American Journal of Orthopsychiatry*, 86(5), p. 477.

Szasz, T.S., 2013. The myth of mental illness. *Perspectives in Abnormal Behavior*, pp. 4–11.

Thornicroft, G., Mehta, N., Clement, S., Evans-Lacko, S., Doherty, M., Rose, D., Koschorke, M., Shidhaye, R., O'Reilly, C. and Henderson, C., 2016. Evidence for effective interventions to reduce mental-health-related stigma and discrimination. *The Lancet*, 387(10023), pp. 1123–1132.

Van Os, J., MacKenna, P., Murray, R. and Dean, K., 2003. *Does schizophrenia exist?* London: Institute of Psychiatry.

Weich, S., Blanchard, M., Prince, M., Burton, E., Erens, B.O.B. and Sproston, K., 2002. Mental health and the built environment: Cross-sectional survey of individual and contextual risk factors for depression. *The British Journal of Psychiatry*, 180(5), pp. 428–433.

Whitaker, R., 2004. The case against antipsychotic drugs: A 50-year record of doing more harm than good. *Medical Hypotheses*, 62(1), pp. 5–13.

Chapter 1

Fear

Fear is an unpleasant emotion that's intense and has a dramatic impact on our bodies, increasing our heart rate, breathing and muscle tension. We don't feel intense fear very often, but we might regularly feel on edge, nervous or anxious. Usually, it's a helpful experience. Before an important meeting, fear encourages us to prepare, think about what questions we might be asked and make sure we arrive on time. In the meeting, it helps us concentrate and improves our performance. Fear can also be helpful in encouraging us to avoid situations that might do us harm. There is a strong link between fear and excitement, and the tension between these two emotions can lead to intensely pleasant experiences like exhilaration and joy.

At other times, fear can become a huge problem. Feeling scared of everyday things, feeling scared most of the time, or feeling easily overwhelmed and struggling to cope can all be extremely unpleasant experiences and can lead to significant problems. It is at these times that the experience of fear can be labelled something else – anxiety – and anxiety disorders might be diagnosed.

This chapter starts with an understanding of fear, its causes, how we learn to fear things and what happens when we are scared in our minds and bodies. It explores the importance of fear in keeping us safe and the tensions with excitement and exhilaration. Next, it looks at how we can tolerate and use helpful responses to fear, with some practical techniques that can help us when we are scared.

The chapter moves on to the fear trap, which illustrates what happens when we feel excessively scared or scared of things we shouldn't be. This covers problems that might be labelled with anxiety disorder diagnoses, including panic disorder, obsessive-compulsive disorder, specific phobias (e.g., of animals and other creatures,

DOI: 10.4324/9781003138112-2

natural environments, flying, dentists and body-based phobias, such as blood), generalised anxiety disorder, social anxiety disorder and post-traumatic stress disorder. The chapter gives illustrations of how the fear trap works for these different fears and how to get out of the fear trap.

Understanding and accepting fear

Like all emotions, fear helps us to respond to what's going on around us. Understanding the causes of fear, the impact it has on the five elements of emotion and its function can help us accept it. This also helps us to think about how we can tolerate and respond to it and to consider some of the difficulties we might have with it. The first exercise in this chapter (Exercise 1.1) will help you to think about what it is that makes you scared.

Exercise 1.1   What makes you scared?

Write a list of your top five fears; things that would make you feel scared if you were to be near them, or to do them; or things that you have worked hard to avoid in your life.

1.

2.

3.

4.

5.

Now think about your early life. What were the adults around you scared of?

Look at your list of your top five fears. Are you right to be afraid of these things – are they as dangerous as you *feel* they are?

What causes fear?

For our ancestors, the most common causes of fear were predators and attack. Today, we still face a variety of threats to our survival, and many of us fear things like terrorist attacks, wars and death. But our modern lives and easy access to information have produced a whole variety of other potential fears – lack of money, social success, intimacy and the future. There are also common fears of spiders, heights, snakes and clowns.[1] Sometimes we can also find ourselves feeling scared about everyday things, like making decisions, answering the phone or going out of the house. Fear can become associated with almost anything.

Natural fears

Most causes of fear fall into four broad categories[2]:

1. **Interpersonal events or situations**
   We can fear criticism, rejection, social conflict, judgement, interaction, displays of sexual or aggressive behaviours.
2. **Death, injuries, illness, blood and surgical procedures**
   We can fear becoming physically and mentally ill, which would include disease, contamination, madness, losing control, fainting and sexual inadequacy.
3. **Animals**
   We can fear creepy crawlies, snakes, dogs and many different animals and creatures.
4. **Agoraphobic**
   We can fear going into shops, crowds or public places; travelling on buses, trains or planes; entering enclosed spaces like elevators or tunnels; or crossing bridges. We can get to the point where we are scared of leaving the house altogether.

Have a look at your fears in Exercise 1.1, and see if you can put them into one of the four groups. Are there any that don't fit? Generally, around 90% of fears fit into these four categories, which suggests that humans are biologically more likely to fear some things over others. In our evolutionary past, fearing particular things probably helped us to survive.

Learned fears

We are not all scared of all of these things, though, so our learning and experiences are also important in shaping our fears.

One of the most powerful situations that teaches us to fear things is the experience of pain. Think of the last time you really hurt yourself. Now think about how you felt in similar situations afterwards. A common example is learning to ride a bike. Falling off a bike hurts, and so once we have fallen off a bike, we've made an association between riding the bike and pain. This results in more fear when we get back on the bike.

Fearing previously painful situations is an example of learning from our own experience, but not all learning is this direct. Monkeys reared in the wild show a fear response to snakes, but monkeys reared in captivity don't. When monkeys reared in captivity see monkeys reared in the wild being scared of snakes, they learn to fear snakes themselves. They continue to show fear in response to snakes even months later.[3] Toddlers who see their mothers responding fearfully to toy snakes learn to fear snakes in much the same way.[4] So not only do we learn to fear things through our own experience, but we can also learn to fear things that those around us seem to fear.

In Exercise 1.1, are there fears that you might have learnt from those around you when you were young? Are there fears that are shared by your family?

Accuracy of fears

All of us have things that we're scared of. We are likely to have learnt to fear these things through our own experience and through watching others. We seem to be more likely to fear certain things than others, which links with evolution and survival.

Importantly, our fears may not be accurate or precise. Consider Exercise 1.1, in particular the question of whether you are right to fear things as much as you do. It is likely that there is at least one fear on your list that you fear more than you should. Most of us fear things that are not as dangerous as we think they are, and many of us will have experienced interference in our lives as a result of strong, unreasonable fears.[5] In fact, if we consider the importance of fear in terms of survival, it is likely that we will 'play it safe'. Missing a real threat may have major consequences for us, whereas responding to a harmless situation as if it were threatening just wastes energy.

We are likely to overestimate threats

Most of the time, we know what is making us feel scared. Sometimes, though, we can find ourselves feeling scared or on edge and not really knowing why or feeling on edge for lots of the time. When this happens, the object of our fear tends to be more abstract, like being out of control or being uncertain. We will return to this in the section on worry.

Exercise 1.2   Feeling scared

Think about a recent time when you felt scared. This is usually easier with an intense feeling rather than a mild one.

How would you describe the experience?
What did you notice/were you most aware of?
What made you feel scared?
How did you respond/what did you do?
What happened afterwards?

What happens when we're scared?

Have a look at Exercise 1.2, which will help you to start thinking about what happens when we feel scared. The Introduction of this book outlines the five different elements of emotions. Fear, like all emotions, arises out of changes in these five different elements, as shown next.

Feelings

We experience fear at different levels of intensity. When we experience a little bit of fear, we are apprehensive, concerned or nervous. With more intense feelings, we are fearful, scared or alarmed, and our most intense experiences of fear are when we are panicked, terrified or petrified. Most of us don't feel scared very often, but when we do it feels energetic and like a 'cold' feeling.[6]

Sometimes people will use words to describe feeling scared like 'anxious', 'stressed' and 'worried'. Each of these three terms usually describes something slightly different than fear, and they are covered separately at the end of this section.

Bodily responses

Fear has a dramatic impact on the body, activating the sympathetic system and suppressing the parasympathetic system.

When the sympathetic (accelerator, or fight-or-flight) system is activated, our heart rate increases, our breathing deepens and our muscles tense. These are the bodily responses we are often most aware of when we are scared. However, there are other important changes too. Our senses are sharpened: our pupils dilate to let in more light, our hearing becomes more acute and our sense of touch is heightened. This is why, if we get scared in a busy place, it feels as though it gets even louder and busier. The sympathetic system also has a powerful impact on our attention, narrowing it and focusing it on the threat. This is why it can be difficult to concentrate on other things when we are scared.

Fear drives an increase in heart rate, breathing, muscle tension and attentional focus on threat

The parasympathetic (brake, or rest-and-digest) system is suppressed in fear. This means that the digestive system slows down, causing a dry mouth and 'butterflies' in the stomach. In extreme cases, we might get rid of food either through being sick or needing the toilet (this is where the phrase 'bricking it' comes from – visiting the brick outhouse before indoor facilities!). The parasympathetic system also controls immunity and libido, so prolonged suppression of the parasympathetic system (see later section on stress) can lead to reduced immune function (and so, getting lots of viruses) and reduced sexual interest.

All of these reactions are fast and often intense; people sometimes talk about an 'adrenalin rush' or 'adrenalin thump'. It usually reduces fairly quickly, but it can be extremely unpleasant if it lasts for a long time.

Facial expression

Fear is an emotion that others can read quickly on our faces. Our facial muscles tense, our eyes widen to allow in more light and our mouths often open. Sometimes this is because we are screaming and shouting;

at other times, it helps us to breathe (and improves our hearing). For lower intensities of fear, our facial expression is often one of thought and consideration.

These facial expressions are linked with the changes in the body outlined in the previous section, but they can also communicate to those around us that we are scared.

Thoughts/interpretation

When we are scared, our thoughts are quick and impulsive rather than slow and methodical. It can feel as though our thoughts are racing or spiralling. Thoughts can be motivating, like "I need to get out of here!" or "Help!", or they might race to find the best response to the threat.

Our attention and thoughts are directed towards the perceived threat, and it is difficult to concentrate on anything else. It is also difficult to use a slow, rational decision-making process. Sometimes this leads to circular processes of thought that are not particularly rational and are also very troubling. This is covered later in the section on worry.

With intense fear, we can find it almost impossible to think clearly at all.

Behaviours

When we are frightened, we often have an urge to do something – usually something quick and physical, like running away. If we resist this urge, we can end up feeling restless and agitated. Another common response is to freeze like a 'rabbit in the headlights': to stop and remain completely still.

Fear and the brain

The Introduction of this book showed how the brain is made up of three parts: reptilian, mammalian and rational. Fear functions to protect us from threat, so it is a quick, instinctive and primitive response driven by the reptilian brain.

Fear activates the reptilian brain

This is important to understand and can help explain a variety of paradoxes with fear. For example, many of us around the world are scared of spiders. Almost all of us are aware that the spiders we frequently come across represent no threat to us whatsoever, and yet we continue to be scared of them. This is because, when we are calm, our rational brains are online, and we can think clearly about threats and risk. However, when we become fearful, our reptilian brains – which are not rational processing organs – take over and we respond as if the spider represents a threat to our lives. This is the 'flipped lid' state mentioned in the Introduction.

What is the function of fear?

Imagine you are walking down the road and suddenly see a tiger. You would want to do something to avoid ending up as tiger food – perhaps turn and run. You would want to make sure that you were aware of where the tiger was and where your best route of escape might be, and that you ran as fast as you could. Your breathing would get deeper to bring in more oxygen, which is pumped around the body through increased heart rate to the muscles that use it for energy and tense up to start running. Your facial expression would be wide to enable good vision and hearing and to take in lots of air. Your attention would be focused on the threat (the tiger) and the escape route, not on the nice car nearby. Digesting your lunch would be stopped and lunch might even be 'dumped' (needing the toilet or being sick), and any energy going to your immune and reproductive systems would be diverted to the most important task of running.

All of the different changes that occur with the experience of fear link directly to its function: the 'flight' response. Our body is geared up for running, our attention is focused on the threat and our senses are sharpened. Other bodily functions are paused. This is all experienced as unpleasant, which motivates us to get away, making us more likely to survive. Sometimes we might freeze, which can be helpful as it reduces the likelihood of detection; many animal species detect potential prey by movement.

The importance of fear to our survival is illustrated by the example of the dodo bird. The dodo lived in Mauritius and had spent much of its evolutionary history living on islands where there were no predators, so it had not learnt to fear other creatures. When sailors arrived in the 17th century, the dodo was easy prey. The lack of predators also meant that the dodo probably nested on the ground, which made the eggs easy prey for other animals that the sailors brought – cats, for example. As a result, the dodo quickly became extinct. An illustration of the importance of fear in humans is found in the case of an individual known as SM. SM had an injury to her brain that caused her to feel almost no fear. This was despite a life in which she was held up at knifepoint and gunpoint, was almost killed in a domestic violence incident, and received many death threats. SM did live in a dangerous neighbourhood, but she also had a tendency to approach rather than avoid potentially dangerous situations because of her inability to feel fear.[7]

**Fear protects us from threat
and helps avoid potential danger**

What is the difference between fear and anxiety?

There is a great deal of confusion about the terms 'fear' and 'anxiety', and some people make a distinction between the two. For example, fear can be described as the emotional response to immediate threat that results in running away, whereas anxiety is the emotional response to the anticipation of future threat that often results in avoidance.[8] Other authors have labelled anxiety as 'unresolved fear', the desire to run away that has not been carried out.[9] Others still have argued that anxiety is a more complex emotion than fear and incorporates other emotions such as shame or guilt.[10]

The situation is further complicated because the words 'anxiety' or 'anxious' are frequently used in mental health diagnosis. Using these terms can lead to a belief that 'anxiety' is a symptom of an illness and is something that we 'have' that can be 'got rid of' or 'cured'. The Introduction of this book emphasised that there is no evidence of a fundamental underlying difference between those diagnosed with an 'anxiety disorder' and the rest of the population.

This book takes the position that distinctions between fear and anxiety are unlikely to be helpful, and so we'll stick with the basic emotion of fear. This emotion can be experienced with varying intensity and can be associated with a present threat and a potential future threat, but the fundamental emotion remains the same. In this context, the experience we might describe as anxiety is an ongoing experience of lower-intensity fear that might well be accompanied by other emotions. In this book, the words 'anxiety' and 'anxious' will be avoided because they are likely to lead to confusion.

Anxiety is best understood as a lower-intensity fear

Fear and worry

Worrying is a repetitive process that involves chains of thought (and images) that go around and around in our minds. Worry is sometimes confused with feelings, as in "I felt worried when you came home late", and is sometimes thought of as an uncontrollable part of fear – "I was so nervous, I worried all night". In fact, worry, while it might seem to be part of the emotion of fear, is actually best understood as a behaviour. Let's look at how it works.

Fear functions to help us respond to threat; it activates the reptilian brain and focuses our attention on the threat to help us protect ourselves. This works well if the threat is immediate – if there is a car coming towards us or a tiger approaching us right now. The problem is that as humans with rational brains as well as reptilian ones, we can think in the abstract, and so we can think about threats that haven't happened yet, things that might go wrong in the future. When this happens, our rational brain is perceiving a potential threat in the future which is often in the form of a 'what if . . . ' thought: 'what if I'm late?', 'what if my child gets ill?', 'what if I've upset them?' or 'what if I make a mistake?'.

In these situations, the rational brain is perceiving potential future threats. This activates the reptilian brain (which responds as if there is a threat *now*) and makes us feel scared, so our bodies get ready to respond to the threat and our attention focuses on it. So now we're experiencing a threat and we feel we need to do something about it, but the problem is that it hasn't happened. As a result, we think about what might happen, how we'd respond to it, what might happen next and what we'd do then. But because none of this has happened, it turns into long chains of potential future threats. This means that we can go from getting a slightly odd text from somebody to imagining a massive argument and feeling really nervous and on edge about it. Or we can go from thinking we might be late for a meeting to imagining losing our jobs. We cannot use our rational brains to problem-solve events that haven't happened yet, but because the reptilian brain has been activated by a potential threat, our attention is focused on the threat, and we feel we need to do something. The problem is that doing something – worrying – leads us to anticipate more threats, so we get more scared and worry more.

**Worry is a repetitive type of thinking
that is caused by – and causes – fear**

For most people, worry is something that is manageable but occasionally spirals in particular situations. Where it starts to interfere significantly with life, we'll be stuck in the fear trap. This is covered later in this chapter, and there is a section on how to apply the fear trap to worry in particular.

Fear and stress

Stress is another common term that is used to describe emotional experiences like fear. What do you think of when you think of 'stress'? You'll probably think about physical changes like muscle tension or feelings in your stomach, maybe aches and pains. These map closely on to the bodily responses associated with fear.

Stress is an ongoing, continuous experience of lower-level fear. It is caused by lots of ongoing threats we respond to with fear and all of the changes in the five elements of emotions outlined earlier. Threats in this case can be repeated demands from work or from others (like family) or changes in circumstances like moving house, getting divorced, illness or injury – any kind of high-level, ongoing demand that feels like an ongoing threat.

Fear functions for quick, immediate action and helps us protect ourselves in situations of immediate danger. If it is activated all the time, then the usual helpful responses become less helpful:

- Muscle tension resulting in aches and pains
- Immune system suppression results in more illness
- Suppression of digestive system results in problems like nausea, diarrhoea, constipation or discomfort
- Suppression of libido results in loss of sex drive and potential relationship problems
- Focus of attention on threat results in difficulty concentrating and seeing the bigger picture
- Urge to run away and avoid things results in unhelpful responses to threats
- High arousal results in exhaustion

Stress can be the result of facing too many actual threats – having too much going on. It can also become self-fulfilling because of the problems in thinking and planning (which are driven by the narrow focus of attention and difficulty seeing the bigger picture). This means that everything feels like a threat, but if we were more able to stop, stand back and think, we'd be better able to prioritise and approach things in a more logical manner. Stress can also be the result of being stuck in one of the fear traps.

Stress is caused by prolonged experience of lower-level fear

Am I scared or excited?

Fear and excitement are very similar and also very different. Have a look at Exercise 1.3 to explore your experience.

Exercise 1.3   Feeling excited

Think about a recent time when you felt excited. It is usually easiest to think about doing something in particular, like going on a roller-coaster.

How would you describe the experience?
What did you notice/were you most aware of?
What made you feel excited?
How did you respond/what did you do?
Were there points when you were scared rather than excited? How did you know?
How did you feel afterwards?

Fear is experienced as unpleasant and the most dreaded emotion. Excitement is experienced as pleasant, and we often go to great lengths to achieve it. Both emotions are prompted by novelty and the unknown. Both are associated with an increase in activity in the body and the mind. The difference can be found in the interpretation. Fear is characterised by a perception of threat and a desire to avoid harm. Excitement is characterised by a perception of potential and a desire to achieve or gain. These differences in interpretation of the situation result in clear differences in behaviours: excitement leads to a desire to approach, whereas fear leads to a desire to avoid.

The similarity of these emotions means that there can often be a swinging between the two, which you may have found in Exercise 1.3.

A roller-coaster ride might be exciting from the back of the queue, but the longer you remain in the queue and the closer you get to the front might mean an increased intensity of fear and an increasing desire to leave. On the roller-coaster itself, there might be a switching between fear and excitement as you gradually make your way to the top or tear down to the bottom.

This tension between fear and excitement is important in our daily lives. Clearly, to keep safe in the short term, we would be best to avoid any potential danger. However, sitting at home and never going out is not going to be the best thing for our longer-term happiness. As a result, we have to learn to tread this line between excitement and fear, and we have to tolerate some level of fear in order to be able to live our lives and explore new things.[11] Children illustrate this as they engage in risky play at height, at speed or 'rough-and-tumble'. They move between fear and excitement, adjusting things by moving lower or higher or going faster or slower to manage this balance.[12]

Refer back to Exercise 1.3 and the feeling *after* the excitement and fear. If we have done something that was difficult, that was new and challenging, we often have an intense feeling following this moment. We might call this feeling exhilaration – a feeling of intense energy and satisfaction, sometimes pride. This feeling comes partly from the freedom from fear but also from the sense of achievement at having conquered something that was so difficult. Children often jump up and down, shout, smile and laugh after doing something that was risky and challenging. There is more on this in Chapter 7 on happiness.

The next time we approach something about which we had this feeling, we might be excited, and so we are more likely to do it. If it all went wrong and we experienced pain, we are more likely to experience fear the next time and so more likely to avoid it.

> **Fear and excitement are both responses to new situations**
> **Fear involves a perception of threat;**
> **excitement involves a perception of potential**

Tolerating fear and using helpful responses when we're scared

Fear is an unpleasant emotion that is driven by the reptilian brain and is not particularly logical. It has a dramatic impact on the body, and we don't like it. So usually, when we feel scared, we try to get rid of it, or at least reduce it. The easiest way to do this is to get away from whatever it is that has made us scared. This is the function of fear: it drives us to get away from danger and protect ourselves.

But we cannot always respond to fear in this way. Sometimes we have to do things that make us feel scared, whether this is going on roller-coasters, doing exams, going to job interviews, doing presentations, going to parties, going on dates or even going on holiday. Many new experiences can make us feel scared, worried or nervous, and if we always avoid these situations, our lives will not be as interesting or fulfilling as we would like. We need to find ways to tolerate fear and helpful ways to respond.

The following pages explore the different ways we can respond to fear – not to get rid of it but to adjust to it and help us better tolerate it. This will help you to think about what to do when you feel scared. Exercise 1.1 at the beginning of the chapter is helpful to refer back to at this point.

Escape and avoidance

If we are scared of ferocious tigers, then running away whenever we see one, and avoiding the kinds of places where they tend to live, helps us to keep our levels of fear in relation to tigers low. In this case, fear is serving its important function of protecting us against the threat that ferocious tigers represent.

This is the most powerful way of responding to fear. If we move towards whatever we are scared of, we feel more scared; as we move away, we feel less scared. The easiest way to make sure we don't feel scared of tigers or roller-coasters is not to go near them – to avoid them altogether and get away if we find ourselves near them.

These responses can be termed 'escape' (running away) and 'avoidance' (not going near in the first place). Both are common responses to fear that lead to rapid reductions in the feeling, which is experienced as relief. However, where they are overused, these responses can lead to significant problems, as we will see in the next section (fear trap).

There are other behavioural responses that are less extreme than avoiding or escaping the situation altogether. These are usually things that modify our experience of the situation, to turn it from something terrifying into something slightly more manageable. Examples of this would include going on a smaller roller-coaster, doing a work or school presentation with somebody else rather than on our own, or going on a bus while wearing headphones. This can help balance the intensity of fear, perhaps moving it closer to an experience of excitement. We will return to this idea later.

Bodily responses

Escape and avoidance are the most powerful responses to fear. But they are not always the best option – sometimes we need to do things even when they make us feel scared.

At these times, we need other ways of responding to fear. Changing our bodily responses when we are scared can adjust the intensity of fear we feel. Remember that the sympathetic nervous system has a powerful impact on the body and is controlled by the reptilian brain, which is outside our conscious control. However, there are three areas of the system that we can override: breathing, muscle tension and the direction of attention. It is these aspects that we can target to change the intensity of fear.

Helpful responses to fear include changing breathing, muscle tension and attentional focus

Breathing

When we are scared, our sympathetic nervous system deepens and quickens our breathing to get more oxygen into our bodies. Overriding and counteracting this process by gently slowing down our breathing influences other parts of our bodies like our heart rate, muscle tension and attentional focus. Bringing the awareness to the breath has been used for centuries and is central to meditation and yoga. It is the out-breath, in particular, that is most calming, so focusing on letting the breath go is a powerful way to reduce the intensity of fear.

Muscle tension

Our muscles tense when we are scared to get us ready to run. Consciously relaxing the tension in our muscles can also reduce the intensity of fear. We can combine this with calming our breathing, by releasing muscle tension on the out-breath. Posture is also an important part of responding to fear. Adjusting our posture can release little tensions that we may not have noticed, so it can be really helpful to sit in a calm, relaxed manner. You can also roll your shoulders back and down or imagine yourself sinking into the chair or the floor.

Focus of attention

When we are scared, our attention is directed towards the threat. If we gently move our attention away from the perceived threat and focus on other things – particularly aspects of the environment and things that are happening in the present – this can reduce the intensity of fear. The practice of focusing the attention on the present moment is called 'mindfulness'. Mindfulness is not trying to get rid of thoughts or ignore emotions but instead is the skill of being able to direct and focus attention and bring it back if it has wandered. It often uses the body and the breath as points of reference, but we can focus our attention outwards too, on what's around us or what's happening now. Developing mindfulness skills can be a really helpful way to improve our response to fear through the body. There are many different options available to practice these skills, including books, apps, online videos and courses. Exercise 1.4 talks you through one exercise that can help you practice moving your attention around.

Exercise 1.4   Mindfulness/attention training

Mindfulness involves developing the skill of focusing and directing attention. One way to do this is to use the senses to pick out different things in the environment and focus the attention on these things. You can do this exercise wherever you are, whatever you're doing. A good time to practice is during 'mundane tasks' like washing up, ironing, eating, walking or showering.

Pick out five things you can see.

Focus your attention on one thing at a time and look closely at each. It might be an object, the way the light shines on something, the way something moves or a pattern on something. Pick out each one of the five in turn.

Pick out four things you can feel.

Focus your attention on four different things you can feel. Perhaps the way the floor or the chair feels supporting your weight, the movement of air on your skin, sunlight or warmth or cold, maybe something you are holding or could pick up? Pick out each of the four in turn.

Pick out three things you can hear.

Notice the sounds around you, sounds that are close or in the distance – traffic, birds, electronics, music, others talking or breathing. Pick out each of the three in turn.

Pick out two things you can smell.

Take a slightly deeper breath in and focus on the smell as you breathe it in. It might be a pleasant smell or an unpleasant one.

Pick out something you can taste.

Notice any tastes in your mouth, focus on that sensation and, if you like, change it by drinking or eating something different and focus on how the sensation changes.

Let's go back to our line for the roller-coaster. We have decided to go on the roller-coaster, but we can feel that we are getting more and more scared. We can feel our breathing getting deeper and faster, our muscles tensing, and we keep looking at the biggest drop and imagining how this is going to feel.

One option is to get out of the line and not to go on. This would bring immediate relief, and we would no longer feel scared. This would be escaping. Another option is to use the bodily techniques outlined here to gently reduce our levels of fear. We could notice our breathing, focusing on the out-breath and gently slowing it down. At the same time, we could notice the tension in our muscles, perhaps particularly in our shoulders, and allow them to drop. None of this would get rid of the feeling of fear, but it might reduce it enough to allow us to stay in the line. We could also gently move our attention away from the most terrifying drop of the roller-coaster, which would increase our sense of fear, and move it towards how happy the people coming off the roller-coaster look, which could increase our sense of excitement.

Calming thoughts and rationalising

Escape and avoidance are almost automatic and link directly to the function of fear. These responses can occur with very little thought or consideration and are driven by the reptilian brain. Responding with the body and calming down the emotional response is an important part of responding to fear without using avoidance and escape. This requires conscious effort and the use of our rational brains to 'override' the automatic response of the reptilian brain.

With a calmer reptilian brain, we can use the rational brain a little more to make sense of the situation. One of the most important tasks to help us respond to emotion is to understand the reason for the emotion, to understand why we are feeling scared. Often when we are scared, particularly in our modern lives, we might have thoughts like "it's all too much", "there's just too much to do" or "I can't cope with it". At these times, it is really important to clarify what the fear is – what we are scared of. We may have lots to do, but which one of these things is it that represents a threat? We may not feel like we can cope, but which thing in particular are we most scared of? Using our rational brains to clarify what the fear is can help us to start to problem-solve in a more detailed way to manage the situation that gives rise to the emotion. Sometimes we might notice that we are overestimating the threat, and we can challenge our interpretation. At other times, there may be particular things that we can do that will help us respond to the fear that can make us feel less scared and more in control. Examples might be finding out how to get to a job interview beforehand or finding out more information about a person we are going to meet before we meet them. At other times, we can't do anything practical but knowing that we are scared because of one particular upcoming event can help us keep other things in perspective.

It is important to remember to approach things in this order. Trying to problem-solve using our rational brains when our reptilian brains are driving our behaviour is not likely to work – it's a bit like trying to talk to a crocodile to tell it to calm down. We need to be calm enough for our rational brains to work properly.

Turning fear into excitement

There is a significant overlap between excitement and fear. If we focus our attention on the things that are likely to go wrong and the pain that we might experience, we are likely to feel scared. If we can move our attention to the things that might go right and the benefits we might get, then we are more likely to feel excitement.

As long as the fear is not overwhelming, it is possible to shift from fear into excitement. Labelling our emotion as excitement, encouraging ourselves to get excited or viewing new situations as challenges and potential opportunities rather than threats can all increase our tendency to experience excitement rather than fear. Interestingly, this shift is linked with improved performance at whatever we are doing.[13]

Helping others with fear

Sometimes we need to help other people when they are scared or frightened. The same techniques can help in these situations. Most importantly, we should remember to respond to the emotion first, before the situation. If we go immediately into problem-solving mode, we can end up trying to rationalise with somebody whose behaviour is driven mostly by their reptilian brain, which is unlikely to work and may instead escalate the situation.

Our first task is to help them to calm, by helping them to feel safe and then using the bodily responses like breathing, muscle tension and attentional focus. With children, we can often do this with bodily contact – picking up a scared child and cuddling them can bring a sense of safety and can help their bodies to calm. Bodily contact is helpful for adults, too – hugs, an arm on the shoulder or a hand in theirs. Remember, though, not to go overboard, as when people are scared their senses are heightened, and a bear hug would likely feel overwhelming in this situation! Even without touch, using our own bodies to model a calmer position – a lower tone of voice, a slower pace of speech, sitting down – can help to reduce some of the tension others feel.

Once the other person is calmer and their rational brain is more engaged, we can start the process of talking about the situation and what they are afraid of, helping them to explore their interpretation and problem-solve the situation.

Fear trap: problems responding to fear ('Anxiety Disorders')

The Introduction outlined how mental health or emotional problems can be understood as difficulties responding to emotions. This section looks at the difficulties we might experience responding to fear, which covers a whole variety of experiences, including everything that might receive a diagnosis of any of the anxiety disorders. This would include specific phobias, agoraphobia, panic disorder, social anxiety disorder (or social phobia), generalised anxiety disorder, illness anxiety disorder (or health anxiety), obsessive-compulsive disorder and post-traumatic stress disorder. This section outlines how the model works in general, using examples. If, as you are reading, you think that the examples are very different from your own experience, keep going, because the model works for different types of fear, and there will most likely be examples closer to your own situation later in the chapter.

The most powerful ways of responding to fear are behavioural: escape and avoidance. These behaviours are closely linked with the function of fear in our lives, which is to protect us from danger and potential threat. The trouble is that our modern lives are associated with continual and powerful representations of potential threats. There are planes, fast cars, potential attackers, disasters and other people and their judgement.

What this means is that, as humans, our fear response can become associated with almost anything and, if we are not careful, we can find ourselves overusing escape and avoidance to respond to fear. This can become a real problem because of the way that the reptilian brain works. Here are two examples:

> Jake had an experience in an elevator that broke down and caused him to be stuck for almost an hour whilst an engineer was called. It was hot and horrible, and he was scared at being there by himself. The next time he thought about going into an elevator, he noticed his heart beating in his chest and he got a horrible feeling in his stomach, so he took the stairs instead. He told himself that it was better for his health anyway. Over time, he found that he had become more fearful of other small spaces like cupboards, tunnels and most recently, subway systems.

> Samantha had never liked dogs. She grew up without knowing anybody with a dog, but there was a loud dog that used to bark at her local park. She became upset and worried when this dog arrived at the park, so her parents used to take her back home whenever it was there. As she grew up, Samantha found that she would avoid going to the park because she was worried about seeing dogs, and whenever she was out, she was constantly on the lookout for dogs. She crossed the road if there was one coming towards her and noticed that she got tense and sweaty whenever she was near one. Recently, she was eating dinner at an outside table, but when a dog came to a nearby table, she moved inside. Her friends told her that she should build up her confidence around dogs, but she said that she hated feeling that way and so it made sense to try to keep away from them.

In these two examples, Jake and Samantha are experiencing all of the elements of fear we outlined earlier in the chapter: the thoughts, feelings, physiology, facial expressions and behavioural urges. These are responses of the reptilian brain that function to help them protect themselves from the danger: elevators and dogs. For both Jake and Samantha, the problem is that they are responding to elevators and dogs as if they represent real and immediate threats to their survival. In their rational brains, both Jake and Samantha know that elevators and dogs, whilst sometimes dangerous, are not as dangerous as they feel they are. In other words, both Jake and Samantha are overestimating the threat. As a result of their overestimate of the threat, they are avoiding aspects of their lives that they don't need to avoid.

This is the point at which the responses to fear have become unhelpful and instead of functioning to protect Jake and Samantha, are now getting in the way of their lives. This is when people may find themselves with a diagnosis of an anxiety disorder. A diagnosis of any anxiety disorder can be understood in this way: there is an overestimated threat that is maintained by an overuse of escape and avoidance, with the result that the problem has a negative impact on life. Neither Jake nor Samantha is experiencing anything fundamentally different from any other human being; they have just gotten caught in problematic ways of responding to fear.

Maintenance

What stops Jake from learning that elevators are – the majority of the time – safe and quick forms of transport? What stops Samantha from learning that dogs – whilst occasionally loud and potentially dangerous – are mostly friendly, harmless creatures?

There are two important factors here. The first is that the reptilian brain is instinctive and not rational; it cannot think things through in a logical manner but instead feels and experiences things. The second important factor is the overuse of avoidance and escape. If we put these things together, we can see that Jake's reptilian brain will never learn that elevators are mostly safe because he avoids them: his reptilian brain never has an experience of a safe journey in an elevator. Samantha's reptilian brain will never learn that most dogs are harmless because her reptilian brain never has an experience of a harmless dog, as she avoids dogs and escapes whenever she finds herself near one.

So our usual helpful, protective fear response can become tangled up in a vicious cycle of overestimated threat, avoiding and escaping the danger, with the result that we never find out that the danger is exaggerated. This is illustrated in the fear trap.

Over time and unchecked, going around and around the fear trap can have dramatic impacts on people's lives. Fear and avoidance can snowball, with the result that there is a greater impact on life and significant problems with functioning. For most people stuck in this fear trap, we can see a gradual deterioration, with increasing use of avoidance and escape, increasingly overestimated threat and an increase in the intensity and frequency of fear.

Jake's fear trap includes an overestimated threat: "I'm not safe in an elevator" or even "I'll die if I go in an elevator", and avoidance of travel in elevators. Over time, the overestimated threat appears to have developed so it might be more like "I'm not safe in small spaces" or even "I'm not safe", linked with avoidance of small spaces and new spaces.

Samantha's fear trap includes an overestimated threat: "I'll be attacked by a dog" or "I'm not safe around dogs", with avoidance of going anywhere a dog might be. She has spent so much of her life avoiding dogs and getting away from them that her reptilian brain (which is active when she feels threatened) has never learned that most dogs are friendly, harmless creatures.

Here is a third example:

Ali worked hard all his life, putting in long hours and taking on lots of responsibility. In his 50s, he had a heart attack. He had a pacemaker fitted and made changes to his diet so that his risk of another heart attack dramatically reduced. However, he remained very scared of having another heart attack, and so had not returned to work and had not left the house for five months. He checked his heart rate frequently and even stopped doing activities around the house, for fear that they would bring on a heart attack.

In this third example, we can see that the difficulties are having a much more dramatic impact on Ali's life, as he is almost unable to function.

The trigger for Ali's experience is a significant life event and the chance that he might experience another heart attack. Importantly, though, the way in which we understand fear and the impact of Ali's responses is exactly the same as the earlier examples, regardless of the severity of the situation or the level of impact it has. Ali is overestimating the threat that he will have another heart attack, and he is overusing avoidance by doing almost nothing. This avoidance stops his reptilian brain from learning that he could manage many aspects of his day-to-day life without having another heart attack.

Subtle forms of avoidance and safety behaviours

Sometimes, there is still an escalation and ongoing problem even without obvious avoidance. This is usually because of subtle forms of avoidance or what are called 'safety behaviours'.

Samantha's example highlights the role of safety behaviours:

> Samantha started to try to overcome her fear of dogs. She started by going to places that she had previously avoided, like parks and the beach. Whilst things felt as though they were improving initially, her progress stalled, and she could not get any further. Samantha explained that she had been wearing boots whenever she went to the park, because they would protect her legs if she were bitten, and she would look carefully at the owners of dogs to see if they looked friendly. Upon more prompting, she also said that she walked in what she felt was a 'confident' way, because she'd heard that dogs responded to confidence. Samantha was pretty sure that these things did not make any difference, but she did them because they made her feel a bit less fearful.

In this example, Samantha is working to reduce her avoidance and escape behaviours by putting herself in situations where she might come across dogs. However, she is doing a whole load of other things that are subtle forms of avoidance. These are called 'safety behaviours' because they make her feel safer, but they stop her reptilian brain from discovering what would happen if she went about her day-to-day life without doing anything differently. Again, the illogical nature of the reptilian brain is important. Wearing boots every time she goes somewhere might seem like a small thing to Samantha's rational brain, but her reptilian brain, in its illogical manner, concludes "it's a good job I wore boots to that park, otherwise that dog would have attacked

me" or "I'm glad I walked in that way, otherwise I would have been attacked". While Samantha's rational brain knows that these conclusions are not logical, her reptilian brain is still avoiding finding out what happens if Samantha goes about her life normally. This is illustrated in Samantha's fear trap.

**'Safety behaviours' are a response to threat and reduce fear
They prevent the reptilian brain from learning
that it is overestimating the threat**

Jake's example provides another illustration:

> Jake was due to start work in an office high up in a building. He spoke to people and read online about how to overcome his difficulties, and he began pushing himself to go in the elevator at work. He did this for a number of weeks but did not find that his fears reduced, and he became angry and frustrated. When asked to explain what he had been doing, Jake said that whenever he had gone in the elevator, he always put his headphones in and looked at his phone throughout his time in the elevator.

In this situation, Jake is working to reduce his avoidance and escape behaviours by travelling in the elevator. However, remember his reptilian brain and its illogical nature? Because Jake is keeping himself almost completely distracted while in the elevator – his reptilian brain's attempt to keep him safe – he is still avoiding letting his reptilian brain connect with the experience of travel in the elevator. Because he is so occupied with other things, his reptilian brain does not have the experience (the sights, sounds, smells, sensations) of travelling in an elevator and it being safe. This is illustrated in Jake's fear trap.

Ali's behaviours are mainly avoidant – he has stopped doing a great many different things. However, he is doing lots of checking of his heart rate. Checking things is a very common thing to do – checking internal bodily states, checking that things are locked or checking for keys on leaving the house. These might not seem like safety behaviours; after all, they are not actually changing anything, and they are so quick to do. But remember the reptilian brain and its irrational ways. Checking results in a small reduction in fear, which means that the reptilian brain is making an association between the check and a reduction in threat: "It's a good job I checked my heart rate, otherwise I'd have had a heart attack" or "It's a good job I checked I had my keys, or I'd have been locked out". These conclusions are clearly illogical, but so is the reptilian brain! The other behaviour that Ali is probably doing without really noticing is focusing his attention. Ali's fears are about his heart, and remember, our attention focuses on the threat. In this case, he is probably paying far more attention to his heart than he did before his heart attack. What might be the result of this? Try Exercise 1.5 to experiment with your attention.

Exercise 1.5 Attentional focus

Think, right now, of your left shoulder, all the muscle around your left shoulder and up to your neck.

Move your attention to this muscle and notice all of the sensations in it.

If you need to move it a little, then do so, and while you do, notice how it feels, whether there is any tension, any discomfort.

Focus your attention in on this muscle; imagine your attention like a spotlight beaming and focusing in on this muscle.

What do you notice as you do this?

Did you become aware of anything that you did not notice before?

Usually, if you increase your attentional focus on a particular thing, you notice things that you did not notice before. If you focus on a part of your body, it is common to notice sensations, maybe even discomfort or pain that you were not so aware of before. For Ali, he is likely to notice changes and sensations in his heart that he would otherwise not notice. This is likely to increase the overestimation of threat and keep the fear trap going. This is all shown in Ali's fear trap.

There is a whole range of other behaviours that might represent an avoidance of finding out what really happens in relation to a whole variety of fears. These include using alcohol, distraction, counting, rehearsing situations, planning, all sorts of bodily things like tensing or looking away, checking, asking others for reassurance and self-reassurance. In general, any behaviour that is done in response to the overestimated threat is likely to be a safety behaviour or a form of avoidance. So our full fear trap (below) has an overestimated threat that is maintained by avoidance and escape, as well as by safety behaviours.

Exercise 1.6 takes you through the process of drawing your own fear trap. It should look like the ones you've seen so far in this chapter.

Exercise 1.6   Draw your own fear trap

If you think you might be stuck in the fear trap, have a go at drawing your own fear trap.

Think about what the fear is: what is it, exactly, that you are scared of? It can often be easiest to think of a recent example when you were scared, which represents the difficulty that you are experiencing. Think about what your reptilian brain was predicting; remember that it is not rational and that it might sound silly or exaggerated to your rational brain. It is also likely to be a statement rather than a 'what if', so it may well start with "I will . . . " or "I am going to . . . "

My overestimated threat is...

The next task is to think about all of the things that you do that are avoidance, escape or safety behaviours. Remember, these behaviours are any behaviours that are responses to the threat and bring relief, at least in the short term. They might be clearly related to the threat or might be almost entirely unrelated but still result in a sense of relief. Think about things that you don't do that you might otherwise do; think about things that you might keep with you, where you focus your attention, or things that you might do with your body (e.g., posture, checking, tensing).

My adoidance, escape, and safety behaviours are...

Don't worry if this is difficult to do at this point. Later in the chapter, there will be examples of all sorts of different fear traps relating to different types of fears, which should help you if you are finding this difficult now.

Getting out of the fear trap

The fear trap highlights what happens when we have difficulties responding to fear. This section outlines the best course of action to tackle these difficulties. It is based on the interventions of CBT and the best available evidence.[14]

Reducing avoidance, escape and safety behaviours

The previous section on the fear trap highlighted the link between an overestimate of threat and an overuse of avoidance and escape in maintaining difficulties with fear.

Returning to this trap helps us to consider the best way out of the trap and to overcome the difficulties. To break the vicious cycle of the fear trap, we need to use different responses to fear and reduce the use of avoidance and escape. Rather than running away and avoiding the things we are scared of, we have to encourage ourselves to tolerate the fear by approaching these things and getting nearer to them.

This focus on our behaviour fits with the way the brain works. Thoughts are a function of the rational brain, but the fear response is driven by the reptilian brain, which is not rational. Trying to think your way out of the fear trap is like trying to explain to a crocodile that it does not need to be scared. The rational brain might be able to understand that the threat is not as scary as it thinks it is, but the reptilian brain has to be shown, has to experience the situation as not as dangerous as it thinks.

> **The only way out of the fear trap is to reduce the avoidance, escape and safety behaviours**

Circles

Doing things that have become the focus for the fear trap is very easy in principle, but actually doing it is very different. Imagine how hard it would be for Samantha, who has spent many years of her life avoiding dogs, to just stop avoiding dogs! Jake might also not respond very well to being told that he just has to get in elevators and stop distracting himself! And how about telling Ali to stop avoiding a heart attack? There are ways to build up confidence and gradually reduce avoidance, escape and safety behaviours over time. The easiest way to understand how to do it is to use the circles.

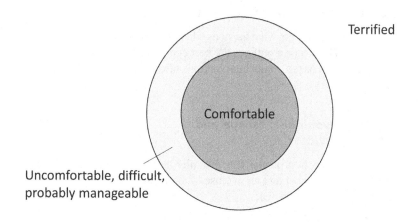

In the diagram, the inner circle includes everything that we find comfortable and not concerning; for example, staying at home and watching TV, reading a book or going to see a close friend. Everything outside the outer circle is terrifying. This might include doing a skydive or a bungee jump but might also include (for Samantha, for example) stroking a dog or (for Jake) getting in an elevator and going up 15 floors. There is a gap between the two circles; the gap between things that are comfortable and things that are terrifying. Activities in this area are uncomfortable and difficult but are probably manageable.

The idea behind these three circles is that humans, like most species, are creatures of habit; we like to do the same things over and over again. Regular activities become comfortable and fall into the comfortable zone, and rare activities fall into the terrified zone. Activities in the uncomfortable zone that are repeated will, over time, move into the comfortable zone. The comfortable zone expands to include these things and eventually, things that were in the terrified zone will move into the uncomfortable zone and then into the comfortable zone.

Returning to the way our brain works can help us further think about what is going on here. In the comfortable zone, we are just doing what we are comfortable with – nothing new is being tackled – so the reptilian brain is offline and can't learn anything new. In the terrified zone, the reptilian brain dominates and is in such a state of panic that it is difficult to learn anything. This is the 'flipped lid' (see the 'hand brain' in the Introduction). In the uncomfortable zone, the rational brain is online and the reptilian brain is also active and scared; the two can operate together to remain in and learn from new experiences.

When we are stuck in the fear trap, what we need to do is to gradually reduce our use of escape, avoidance and safety behaviours by doing things that are in the uncomfortable zone. Over time, these things will become increasingly comfortable, and we can then step things up and start on things that might now feel uncomfortable that would previously have felt closer to terrifying or overwhelming. There are a number of other considerations to ensure that you manage to do this properly.

Remember that you are trying to teach your reptilian brain new information – that it is overestimating the threat, that the threat is not as bad as it thinks it is. Repetition is an important part of learning, and so you will need to do this regularly. Also, you will need to do things for long enough for your reptilian brain to have an experience of it being safer than it thinks it is, rather than concluding that something dreadful would have happened if you had stayed or done the activity any longer. The best way to judge how long is long enough is to notice how it feels. When your reptilian brain has calmed a little, this usually indicates that it has had a different experience.

**To reduce the overestimate of threat,
regularly do things in the uncomfortable zone**

Exposure and reducing avoidance

There are two ways to think about organising the tasks that will push you into the uncomfortable zone. The first is to approach things that you normally avoid – a process known as exposure – which might involve doing things that are slightly artificial purely for the purposes of teaching your reptilian brain. For Samantha, this might mean going near parks where lots of dogs go and building up to visiting a friend's dog. For Jake, this might mean watching videos about elevators and working towards the point where he can take a ride in a high elevator. For Ali, this might involve going slightly quicker up the stairs and working towards going out for a run. These are activities that they have decided to do to challenge themselves and to teach their reptilian brain something new. Sometimes they can be thought of as experiments that push us and make us do things that we would otherwise avoid.

Another way to think about doing these tasks is to stop doing the things that you normally do to avoid your fears. This might mean stopping doing safety behaviours and stopping avoiding usual activities. For Jake, this might mean not getting his phone out as soon as he gets in the elevator, or not checking in advance what floor the office he is visiting is on. For Samantha, this might be choosing a route to walk without taking into account how likely it is that she would meet a dog and not crossing the road if she does see one. Ali might need to reduce how often he checks his heart rate.

The tasks in the first group are artificial and are challenges to teach the reptilian brain something new. These should be planned and organised in advance, and then done only a few times. The tasks in the second group involve stopping doing things that you do to prevent coming into contact with the fears, and these should all be stopped so that you move towards 'normal' living. Exercise 1.7 helps you make your own plan to get out of your own fear trap.

Exercise 1.7   Breaking out of your own fear trap

When you have drawn your fear trap, have a go at thinking about what kinds of behaviours you might need to stop doing to get out of the fear trap.

You might need to stop avoiding things, so your first task might be to push yourself to do things that you don't usually do. These will be like experiments or challenges to see 'what happens if...'. Remember to make sure that these activities make you feel uncomfortable, but that you think you can probably tolerate them. If they are too easy, they will be in the comfortable zone and your reptilian brain won't learn anything new. If they are too difficult, your reptilian brain will be too overwhelmed to learn, and you will just have a horrible experience. You want to push yourself to the edge of the uncomfortable zone – to see how much you can manage. Then, think about how you can build on each one.

You will probably also need to stop doing things that you do to avoid feeling scared – your safety behaviours. You'll need to think about which things you could stop doing, so that it would feel uncomfortable but that you could probably cope with. If you make too-small changes, your reptilian brain won't learn anything new; if you try to stop everything all at once, your reptilian brain will be overwhelmed. You want lots of repetition, so pick things you can do at least once every day, more often if possible.

Different types of fear traps

There are many different things that we can find ourselves afraid of, and there are a whole variety of different mental health diagnoses that relate to difficulties with fear. These emphasise the differences between fears and downplay the similarities. This chapter highlights that underneath it all, the experience of fear, the ways we can respond to it and the difficulties we might have in responding to it are always the same. As long as the two aspects of the fear trap are clear – the overestimated threat and the avoidance, escape and safety behaviours – this is enough to work with problems with fear, regardless of the type of fear experienced.

This section outlines many common fears and provides examples of what the overestimated threat and associated behaviours might be, to help you identify your own experiences.

Particular groups of fears are highlighted:

- Fears of specific creatures or situations (specific phobias)
- Social fears (social anxiety disorder or social phobia)
- Bodily fears, which include panic attacks, fears of panic attacks (panic disorder and panic disorder with agoraphobia), fears about illness (illness anxiety disorder or health anxiety disorder, and eme-tophobia or vomit phobia)
- Worry (generalised anxiety disorder)
- Obsessive-compulsive fears (obsessive-compulsive disorder)
- Trauma (post-traumatic stress disorder)

Fears of specific creatures or situations, e.g., small creatures, thunder, water, blood, elevators or clowns (specific phobias)

Many of our fears link with specific situations or objects, and many people in the fear trap have overestimated fears of particular creatures or situations. Two of our earlier examples were fears of specific situations: Jake had a fear of elevators, and Samantha had a fear of dogs. Their fear traps and the things they need to do to get out of these fear traps are out-lined earlier in this chapter.

Most fears of specific objects or situations will follow the process in exactly the same way as Jake and Samantha. There are some, though, where there is disgust as well as fear. The main examples of these are fears of small creatures (like spiders, rats, mice and insects) and fears of blood-injury and injection, as well as of particular types of food. For these kinds of fears, the fear trap works in exactly the same way, as does the way out of the fear trap. Understanding the role that disgust can play is helpful, though, and there are examples of these kinds of fear traps in Chapter 4 on disgust.

Social fears (social anxiety disorder or social phobia)

Fear of social situations is one of the four groups of common fears for humans. We are social beings and being included in social groups is very important to us. Most fears in social situations relate to something about the way in which we will be perceived by others. Here is an example:

> Michelle had always been a shy person, but she was able to make friends at school and managed to get a job she enjoyed. As she developed in her job, she started to have to attend more meetings and give presentations, something she never found easy and started to dread. On one occasion, she got so stressed that she couldn't get her words out and excused herself from the meeting. Ever since then, she's been convinced that this will happen again and that everybody will think she's an idiot and no good at her job. She's tried to avoid meetings, and when she has gone, she's made sure she's sat down, written out everything she's going to say and has water with her to drink.

Remember, the fear trap has two main components: an overestimation of threat and avoidance, escape and safety behaviours. See if you can spot Michelle's overestimation of threat and her avoidance, escape and safety behaviours.

Michelle's fear trap includes an overestimation of threat, something like: "I'm going to panic, and everybody will think I'm an idiot". Her avoidance, escape and safety behaviours include avoiding the meeting, sitting down, writing down everything she's going to say and having water to drink. These are the things she notices, but she may also do other things like avoiding making eye contact, concentrating on her paper and speaking more quickly. Remember, too, that our attention follows what we believe to be the threat, which in this case is that she is going to panic and people will then think she's an idiot. For Michelle, it is likely that her attention is focused on herself and trying not to panic and look like an idiot. She might even have a picture of herself in her mind that represents what she thinks she looks like.[15]

Importantly, Michelle's sense that she'll look like an idiot and her attentional focus on herself are also consistent with shame. Shame – and less intense embarrassment – are characterised by a sense of feeling inadequate or flawed, particularly in front of others. Feeling embarrassed or ashamed leads to an intense attentional focus on ourselves that can result in losing our ability to think clearly or to perform. So Michelle's fear that she will embarrass herself focuses her attention on how she is coming across, which makes it more likely that she will feel embarrassed or ashamed. For this reason, there is an overlap with embarrassment and shame in social fears,[16] and it is worth reading the chapter on shame (Chapter 6) to better understand the whole experience.

We can see how this looks in Michelle's fear trap.

Michelle is working really hard to try to make sure that she does not panic and look like an idiot, and all of these behaviours might feel like they are helping her. But the problem is that she is preventing her reptilian brain from finding out what happens if she does not do these things, what happens if she gives her presentation without doing all of this.

What does she have to do from here, then?

The fear trap always works in the same way, so Michelle has to try to reduce all of the behaviours on the right so that her reptilian brain learns that it is overestimating the threat. She has to give some presentations whilst not doing all of the other things at the same time. One way to make this feel less overwhelming would be for her to experiment doing presentations not at work – maybe with friends or family, or even in front of a mirror. She could stand up, not write down everything she's going to say, not have water with her, make eye contact, and focus her attention outwards on what she's talking about rather than on how she thinks she's coming across to other people (see Chapter 6 for this too). She can find out how much she panics and whether she does look like an idiot. She

"I'm going to panic and look like an idiot"   **MICHELLE'S FEAR TRAP**   Avoid meetings
Sit down
Write everything down
Have water
Avoid eye contact
Speak quickly
Focus attention on self

could even record a video of herself doing this, so she can see herself afterwards and determine whether she really looks as bad as her reptilian brain thinks she does.

Of course, none of this is easy, and it will be very difficult for Michelle to do these things, but if she can build up from a couple of minutes in front of a friend, over time she will find that her reptilian brain learns that it is overestimating the fear, and her confidence will grow.

If the fears are about more general social situations, the process is basically the same, and the task is to gradually increase social inter-actions whilst not doing all of the safety behaviours. Examples would include talking to people in shops, saying just a little bit more when talking to other people, asking one extra question or approaching people rather than waiting to be approached. Attention would need to be focused on the conversation and not on how you're coming across to others, and all the safety behaviours would need to be reduced.

Bodily fears (panic attacks, fears about illness, fears about being sick)

Fears about death and injury are common among the general population because these are very real threats to our existence. It makes sense to be concerned about our health and potential dangers to our health. Like with other fears, though, responding with too much avoidance, including safety behaviours, to these fears can lead us into the fear trap.

Ali's example illustrates a common cycle in panic attacks. Following Ali's heart attack, he overestimated the threat that he would have another. He linked this threat with monitoring his heart rate. Fear is linked to an increase in heart rate, and so monitoring his heart rate and noticing the increase in heart rate linked with his fear is likely to fuel his overestima-tion of threat. So the more that Ali thinks he's having a heart attack (his overestimated threat), the faster his heart beats (the fear response). The faster his heart beats, the more that Ali is convinced he's having a heart attack. This is a common pattern seen in fears about the body: the bodily response to fear is misinterpreted to mean something else and fuels the fear trap.[17]

Ayesha provides another example:

> Ayesha had disliked the idea of being sick for many years, and her fears about it had gradually got worse. Over time, this fear had come to dominate much of her life. She did all of the cooking at home and spent lots of her time cleaning the house. She did not like going out

to eat and would only go to the same three restaurants; she did not like going to her children's schools and tried to get her husband to go instead; and she could not watch programmes on TV about health or hospitals. When her children came home from school, she would ask them questions about whether there was anybody at school who had been ill. When Ayesha felt sick, which was three or four times a week, she would spend hours sitting in the bathroom, doing breathing exercises and holding her stomach. All of this was despite the fact that she had not been sick since her pregnancy some years ago, and even then, it had not been that bad.

Ayesha's fears are longstanding and have grown over time. What kinds of things does she do that keep her stuck in the fear trap? What is the overlap between the bodily response to fear and feeling sick?

Ayesha does many things that keep her stuck in the fear trap in the longer term, which include avoiding eating food that others have cooked, probably overcleaning the house and asking her children about other children who might have been ill. These are some of the things that Ayesha is most likely to be able to notice. But like Ali and his heart, Ayesha is also likely to be doing more subtle things that keep her stuck in the fear trap. The most likely one is focusing her attention on how her body feels, noticing the changes in her stomach. As a result, she is likely to be misinterpreting her bodily response to fear as a sign that she is going to be sick. Remember the changes to the 'rest-and-digest' system, the slowing down of digestion and the uncomfortable feelings that come when we are scared? This does feel a bit like sickness, but for Ayesha, who hasn't been sick for some time, it is likely to be fear rather than sickness she is feeling. But Ayesha is doing lots of things that prevent her reptilian brain from finding this out. She is staying in the bathroom, doing things with her breathing and tensing her muscles. All of this means that her reptilian brain is learning that doing these things is what stops her from being sick, and so she is left with her overestimation of the likelihood of being sick. Ayesha's many behaviours also fuel the sense that being sick is awful, even though the last time she was sick, it wasn't that bad. This is shown in Ayesha's fear trap.

So Ali's and Ayesha's fear traps are the same as all of the other fear traps in this chapter. An overestimated threat is maintained by avoidance, escape and safety behaviours. The only difference is that they also include a misinterpretation of the body's response to fear, which is linked with the overestimation of threat. Ali misinterprets the changes

"I'm going to be sick and it will be terrible"	**AYESHA'S FEAR TRAP**	Avoid eating out and schools Avoid thinking about sickness Overclean house Check with children Focus attention on stomach Change breathing and muscles when feeling sick

in his heart rate driven by fear as a sign that he is having a heart attack. Ayesha misinterprets the sensations in her digestive system driven by fear as a sign that she is going to be sick. If Ali and Ayesha reduce their avoidance, escape and safety behaviours, their reptilian brains will find out that these are the result of fear and not of heart attacks or sickness.

Fear traps that are based on being ill or having a particular disease follow the same pattern as all the other fear traps in this book, and again, the extra attention paid to the part of the body where there is overestimated threat will result in more sensations being noticed in these areas and these sensations being interpreted as signs of illness.

Worry (generalised anxiety disorder – GAD)

Earlier in the chapter, we highlighted that most fears were clearly linked with a particular cause or object. We also discussed how some fears were more abstract and resulted in worry linked to all sorts of things. These kinds of fears are usually at lower levels of intensity, but there may be times where these fears feel overwhelming. Often, people talk about never really being able to relax or generally feeling stressed about everything for most of the time. An example will illustrate:

Emily was described by her friends as an organiser and described herself as an overthinker. Whenever she was doing something unusual, like going on holiday or attending an important meeting at work, she would think about it in detail, go over all the things that might happen and often think about the worst-case scenario. She would organise and plan everything in advance, so her family and friends often expected her to do the planning for larger events. Because doing new things needed so much planning, Emily tended to stick to a routine, doing similar things on weekends and going to similar places. She would say to her family, "It just makes things easier – we know what to expect." Emily found that most of the time, things were okay, but when things did not happen how she expected – somebody at work made a negative comment, for example – she found herself dwelling on it and thinking about it so much that she felt very stressed and could not sleep. When she had children, she found that there were more things to worry about, and when they went to daycare she was preoccupied all day wondering what might happen to them.

For Emily, there is no particular thing that she is finding difficult to manage, no specific fear she is avoiding. However, she is experiencing ongoing lower levels of fear throughout her life. How can we use the fear trap to help Emily understand what is going on and help her to better manage things?

Emily's fear is more abstract than the others in this chapter. Her fear is of uncertainty, of not feeling in control.[18] For Emily, new situations bring the potential for uncertainty and not knowing what's happening. She may well say things like "Once I know what's going on, I'm fine, it's the not knowing that's difficult." So if Emily has a fear of being uncertain or not being in control, what kind of things is she doing to try to manage this fear?

The first is avoidance. Emily avoids situations that are uncertain. She tends to go to the same places, sticks to the same routines and tries to avoid new things. When she does do new things, she tries to reduce the uncertainty by planning and organising. If she can find out about things in advance, plan routes, book things and organise what everybody is doing, then uncertainty is reduced. Emily also worries. Worry is a particular type of thinking where thoughts tend to go around and around, going through many different "what if . . ." situations, often with a negative focus. This type of thinking can make Emily feel that she is reducing uncertainty because she has been through all of the different situations in her mind beforehand. For some situations, thinking and planning in advance can help – for example, booking flights and finding routes from an airport to a hotel. For other situations, though, thinking in this way fills Emily's head with all sorts of disastrous outcomes, like "What if my child falls ill?" Worrying about things that haven't happened yet – which are often "what if . . . " thoughts – can produce more worries and make Emily feel even more uncertain and out of control.

This is shown in Emily's fear trap.

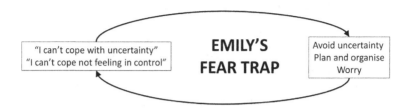

"I can't cope with uncertainty"
"I can't cope not feeling in control"

EMILY'S
FEAR TRAP

Avoid uncertainty
Plan and organise
Worry

Her overestimated threat is that she cannot cope with uncertainty or not feeling in control. This threat is maintained by avoiding uncertainty, planning, organising and worrying. These behaviours stop Emily from finding out whether she cope with uncertainty, whether she would be okay not always feeling in control.

Now that we have Emily's fear trap, we can think about how she might start getting out of it. The first thing for Emily to do is reduce her avoidance of uncertainty. Emily needs to find something she can do that is in the uncomfortable zone of the circles. This is likely to be an experiment to test how well she actually copes with uncertainty – something small, like sending an email without checking it or going to a new restaurant without looking at the menu beforehand. Over time, Emily can build up the level of uncertainty she is trying to cope with – for example, by letting somebody else organise something without telling her what they are going to do – and this can help to adjust the overestimation of threat. Emily should find over time that she can cope with uncertainty and not feeling in control better than she thought (i.e., that she was overestimating the threat) and she can continue to reduce her planning and organising by allowing other people to do some of it.

One of the problems Emily might face in doing this is with her worries. Worrying is something Emily does in response to her overestimation of threat that she cannot cope with uncertainty or not feeling in control. But worrying might not *feel* like something she chooses to do. Worrying can become such a habit that it feels like it just happens by itself and there is nothing we can do to stop it. This is particularly true because, when we are scared, our attention is drawn towards the threat, and trying to move it away can be difficult. In this case, there are some tricks that can help to reduce worry.

The first is 'worry time'.[19] Worry time is a scheduled part of the day devoted to worry, just worry and nothing else. It is usually best to pick a period of about 20–30 minutes, towards the end of the day but not too close to bedtime. Throughout the day, any worries that pop into Emily's head can be worried about not then and there, but during the worry time. She can make a note of the worry (just a headline) and then review it during the worry time, or she can trust that she will remember the worries during the worry time. During this time, Emily just worries, nothing else, and she makes sure that she worries for the whole time – otherwise, she won't believe herself the next day when she says she can push her worries to the worry time. This process can help Emily feel more in control of her worries, evaluate her worries better and explore what it is like to have periods when she worries and periods when she doesn't.

If Emily's worries are almost continuous and it feels too difficult to squash them into a worry time, she can instead book into her diary 'worry-free time'. These are particular times in the day when she says that she will not worry. If any worries pop into her head at these times, she can remind herself that she can worry about them after the worry-free time. As she gains more control over her worries, she can swap to having worry time rather than worry-free time.

Another common problem linked with worry, although less so in Emily's case, is that of making decisions. Deciding between different options leaves open the possibility that we've chosen the wrong one, and a whole load of uncertainty and potential unknowns. If you find decisions difficult, then the overestimated threat might be "I'll make the wrong decision" or "I'm not capable of making decisions"; the behaviours will likely be avoidance of decisions and lots of worry about whether you've made the right decision and what might have happened if you'd made a different one. The fear trap works in the same way, and you'll have to approach decisions that are uncomfortable but manageable without doing the worrying and, over time, challenge the overestimated threats that you cannot make decisions or that you'll always make the wrong decision.

So even though the fear is slightly different for worry, the fear trap is the same, and the intervention is the same. The avoidance, escape and safety behaviours have to be reduced in order to reduce the overestimation of threat and get out of the fear trap.

Obsessive compulsive fears (obsessive-compulsive disorder – OCD)

Sometimes fears of unlikely events, that we know to be unlikely, can still drive our behaviour. When this happens, our thoughts often fit a pattern like "if I don't do x, then y will happen"; for example "If I don't wash

my hands for a full minute, I'll get ill", or "If I don't step in this particular way, then my mum will have an accident". These difficulties are
often called obsessive-compulsive, where the obsession is the thought
and the compulsion is the behaviour. Obsessions are repeating patterns
of thought, and compulsions are repeated patterns of behaviour. This is
where the term 'obsessive-compulsive disorder' comes from. Here is an
example:

> Ever since her grandmother died, Sofia worried about something
> happening to her family. She was close with her family and even
> though they were all healthy, she still found herself imagining some-
> thing terrible happening to them. When she was younger, she had
> taken on some of her mother's superstitions and had touched wood
> whenever she'd had a thought like this. Over time, this had grown,
> and she found herself touching things in a particular order whenever
> she had a horrible thought and having to do it again until she got rid
> of the thought. This had got gradually worse so that she tended to
> avoid going to places or watching programmes that might trigger off
> these thoughts and was spending increasing amounts of time touch-
> ing things or thinking about each thing in her head, if she could not
> touch them directly. Sometimes she asked her mother to tell her that
> things were going to be okay, or asked her mother to touch things
> for her.

In this example, Sofia is having lots of thoughts about terrible things
happening to people. These kinds of thoughts can be called 'obsessions'. Thoughts like these tend to pop into all of our minds from time
to time – thoughts about our own death, thoughts about other people
dying or sexually inappropriate thoughts. These kinds of thoughts are
quite normal in the population and are just the result of our brains throwing ideas together to see what happens. The problem for Sofia is that
these thoughts scare her, and she perceives them as threatening. Why
might Sofia find thoughts like these threatening? At some level, Sofia
believes that that having these thoughts or obsessions will somehow lead
to these things happening. This is Sofia's overestimated threat: "having
these thoughts makes it more likely that these bad things will happen".
As a result of this overestimated threat, Sofia engages in lots of avoidance and safety behaviours, like tapping things or thinking about things.
The tapping and repetitive thoughts are called compulsions. So Sofia
has a strong link between the obsessions and the compulsions, and it

is this link between obsessions and compulsions that leads to the term obsessive-compulsive disorder. This is shown in Sofia's fear trap.

In this example, we can see that Sofia does some of her behaviours or compulsions in her head. This is common, and just because she's doing something in her mind doesn't make it any different – it is still a behaviour carried out in response to the overestimated threat and it still fuels the fear trap in the same way. She also needs to reduce and then stop doing it if she is ever going to get out of the fear trap.

We can see that Sofia's fear trap is just like the others in this chapter, and the things that she needs to do are the same if she is going to get out of the fear trap. Something that can add a slightly different dimension is that the kinds of thoughts that Sofia is having will make her feel scared, but they may also make her feel guilty. This is because Sofia's ideas about her family and her role in keeping them safe make her feel responsible for her family. Chapter 5 explores guilt and shows how overestimations of responsibility lead to feelings of guilt that can make people work hard to try to make things better. For Sofia, this might lead to feelings of both fear and guilt driving the behaviours on the right of the fear trap. In this case, reducing the avoidance, escape and safety behaviours will reduce both the overestimate of threat and the overestimate of responsibility.[20] Still, it would probably help Sofia to understand how guilt works too by reading Chapter 5.

The term OCD is often used to describe excessive tidiness or cleanliness, and sometimes the behaviours or compulsions are to keep things in order or to keep things clean, but this is not always the case. Any kind of thought can become an obsession, and any kind of behaviour can become a compulsion. The overestimated threat is always what the obsessions mean and why they are threatening, and the compulsions are the behaviours on the right that keep the overestimated threat going.

Difficult memories (post-traumatic stress disorder – PTSD)

During the course of our lives, we will all experience difficult events. We will lose pets, relatives and friends; we will have accidents and injuries; people close to us will be injured or hurt. We may also experience hurt and harm at the hands of others – insults, burglaries, thefts and assaults. We might experience natural disasters and events that are random and unexpected. All of these things are a fact of life, but they are painful and difficult to deal with.

Following these kinds of events, we usually experience a variety of emotions: maybe fear but also anger, sadness or guilt. Often, the memories of these events keep popping into our minds following the events, and we might have regular experiences of intense emotion at these times. We might talk about these events with others, think about them in different ways, have new experiences in the same places or different experiences that overlay the previous experience. This means that the memories of the events get organised or 'processed'. As they are processed over time, these memories pop into our minds less and less often and the emotions linked with the events will fade and reduce over time. Eventually, we get to the point where we can remember a difficult and painful time in our lives without feeling intense emotion at the time we think about it.

Sometimes, though, memories of difficult events don't fade in this way.

> Scott was mugged by two men at knifepoint while walking down a quiet street at night. They took his phone, but he returned home safe and unharmed. Following this event, he found himself feeling on edge whenever he left his house. He never went down that street again, preferring to take large detours instead, and he avoided going out on his own at night. He also didn't talk about the event after it happened and tried very hard not to think about it, avoiding TV shows or conversations that reminded him of it and pushing it out whenever it popped into his mind. Even though Scott tried not to think about the event, he found that he had lots of dreams related to it and vivid memories of it that made him feel scared.

Scott found the experience of being mugged at knifepoint intensely difficult and distressing. As a result, he tried not think about it and avoided

reminders of it. The problem for Scott is that the memories of the event get stuck; they are not processed (instead remaining 'unprocessed') and do not fade or change over time. This brings with it extra difficulties, as the unprocessed memories of the event, although in reality in the past, *feel* as though they are relevant to the present. Unprocessed memories of this type can produce 'flashbacks' and nightmares, and it can feel as though it is very likely to happen again. The presence of unprocessed memories of difficult events is often given the label post-traumatic stress disorder.[21]

How would Scott's experience fit into the fear trap?

Scott is overestimating the threat of the memories of the past event. He experienced a very real threat, a very scary situation, but this was in the past and he survived it. Yet he is responding to the memories of the event as if they represent a current threat to him. As a result of overestimating the threat of the memories, he is avoiding a great deal: avoiding thinking about it, talking about it, feeling any of the emotions relating to it and trying to avoid reminders. But Scott isn't only over-estimating the threat of thinking about the memory; he is also over-estimating the threat that it will happen again. This is very common following a difficult event but particularly where the memories of the event remain unprocessed. As a result of overestimating the threat that it will happen again, Scott is also avoiding going to the place where it happened, and avoiding going out at night. All of this is shown in Scott's fear trap.

Scott's fear trap works in exactly the same way as the other fear traps in this chapter. He is overestimating the threat, and he needs to reduce his avoidance, escape and safety behaviours to allow his reptilian brain to find out that the threat is not as great as he thinks it is.

What does Scott need to do to get out of the fear trap?

Scott can approach his fear trap in the same way as all of the others; he can reduce the behaviours on the right to reduce the overestimated

threats on the left. If Scott works to reduce his avoidance of the memories of the event, thinking a bit about it and talking about it, this will be
difficult and distressing, but over time it will also allow him to process
the memories, which will support him to reduce the overestimations of
the threat of it happening again. Scott can approach all of this in the same
way, using the circles to consider what would be uncomfortable but manageable in terms of talking about it – perhaps saying a little bit more to
people he's close to, or doing an experiment where he talks all the way
through it with somebody he trusts. He could also reduce his avoidance
of reminders like TV shows and start to go out to different places with
other people when it's getting dark. Scott's aim is to reduce his avoidance of the memory and the things associated with it so that his reptilian
brain can learn that it is overestimating the threat of the memory and of
his being mugged again.

For some difficult events, people will be left not only with intense
feelings of fear but with other emotions too. Another example of a difficult event that results in problems with overestimations of responsibility
and intense guilt is provided in Chapter 5.

Summary

This chapter began with an understanding of fear: that it is a common
human emotion that uses the sympathetic nervous system to gear up the
body and the mind to respond to threat. It is an important emotion that
serves to protect us in a great many situations.

The most common response to fear is escape and avoidance, but there
are also more subtle ways we can respond; for example, by gently countering three parts of the sympathetic nervous system: breathing, muscle
tension and attentional focus. Responding in this way can allow us to go
through with actions or remain in situations that make us feel nervous
or scared, and so allow us to experience excitement, exhilaration and
achievement.

Fear, however, is not always helpful, and if we overuse escape and
avoidance, we can find ourselves having difficulties with fear in a variety
of different situations. The fear trap illustrates the links between overestimated threat and the overuse of these responses and shows how reducing avoidance, escape and safety behaviours can break the fear trap. This
chapter has provided examples of using the same basic fear trap with lots
of different fears. The same trap works, and the ways out of the fear trap
are all the same, no matter what the fear.

Notes

1 An analysis of online searches for "fear of . . . " in 2008 found that the top ten were flying, heights, clowns, intimacy, death, rejection, people, snakes, failure and driving (Tancer, 2008). In 2005, adolescents in America were asked what they feared most and reported terrorist attacks at number one, shortly followed by spiders, death/dying, failure, war and heights (Lyons, 2005).

2 In one review, 39 different studies were brought together to test how well these four factors accounted for all the various fears that individuals identified. They found that over 90% of fears fit into one of the four categories (Arrindell et al., 1991).

3 For the full study, please see Mineka et al. (1984).

4 Gerull and Rapee (2002)

5 In a study in the Netherlands of a random community sample, over 40% of people surveyed reported that they had experienced a strong, unreasonable fear at some point in their lives. The highest rated were heights, animals, enclosed spaces and blood (Depla et al., 2008).

6 A fascinating study of emotional experience across 37 countries and five continents reveals remarkable similarities in the experience of the basic emotions (joy, fear, anger, sadness, disgust, shame and guilt) across the world. These conclusions come from Scherer & Wallbott, 1994.

7 Tranel et al. (2006).

8 APA (2013).

9 Epstein (1972).

10 Izard (1991).

11 Izard (1991)

12 Sandseter (2009).

13 An interesting study by Alison Brooks included four different studies exploring the impact of moving from fear to excitement in areas like public speaking, mathematics tests and karaoke singing. In each study, those participants who were encouraged in various ways to view themselves as excited rather than scared, increased their excitement, which helped them view situations as opportunities rather than threats and improved their performance (Brooks, 2014).

14 Meta-analytic reviews support the use of CBT for those diagnosed with anxiety disorders, whether adults (e.g., Hofmann et al., 2012) or children and adolescents (James et al., 2015). Despite the variety of models available, there is little evidence to support the use of one model of CBT over another; a recent meta-analytic review found no evidence that disorder-specific CBT was more effective than generic CBT for children and adolescents (Oldham-Cooper & Loades, 2017). In adults, there is evidence to support the use of the Clark and Wells (1995) model of social anxiety over more generic models, but this should be interpreted with the caution that all trials were conducted by the developer. This chapter outlines a generic CBT formulation for fear-based difficulties that leads to interventions that are consistent with the evidence base: a focus on behavioural intervention and behavioural experimentation that is designed to target specific fears. The resulting interventions are consistent with disorder-specific interventions, as outlined in the section on specific presentations.

15 The internal focus of attention and a worst-case scenario image are important parts of the Clark and Wells (1995) model.
16 For example, Hedman et al. (2013) found higher levels of shame in those experiencing social fears, and noted that shame was reduced alongside fear as a result of CBT intervention.
17 The misinterpretation of bodily signals is a central part of one model of CBT for working with panic attacks (Clark, 1986).
18 The link between worry and uncertainty is a core part of the formulation for one evidence-based model of working with worry. The associated behaviours and intervention outlined in this chapter are consistent with this model (Robichaud & Dugas, 2015).
19 Worry time and worry-free time are concepts outlined in a different treatment manual for difficulties with worry (Borkovec & Sharpless, 2004).
20 The ideas included here are consistent with the cognitive model of OCD (Salkovskis, 1999). There is also evidence of increased experience of guilt with these kinds of difficulties (Geissner et al., 2020).
21 These two constructs are important parts of CBT for PTSD programmes (Ehlers & Clark, 2000).

References

APA, 2013. *Diagnostic and statistical manual of mental disorders* (5th edn.). Washington, DC: Author.
Arrindell, W.A., Pickersgill, M.J., Merckelbach, H., Ardon, A.M. and Cornet, F.C., 1991. Phobic dimensions: III. Factor analytic approaches to the study of common phobic fears; An updated review of findings obtained with adult subjects. *Advances in Behaviour Research and Therapy*, 13(2), pp. 73–130.
Borkovec, T.D. and Sharpless, B., 2004. Generalized anxiety disorder: Bringing cognitive behavioral therapy into the valued present. In S. Hayes, V. Follette, and M. Linehan (eds.), *Mindfulness and acceptance: Expanding the cognitive behavioral tradition*. New York: Guilford Press, pp. 209–242.
Brooks, A.W., 2014. Get excited: Reappraising pre-performance anxiety as excitement. *Journal of Experimental Psychology: General*, 143(3), p. 1144.
Clark, D.M., 1986. A cognitive approach to panic. *Behaviour Research and Therapy*, 24(4), pp. 461–470.
Clark, D.M. and Wells, A., 1995. A cognitive model of social phobia. In R.G. Heimberg, M. Liebowitz, D. Hope, and F.R. Schneier (eds.), *Social phobia: Diagnosis, assessment, and treatment*. New York: Guilford Press, pp. 69–93.
Depla, M.F., Margreet, L., van Balkom, A.J. and de Graaf, R., 2008. Specific fears and phobias in the general population: Results from the Netherlands Mental Health Survey and Incidence Study (NEMESIS). *Social Psychiatry and Psychiatric Epidemiology*, 43(3), pp. 200–208.
Ehlers, A. and Clark, D.M., 2000. A cognitive model of posttraumatic stress disorder. *Behaviour Research and Therapy*, 38(4), pp. 319–345.
Epstein, S., 1972. The nature of anxiety with emphasis upon its relationship to expectancy. In C.D. Spielberger (ed.), *Anxiety: Current trends in theory and research* (Vol.). New York: Academic Press.

Geissner, E., Knechtl, L.M., Baumert, A., Rothmund, T. and Schmitt, M., 2020. Guilt experience in patients with obsessive-compulsive disorder. *Verhaltenstherapie*, pp. 1–8.

Gerull, F.C. and Rapee, R.M., 2002. Mother knows best: Effects of maternal modelling on the acquisition of fear and avoidance behaviour in toddlers. *Behaviour Research and Therapy*, 40(3), pp. 279–287.

Hedman, E., Ström, P., Stünkel, A. and Mörtberg, E., 2013. Shame and guilt in social anxiety disorder: Effects of cognitive behavior therapy and association with social anxiety and depressive symptoms. *PloS one*, 8(4), p. e61713.

Hofmann, S.G., Asnaani, A., Vonk, I.J.J., Sawyer, A.T. and Fang, A., 2012. The efficacy of cognitive behavioral therapy: A review of meta-analyses. *Cognitive Therapy and Research*, 36(5), pp. 427–440.

Izard, C.E., 1991. *The psychology of emotions*. New York: Plenum Press.

James, A.C., James, G., Cowdrey, F.A., Soler, A. and Choke, A., 2015. Cognitive behavioural therapy for anxiety disorders in children and adolescents. *The Cochrane Library*.

Lyons, L., 2005. What frightens America's youth? *Gallup.com*. March 29.

Mineka, S., Davidson, M., Cook, M. and Keir, R. (1984). Observational conditioning of snake fear in rhesus monkeys. *Journal of Abnormal Psychology*, 93(4), p. 355.

Oldham-Cooper, R. and Loades, M., 2017. Disorder-specific versus generic cognitive-behavioral treatment of anxiety disorders in children and young people: A systematic narrative review of evidence for the effectiveness of disorder-specific CBT compared with the disorder-generic treatment, Coping Cat. *Journal of Child and Adolescent Psychiatric Nursing*, 30(1), pp. 6–17.

Robichaud, M. and Dugas, M.J., 2015. The generalized anxiety disorder workbook: A comprehensive CBT guide for coping with uncertainty, worry, and fear. Oakland, CA: New Harbinger Publications.

Salkovskis, P.M., 1999. Understanding and treating obsessive—compulsive disorder. *Behaviour Research and Therapy*, 37, pp. S29–S52.

Sandseter, E.B.H., 2009. Children's expressions of exhilaration and fear in risky play. *Contemporary Issues in Early Childhood*, 10(2), pp. 92–106.

Scherer, K.R. and Wallbott, H.G., 1994. Evidence for universality and cultural variation of differential emotion response patterning. *Journal of Personality and Social Psychology*, 66(2), p. 310.

Tancer, B., 2008. Click: What millions of people are doing online and why it matters. New York, NY: Hachette Books.

Tranel, D., Gullickson, G., Koch, M. and Adolphs, R., 2006. Altered experience of emotion following bilateral amygdala damage. *Cognitive Neuropsychiatry*, 11(3), pp. 219–232.

Chapter 2

Sadness

Sadness is an important human emotion, common following a loss, that makes our bodies slow down and makes us want to turn inward and withdraw from the world. Even though sadness is widely recognised as a basic emotion and is common amongst users of emojis, it has not received the same scientific attention as some of the other emotions in this book. Online searches for 'sadness' bring up results about depression and grief, but sadness in its own right has been relatively neglected.

Although most of us don't feel sad very often, when we do, it feels intense and unpleasant. It is the longest lasting of the common emotions, often continuing for days or more. Most of the time, when we feel sad, we can respond in healthy and helpful ways, making changes and adjustments to how we live. Noticing how sad we feel in our current situations can prompt us to make important changes, like starting and ending relationships, changing jobs or moving house. The threat of sadness bonds and holds communities together. This chapter also highlights the links between sadness and other emotions, particularly guilt and shame.

When we find sadness difficult, though, it can send us into spirals that can lead to intensely difficult feelings, negative thoughts, problems in many aspects of life and dramatic reductions in energy levels and motivation. It is this bodily response that gives rise to the diagnostic term 'depression' for problems with sadness. Problems with sadness can have a significant negative impact on all aspects of life, ranging from reduced interest and enjoyment to problems in relationships and work, to an almost inability to function and even to suicide. This will be an important chapter for many readers and should provide useful information to help think about experiences ranging from everyday sadness and disappointment all the way up to experiences given a diagnosis of depression.

DOI: 10.4324/9781003138112-3

This chapter explores sadness, what causes it, what it is and why humans experience it. It then looks at some helpful ways of responding when we are feeling sad. Next, it looks at some of the problems that might arise with sadness, using the sadness trap, and ways out of the sadness trap. It highlights how difficulties with sadness often overlap with difficulties with shame and guilt and how the diagnosis of depression fits with all of this. There are lots of examples to illustrate the ideas, and you can think of your own example by doing Exercise 2.1.

Exercise 2.1   Feeling sad

Think about a recent time when you experienced sadness. This is usually easier with an intense feeling rather than a mild one.

How would you describe the experience?
What did you notice/were you most aware of?
What made you feel sad?
Were there other feelings in addition to sadness?
How did you respond/what did you do?
What happened afterwards?

Understanding and accepting sadness

Sadness is an important human emotion, one that we all experience and recognise. Imagine, though, that you have to explain to somebody else what sadness is and what it is for. Most people are surprised at how little they actually know about sadness, and they are often stuck when thinking about why it might ever be a helpful feeling. The next section explores these questions using research from CBT and psychology.

What causes sadness?

The third question in Exercise 2.1 asks what made you feel sad. Can you identify what prompted this feeling? We usually find that feelings of sadness are prompted by loss. It might be the loss of something we had, or it might be the loss of something we wanted or expected. The most obvious loss is of something or someone close; for example, a relative or a pet.

Losing such important parts of our lives can produce intense feelings of sadness that can last for weeks and months at a time. Other situations that might prompt sadness are not getting the grade we worked for or the job we applied for. Less-intense feelings – which we might call disappointment, for example – might come when we find out that our favourite food is off the menu or that our friend cannot meet us as arranged.

We usually feel sad when we lose something we had or we wanted, but we might also feel sad when we have something we did not want. For example, being the last person picked for a team, or having to do something we do not want to do, might make us feel sad.

So sadness is prompted by losing something we want, or having something we don't want. But these situations can also prompt other feelings. Have a think back to Exercise 2.1. Were there other emotions that you experienced as well as sadness? Anger or guilt, perhaps, or maybe shame?

Guilt, anger and shame, which are covered in other chapters in this book, can be prompted by similar situations to sadness – situations where things did not go our way or happen as we had hoped. So why might we feel sadness in some situations, anger in others, and sometimes both? Exercise 2.2 should help us think about this. We'll come to guilt and shame later.

Exercise 2.2   Sadness or anger?

Think about a possession that is important to you, perhaps one you have worked hard for or that means something to you. Now imagine that somebody has taken it, and you think you know who.

What do you think you would feel?
If you felt anger, what would that anger prompt you to do?
If you felt sadness, what would that prompt you to do?
How would you have to view the situation to feel sad?

Anger is an activating emotion that drives us to try to sort things out, to fix the thing that has not gone our way. In this case, we would expect that anger would drive you to try to get your possession back. You might go to see the person and demand your possession back, or you might involve other people to try to help you get it back. Anger might also drive you to seek compensation from the person or even to take revenge on them.

We would expect sadness to come when you accepted the loss of your possession, when you got to the point that you had to give up trying to get it back. Sadness is prompted by a loss of something we wanted (or being stuck with something we don't want) combined with an acceptance that we cannot change the situation. Anger may be prompted by similar situations, but in these situations, we would be working to change the situation and recover what we had lost. As a result, some situations will prompt anger initially and sadness over time, as we discover that we cannot change the situation.[1]

Sadness is associated with both loss and limitation

So even though sadness can be prompted by the loss of something, like a possession, it might result in something much more significant, like the loss of an idea about ourselves or the way the world works. Think again about your possession. If this possession was taken by somebody you thought was a friend, and nobody around you helped you to get it back, you would have lost more than just your possession. You would have lost your possession and a friendship, you might have lost confidence in your own ability to stand up for yourself and you might have lost confidence in your sense that the world is a fair place and that people are generally nice to each other. An example illustrates this:

> Maisy had worked in the same job for almost three years before she decided to try for a promotion. Her colleagues had encouraged her to apply and said that she would be great at it. She worked hard towards it, doing everything expected of her and got some positive feedback from colleagues. When it came to it, though, the promotion was offered to somebody else who hadn't been there as long as she had. She was angry initially, because she couldn't understand why this other person had got the job. Over time and as the news sank in, she started to feel sad that she didn't have the new job and the extra money she'd been hoping for. What really made her the saddest, though, was feeling that perhaps she wasn't as good at her job as she thought she was.

In this example, we can see that Maisy is sad because she lost something she hoped for and maybe even expected. But this loss is also linked with an experience of her own limitation, the idea that she was not as good as she thought she was. The sadness she feels is not just for the job but also for herself and what not getting the job means about her. Every time we lose something we want, or we have something we don't want, accepting this situation means that we have to accept our own limitations. Sometimes this feels even worse than the loss itself.

In Exercise 2.1, you were asked to think about an intense feeling of sadness. Usually, intense feelings link fairly clearly to a cause. Sometimes less-intense feelings, particularly of sadness, can arise without a known cause; we can just feel 'not quite 100%', 'blue', or 'down'. Sadness of this type can feel more difficult because it is harder to explain to ourselves and to others. In some cultures, there are not even words to describe this experience; this diffuse sadness is largely ignored and not discussed, perhaps out of fear about its links with passivity (see later in this chapter).[2] Sometimes, thinking about sadness not just as a response to a loss of something but as relating to limitation too can help us make more sense of it. If we are feeling sad or down and we can't identify the reason, or the loss doesn't seem big enough to justify the feeling, it may be the sense of limitation that we are feeling the most. It may be that we haven't got the bread we wanted from the shop, but against a background of a day where lots of things went wrong, we are left feeling like we can't do anything right and that makes us feel so sad.

One of the most common causes of sadness is death. Losing somebody we care about is a powerful experience and generates lots of emotions. Initially, we are likely to feel shock and to find it difficult to adjust to the idea of the loss. We might feel angry, leading us to try to prevent or reverse the loss. We might also feel guilt, wondering if there was something we could have done, should have done, or could be doing to make things better. Over time, we are likely to start to feel sadness and when we do, we have to accept our limitations. We have to accept that we are powerless and helpless in the face of one of the most painful and difficult experiences of our lives.[3]

With intense feelings of sadness come intense feelings of limitation. We might get to the point where we feel useless, powerless and utterly hopeless. Experiencing our limitations in this way can cause shame, which is caused by a sense of ourselves as inadequate, defective or lacking in some way. If Maisy, for example, dwelled on missing out on the promotion and started to think that she must be useless at her job and nobody wanted her to work there, she would feel shame. Shame is covered in detail in Chapter 6.

What happens when we're sad?

Previous chapters showed that all emotional experience arises out of changes in five areas. The next section goes through each in turn in relation to sadness.

Feelings

For most of us, sadness is uncommon but the longest lasting of the main emotions, often continuing for days or more. Most people say that sadness feels cold, and they associate it with cold colours, like blue. Usually, sadness feels intense and unpleasant.[4] Sometimes, though, sadness is enjoyed or pleasurable. Can you think of a time when feeling sad was not unpleasant? Perhaps you enjoyed feeling sad or at least it felt 'right'?

There is a big industry in producing films that make the audience cry (so-called 'tear-jerkers') which indicates that maybe, at times, we do like to feel sad. Likewise, much of the most popular music in many genres has sadness as an important theme. Across cultures, too, sadness is an emotion that has been linked with valued characteristics like virtue (in 17th-century England), generosity and maturity (in the Ifaluk Pacific islanders) and depth (in Sri Lanka).[5] Some of the pleasant aspects of feeling sad may relate to aspects of its function, discussed later.

The word 'depression' comes from the Latin *deprimere*, meaning to press down or depress. The medical profession has used this term to describe the slowing down often seen in cases of extreme and prolonged sadness. Depression is a word that is used in both medical and emotional fields and is sometimes given extra weight by adding the word 'clinical', such as 'clinically depressed'. In this book, we will avoid the word depression because it makes us think of our emotions in medical terms (see the Introduction). Viewing sadness in this way makes us think that we 'have' something that we can 'get rid of'. There are similar problems with using the term 'mood', which makes us think about 'low mood' or 'bad mood' and gives us the sense that we should be working to prevent or get out of them. In this book, we will consider the experiences that are sometimes called 'depression' or 'low mood' as times when people are stuck in traps – often the sadness trap, but sometimes also guilt or shame traps. It is not possible to get rid of the emotions themselves but changing the responses to the emotions can help us get out of the trap. The later part of this chapter focuses on how to get out of the sadness trap. Chapter 5 covers the guilt trap, and Chapter 6 discusses the shame trap.

Have a look back to Exercise 2.1 and the words you used to describe how you felt. Perhaps you used the word 'depression', but what other words did you use, or could you use? In increasing intensity, a sadness scale might include words like blue, disappointed, gloomy, miserable, despondent, forlorn, dejected, bleak, heartbroken, despairing and wretched.

As outlined earlier, sadness is an emotion that is associated not just with the loss of something or someone but also with an experience of limitation and lack of power. As the level of sadness intensifies, the experience of this sense of limitation and reduced power also intensifies, with the result that extreme sadness is usually associated with feelings of powerlessness and hopelessness. This combination of loss and powerlessness, as well as a lack of hope, often also leads to a sense that there is no point or purpose to anything. At this point, it may be helpful to think about whether you are stuck in the sadness trap.

Bodily responses

Sadness has a dramatic impact on the body, and in Exercise 2.1, you probably wrote down something about how your body felt. The Introduction outlined the two systems of the nervous system: the sympathetic and the parasympathetic. In sadness, the parasympathetic system – the brake system – is activated.

Parasympathetic activation means that the body is slowed down to conserve energy and to allow the slow, gradual processes of digestion, absorption and expulsion. Our heart rates are slowed, our muscles relaxed and heavy, the pupils of our eyes contract and the lens is near-focused. The energy of our bodies is focused inward. We can call this a 'rest-and-digest' state.

Sadness is the only emotion dominated by parasympathetic nervous system activity (the rest-and-digest or brake system)

The intense impact that sadness has on the body is one of its defining characteristics and leads to the label 'depression' for intense sadness, almost as though it were an outside force pushing down on us. In some cultures, there appears almost deliberately to be no emotion word for the experience, as it is viewed as a dangerous external force that has to be fought off.[6]

Facial expression

We often express sadness through our faces. When we are sad, our faces lower and draw down, our features are reduced in form and no particular aspect is highlighted. Our face displays this withdrawal of the senses but also communicates sadness to others. A sad face tends to encourage others to approach, which links to the function of sadness, explored later in the chapter. One of the most characteristic facial traits associated with sadness is crying. The tears associated with sadness are unique to humans and are a powerful signal of the emotion.

Thoughts

Sadness is an emotion that makes us turn inward and search for meaning. The slow burning intensity of sadness leads to long periods of thought. In Exercise 2.1, thoughts would most likely have been an important part of the experience when you felt sad.

Many of our thoughts centre on the loss itself. We might go over memories, reminisce, remember how things were and think about what might have been. We might think about the moment of the loss, the reasons for the loss, perhaps whether the loss was deserved, and whether anything might have been done to prevent it.

We might also think about our limitations, focusing on the things we did wrong, couldn't do, couldn't stop. We might have lots of thoughts about what this loss means about us, thoughts like "I'm not as good as I thought I was". More global thoughts about our own limitations, like "I'm useless" or "I'm uninteresting", would lead to shame as well as sadness (see Chapter 6).

As we've said, sadness prompts a search for meaning, and many of our thoughts in sadness can be about sadness itself – thoughts like "Why am I so sad?" or "Why do I feel like this?"

Not only do we have different thoughts when we're sad, we also think in different ways. For example, we are more likely to remember times in our past when we were sad, we are less able to read others' emotional expressions, and we are more likely to think about the detail of things rather than the bigger picture. When we look to the future, we are also more likely to predict failure rather than success and have a negative view of our abilities. These effects are sometimes called 'cognitive biases' or 'negative thinking styles' and are often spoken about as a part or result of depression. But these findings relate to sadness, not just to the more extreme experiences that might be labelled depression. These ways of thinking can be produced in any of us, simply by making us feel sad.[7]

At higher levels of intensity and as a result of these ways of thinking, we can have more extreme thoughts, like "nothing will ever turn out right" or "I would be better off dead". These thoughts are fairly common with intense sadness, particularly if the cause of the sadness was a death. If these thoughts are intense or prolonged, and if plans are made to act on these thoughts, this suggests problems with sadness that will be covered in the section on the sadness trap.

Behaviours

When you thought about the time when you were sad in Exercise 2.1, what did you do? Usually, when we're sad, we withdraw. We often cancel our plans, avoiding meeting up and stay home, perhaps even stay in bed. We want to move away from stimulation and people and to seek out quiet and solitude. A powerful example of this withdrawal can be seen in football. At the end of an important match, the winning side come together as a team and join together in their happiness. The losing side sit down on the pitch, looking downward at the grass and turning in, alone.

While we often withdraw from others when we're sad, sometimes we turn to others for comfort – usually those closest to us, maybe family or close friends. There is a tension between these two behaviours – the desire to be alone and the desire to seek refuge and help from others. We may often feel this tension when we feel sad, seeking solitude but then feeling lonely or angry with others for ignoring us. This tension is partly driven by our own desires but also by our expectations of others. Some people and some cultures are more likely to respond to sadness with care, compassion and empathy, whereas others are more likely to respond with rejection and anger. There is more on this in the section on the sadness trap.

When sadness becomes intense and powerlessness and hopelessness really take hold, thoughts of ending life might lead towards suicidal behaviour. This is covered in the section on the sadness trap.

What is the function of sadness?

Sadness is important, because it signals to us and to those around us that all is not well. Sometimes, it makes other people feel for us, and they might look after us or do something nice for us. When we withdraw when we're sad, we usually withdraw back to a place of safety where we can get comfort and care. This is particularly true for children, in which sadness – often demonstrated by crying –– brings adults fairly quickly to the rescue.[8]

In short, sadness makes us slow down, turn inward and think. Withdrawing and reducing our usual activity to take stock and reevaluate can lead to important changes in our approach to life. Think about the last time you made an important decision in your life: to change school, to change job, to move house or to begin or end a relationship. What prompted you to make this decision? How did you feel before you made the decision? Many of the most important decisions in our lives are made following a period of sadness. Making these changes often makes us feel more connected with the people and things that are important to us. In this sense the experience of sadness, with its tendency for withdrawal and thought, is extremely important and if we try to dampen or lessen it without properly understanding it, we might prevent or delay important decisions.

Sometimes, sadness is a shared emotion. Many things that make us sad will also make others sad; perhaps this is true for your example in Exercise 2.1? When sadness brings us together, it can lead to deepened feelings of connection – for example, through empathy. Perhaps this is why sadness sometimes feels good, healthy or needed. A good cry with somebody else – whether a relative, a friend or even a character in a film or book – makes us feel less alone and more connected with those around us. In this context, the joy and the happiness we feel at connection with others (see Chapter 7) has its opposite in the sadness we feel when these connections are broken. This threat of sadness holds us together and maintains our social bonds.

All of these ideas are evident in relation to the most obvious cause of sadness – death. Ceremonies and rituals take place in all cultures around the world to commemorate the death of loved ones. Those close to the deceased come together to mourn their passing, remember their lives and reconnect with each other. It is a time of sadness but also a time of connection and reflection. Losing loved ones makes us think about our own mortality, the people important to us and the time we have left, and it often prompts us to change the ways we live and our priorities.

**Sadness signals that all is not well,
driving us to make important life changes
It brings us together, deepens bonds and
encourages care and support**

Tolerating sadness and using helpful responses when we're sad

Sadness is a response to loss and limitation that functions to encourage us to pause and reflect. We have lower energy levels, we withdraw from our usual activities and we think.

In Exercise 2.1, you were asked to think about a time when you felt sad. What did you do? What was the result? This section will outline a number of options to respond to sadness. These are some of the helpful ways in which you can respond. If you found yourself doing less helpful things, you may have been moving into the sadness trap, which is illustrated later in the chapter.

Sadness is an invitation for us to pause and think about the way we are living and the things we are focusing on in life. Carrying on as if everything is okay is like ignoring a warning flag. So we need to accept and tolerate the feeling of sadness and allow time to consider and think about how to respond. We also know that the way we think can be affected by feeling sad. We are more likely to remember other difficult times, to think about the detail rather than the bigger picture, and to predict difficulties in the future. Thinking too much might lead us in unhelpful directions or, as you've most probably experienced, around and around in circles. So we also need to have a break from thinking to do something. Following a difficult experience that makes us feel very sad, we can try to follow a pattern of thinking, doing, thinking, doing, thinking, doing. This means that we can respect the importance of sadness by thinking about it but also not get too lost in it or overwhelmed by it.

Withdrawing from the world is entirely consistent with the experience of sadness. It makes sense to reduce activity and not to push on at the same pace as before. It might make sense to head back to places of safety and to spend more time around loved ones and more time at home. These behaviours can bring comfort and solace. But again, we need to make sure we don't go too far, so we need to hang on to some connection with others and talk to them about what we're doing and how we're feeling.

Thinking should also move us in a different direction, and we need to act on the thoughts and ideas we have. We may need to work less, to spend more time with family, to make space for interests or to take a different approach to our health. It might also lead, gradually, to more significant life changes, like starting or ending relationships or changing jobs.

Exercise 2.3   Responding to sadness

These example questions should help you to respond to sadness. They are grouped according to what we know about sadness and its importance but also according to the impact it can have on how we think and behave.

Exploring the feeling:

This feeling is important, and I need to think about what it means for me.

What am I feeling?
What is it that has made me feel this way?
What is it in particular about this situation that links to this feeling?

Getting bogged down:

I know that sadness has an impact on how I think, and I might not make sense of everything how I normally would.

Is there any other way to view this situation?
What might someone else say to me (or might I say to someone else) about this situation?
Is there a bigger picture?
What is going well/what am I doing right?
What can I do to have a break from thinking about it?

Connection:

Sadness will make me want to withdraw. To avoid withdrawing too far, I might need to seek certain people out.

Who could I talk to about this?
Who could I see without having to talk to them about this?
Who might be able to help me?

Response:

This feeling is important, and I need to think about how to respond.

Is there anything I can do?
What are ALL the options, no matter how silly?
Which is the best of these options and why?
Do I need help with this process?

Exercise 2.3 puts these ideas together so that you can use them practically at times when you are sad. It will help you acknowledge the importance of sadness and allow time and space for reflection and connection with those with whom you are close. It will support you to emerge feeling a little stronger and clearer about what is important to you and help you head off in a slightly different direction as a result. Here is an example of how it can work:

George lost his father, with whom he was very close, after a short illness. Initially, he felt completely overwhelmed and did not know what to do with himself. He found himself staying up all night, crying and wondering how on earth he was going to cope. The following morning, his mother called asking him to help her, because she was being asked to do things and she was feeling overwhelmed. George, priding himself on his practical nature, much like his father, stepped in and started to organise things and help his mother. These things kept him busy for parts of the next few days, and he felt that he was doing something helpful for his mother and something respectful for his father. He continued to have times where he felt very sad for his father's loss but began to think about what he wanted to say at the funeral, which helped him to organise his thoughts a little more and gave him more direction and purpose. George was pleased with how the funeral went; he saw lots of family and friends he had not seen for a while and had lots of conversations about his father and the kind of man he was. George continued to have moments of intense sadness over the coming months, but he also began to think a little about his life and his values and some of the things he might start to do a little differently to make sure he was living a life that he and his father would be proud of.

Sadness trap: problems with sadness ("depression")

In this book, mental health 'disorders' and emotional difficulties are understood as problems responding to emotions. This section looks at the problems we might experience with sadness. This will be relevant to a whole variety of difficulties with sadness, including experiences that might receive a diagnosis like depression, major depressive disorder, bipolar disorder, cyclothymic disorder, seasonal affective disorder or persistent depressive disorder. All of the experiences given these labels will involve significant difficulties with sadness, although some might also involve difficulties with other emotions, like guilt (Chapter 5), shame (Chapter 6) or a lack of happiness (Chapter 7).

The most common response to sadness is withdrawal. When we feel sad, our energy levels drop, our motivation falls and we often feel like being alone. This serves an important function in our lives and can enable us to reevaluate our priorities, deepen our connection with others and lead fulfilled and happy lives. If we are not careful, though, we can find ourselves withdrawing too much, isolating ourselves and disconnecting from the people around us. This excessive withdrawal can lead to increasing loss and limitation through two processes: magnification and multiplication.

Magnification

Sadness has a powerful impact on the ways in which we think. When we are sad, we are more likely to remember bad times in the past, to predict bad times in the future, and to believe ourselves to be less capable. If we withdraw excessively and spend too long thinking, it can snowball so that our losses seem more important and our limitations more significant. Excessive withdrawal leads to a magnification of our losses and our limitations.

Multiplication

Excessive withdrawal can mean that we end up losing more and limiting ourselves more than we have to. If we withdraw from everybody because of the ending of one relationship, then we have lost all relationships rather than just one. If we view ourselves as unable to do things and thus stop trying, then we can make ourselves more incapable and multiply our limitations.

Unchecked, excessive withdrawal can lead us into a spiral of increasing loss and limitation, increasing sadness and excessive withdrawal. This is a cycle we call the sadness trap.[9]

Some examples will highlight how the sadness trap works.

Conrad was a sociable man who enjoyed the company of his family and friends. He was popular because he brought people together, organising events and making suggestions of things to do. The company Conrad had run for almost 10 years folded, and Conrad had to let his two employees go and was left unemployed. His two employees quickly found new jobs, but Conrad struggled and had been out of work for months. Running his own business had taken a great deal of his time and he found himself thinking a lot about what he could have done differently. He did things around the house in the mornings and told himself he'd work on another business or apply for jobs in the afternoon, but he had lots of concerns about whether he'd be able to manage a job after such a long time and watched television instead for the rest of the day. While he still saw his family and friends, he didn't arrange things like he used to, and he was much quieter around others than he used to be. He said this was because he didn't have much to offer and had little to talk about.

Conrad's loss of his company and his job are significant and lead to high levels of sadness. Many people who experience difficulties with sadness can trace the beginning of the process back to a significant loss in their lives.[10] Conrad has responded to sadness as we'd expect; he has withdrawn and spent his time thinking about what happened and why. But Conrad has found it difficult to reemerge from this withdrawal, with the result that his losses have multiplied – his company and job but now also his connections with those around him and his sense of himself as interesting and having something to offer. His withdrawal also feeds his sense of himself as not able to work (a limitation), which further fuels the sadness trap. Conrad's sadness trap highlights these links.

"I've lost everything"
"I can't work like I used to"
"I don't have much to offer"

CONRAD'S SADNESS TRAP

Withdraw from people
Watch TV
Avoid applying for jobs

Here is another example:

> Jenny lived with her mother and sister. She'd always had a busy life and valued her ability to get things done and always be on the go. She had a job she enjoyed, regularly went out with friends and was on a local hockey team, going to training and playing regular matches. Over the past few months, Jenny had been feeling less motivated, and so she'd been going out less and spending more time at home. Once or twice, she called in sick to work because she just couldn't face going, but she had been able to go back the following day. She had been feeling lower and more disconnected from others, and even though people invited her out, she thought she probably wouldn't be her usual happy self and stayed home. Over time, Jenny had been missing more and more of her activities, seeing friends less and missing lots of hockey, and her manager asked for more information about her increasing time being sick from work. Jenny felt she had 'lost her confidence' and had lots of thoughts about not being able to do things at work and not being any good at hockey. She also didn't feel like herself, feeling that she couldn't do things and didn't have energy like she used to.

In this second example, Jenny's difficulties with sadness cannot be traced back to a single significant loss but instead to a reduced sense of motivation leading to increased withdrawal from others, in turn leading to increasing sadness and increasing loss and limitation. The more she felt different from how she used to and the less capable she felt, the sadder she felt and the more she withdrew. Having previously had a busy life, she had lost lots of social contact, lost her identity as a busy productive person and had a sense of limitation, that she could not do the things she used to do. Jenny might find it harder to explain to herself and others what has happened to her because the trigger does not appear significant

| "I'm not close to people"
"I can't do things like I used to"
"I'm not the same person I was" | JENNY'S
SADNESS
TRAP | Stop socialising
Withdraw at work
Stop playing hockey |

enough to explain her feelings, but her sadness, withdrawal, and the losses and limitation she is experiencing are no less real. Jenny's sadness trap highlights these links.

Here is a final example:

> Kwame had been married for 10 years before, out of the blue, his wife told him she was leaving. She left the following week, and Kwame felt bereft and as though his whole life had changed overnight. He had long periods where he did not know what to do with himself because he and his wife socialised together, and he found himself thinking a lot about why his wife had left and going over all of the things he had done wrong in the past. Kwame did not know how to tell his friends about what had happened, and he put off meeting them until it began to feel more and more difficult to see them. He withdrew from household tasks, so the dishes piled up and the house got messier, and he didn't want people around because he was embarrassed about how untidy it had got. When Kwame's mother came to visit, she had a go at him for being lazy and not doing enough around the house. She also said that he should be over it by now and he should get on with his life, and she saw less of him because she found him frustrating. Kwame kept working but began to think that he could not manage on his own, and he started to think that maybe he was lazy and not worth spending time with.

In this example, Kwame experiences a loss that makes him feel sad, and things escalate from there. Kwame's sadness following this loss leads him to withdraw from his usual activities. In trying to understand the loss, he finds himself focusing on his limitations, which magnifies them and increases the intensity of his sadness, leading to further withdrawal. This withdrawal leads to multiplying losses – for example, contact with his friends and family. His withdrawal from household tasks multiplies his limitations and feeds his sense that he cannot manage on his own.

KWAME'S SADNESS TRAP

"My life is over"
"I can't cope on my own"
"I'm lazy, not worth others' time"

Withdraw from friends
Avoid household tasks

Kwame's sense of himself and his limitations will also likely lead him to feel shame; he has been rejected by his wife and has a sense of himself as inadequate. Difficulties with sadness often overlap with difficulties with shame. Fortunately, many of the things that help with sadness also help with shame and vice versa, but it is important to understand both emotions (Chapter 6 covers shame in detail).

In each of these examples, the sadness trap leads to a spiral of increasing withdrawal, increasing loss and limitation, and increasing sadness. Jenny and Kwame have found that they have withdrawn too much from their lives, with the result that the losses and limitations they have experienced have magnified and multiplied. Jenny has not only lost the close relationships with her friends and colleagues but also has a strong sense of her limitations, which has become generalised to all aspects of her life. Kwame has not just lost his wife but, as a result of going around the sadness trap, also feels as though he has lost his friends, his family and his confidence in his own ability to manage. He is also getting some negative comments from others, like his mother.

Sadness becomes a problem when we excessively withdraw which magnifies and multiplies losses and limitations

Jenny, Conrad and Kwame might all receive a diagnosis of depression and be offered some kind of treatment. They are not fundamentally different from other people, nor are their brain chemicals any different. The issue for all of them is that they are overusing withdrawal to cope with sadness, which has led them into the spiral of the sadness trap. They might also be struggling with other emotions, like guilt and shame (which are covered in other chapters of this book).

Earlier in this chapter, sadness was linked with empathy and seeking care from others. Often, though, sadness can elicit the opposite response in others, and people can reject sad people or get fed up with being around them. There are a number of ideas about why this might be, but the main one appears to be the link between sadness and withdrawal and what others might perceive as passivity. When we are sad, we withdraw and reevaluate. People appear to have a sense of what is a 'reasonable' amount of withdrawal and of when we should be moving forward and getting going again. When we seem to take too long, or get too stuck in a passive role, people can get frustrated and respond with frustration rather than care. This is most likely to happen in the sadness trap, where there is excessive withdrawal, but the responses of others can fuel the trap further, perhaps highlighting our limitations or adding to losses. For Kwame, his mother magnifies his limitations and withdraws herself from him, multiplying his losses. Exercise 2.4 helps you to draw your own sadness trap.

Exercise 2.4 Draw your own sadness trap

If you think you might be stuck in the sadness trap, have a go at drawing your own.

Think about the losses first. Was there a trigger to how you felt? Did you lose something that was important to you? Or did you have to accept something that you did not want? If there was no particular trigger, that's fine, just move on to the next section.

Think about what you might have lost over time. What do you not have that you used to have? How is your life different from before you felt this way?

What have you withdrawn from? Are there things you used to do that you no longer do? Are there people you used to see whom you now don't see as much or at all? Have you changed the way in which you interact with others – are you more distant or reserved, for example? Have you quietly withdrawn, not being so proactive, or are waiting to be approached rather than approaching others?

Now think about your limitations. What kind of thoughts do you have about yourself? Are you thinking that you are less capable than you would have thought before? In what areas do you feel, you are not good enough or lacking? What do you give yourself a hard time for or wish you were more able to do?

Think about the links between the different parts of the trap to make sure you capture everything.

Getting out of the sadness trap

The sadness trap outlines what happens when we get stuck in a spiral with sadness, withdrawal, loss and limitation. The point of understanding this process is to help us to think about what we can do to get out of this trap. It is based on the best available evidence from CBT.[11]

Reducing excessive withdrawal: doing more

The sadness trap highlights the link between excessive withdrawal and increasing loss and limitation. If we can reduce the excessive withdrawal and do more, we can start to reduce the impact of this link and start to turn things around. Of course, this is far easier said than done, and doing more is one of the most difficult things when we are stuck in the sadness trap, feeling terrible. Yet doing more is the most important way to start to improve things. It may not be enough on its own, but it is the best place to start.

> **Doing more is the most important first step in getting out of the sadness trap**

There are a number of steps we can follow to help us to do more, even when it is probably the last thing we feel like doing. This process is a commonly used intervention in CBT that has shown to be helpful, known as behavioural activation.[12] Exercise 2.5 helps you apply these ideas.

Setting expectations

The aim of doing more is to *do more*. Sometimes we will start to do more in the hope that it will make us feel better, or that other people will stop giving us such a hard time, or that we'll feel less tired. All of these things are longer-term aims, not short-term ones. When we are trying to do more, if we manage to do more, we have succeeded. Think of a train going along the track. We can only have control over the engine; the carriages just follow along behind. The engine is our behaviours, and this is what we are trying to change. The way that we feel, how our bodies feel, what we think and what other people think are all like the carriages – they will follow along behind. So when we are trying to do more, doing more is a success. The rest will come later.

Activity monitoring

The next step is to take account of what we already do. Remember the way that our minds work when we're sad? We are likely to get caught up in the detail of things, to remember negative events, to expect negative outcomes in the future and to view ourselves as less capable. All of this means that when we think about what we do, we are likely to underestimate our activity or to discount many of the things that we do. If we have been stuck in the sadness trap for a while, this is likely to magnify our losses and limitations. Getting an accurate sense of what we are actually doing can counter some of this magnification and help us realise, for example, that we are doing more than we think we are.

Problem solving

Once we have a sense of how we are spending our time, our next task is to think about the main issues with what we are doing. It is likely that we are withdrawing from a variety of activities, but we need to understand this in more detail. There are three main principles that can help us think about this[13]:

Right amount of activity

Excessive withdrawal will commonly involve us doing too little. However, it can sometimes involve the opposite – throwing ourselves into work, for example, and having no time left to engage in other things that are important. There is a balance where we feel busy enough but also have time available for things not to go to plan or to adjust or rearrange things where needed.

Balance of different activities

Not all activities are equal, and different activities fulfil different needs. We can separate activities into three separate categories (ACE for short): those that bring Achievement (A), those that are Connected (C) with others and those that are Enjoyable (E). Activities that bring a sense of **Achievement** are those that we don't necessarily enjoy doing but are pleased with afterwards. These can range from things like washing up to tidying to going to work. Activities that are **Connected** involve connecting with other people. This could involve talking to people in the supermarket, communicating with family or going to a party. Activities that are **Enjoyable** are those that we do for their own sake, that we tend to enjoy whilst we are doing them. These might include watching TV, reading, walking or doing sports. Of course, some activities will fall into more than one category – sports training, for example, might fulfil all three. We all need a rough balance between these three groups of activities (ACE) in our daily lives.

Routine

Routine and structure are very important to us as human beings. In a world of chaos where anything can happen at any time, we have no influence and no control. The repetition that comes with structure and routine allows us to feel that we can influence things and that we have some control and power. The sadness trap is linked with a sense of limitation, so making sure that we have a sense of routine and structure can be an important way to help us feel more able and capable. With routine, too, there is a balance. Too much routine can make us feel stifled and controlled and as though there is no space for fun.

Scheduling activities

Looking through our diary and thinking about these three principles should help us identify what we could change to improve things. If are not doing enough, we can try to do more. When we do this, though, we want to make sure we are asking ourselves to do some Achievement things, some Enjoyable things and some Connection things. If we get this balance wrong, we may find it is too difficult.

The sadness trap also magnifies our limitations and makes us feel that we're not as good as we might really be. As a result, when we do more, we want to **aim small** to set ourselves up to achieve what we've set out to achieve. If we have some successes, this will start to rebalance our sense of ourselves and reduce the limitation that we feel. It is better to set the target too low and find it easy, rather than to set it too high and give ourselves a sense of failure.

We also need to **be specific** about what we're asking ourselves to do and when. Doing more is difficult, so breaking things down and being clear about our expectations is really important in helping us to achieve what we've set out.

One of the best ways to tell whether the balance is right is to ask how we feel when looking at the list of things we've planned. We should feel fairly positive and have thoughts like "I think I can do that" and "That doesn't look too bad". If looking at the list makes us feel heavy, overwhelmed and demotivated, we have asked too much of ourselves and we need to rebalance or reduce it. Exercise 2.5 helps you apply these ideas.

> **We need a balance of achievement, connection and enjoyment, and we need to aim small and be specific**

Exercise 2.5   Doing more

Use a diary or table to record your activity during the course of a week. It is best to do this as you go along, as the way our minds work when we are sad is likely to mean that you have a more negative memory of events than is actually the case. You can use a diary; or a table with the days of the week and morning, afternoon, evening for each day; or you can write it some other way or use an app. Whatever you use, keep it brief, and do it as you go along.

Have a look through the diary and think about the amount of activity, the type of activity and the routine of your activities. Which areas need the most work? What do you need to do to make some changes? Consider whether you are doing too much or too little, whether you have the right balance of Achievement, Connection and Enjoyment (ACE) and whether you have enough routine.

Now, using another copy of the record, write in what you are going to ask yourself to do next week. Remember to **aim small**, so that you are only asking yourself to make minor adjustments to what you did last week – perhaps just one or two different things. Also remember to **be specific**, deciding when, where, how and with whom you are going to do these things. Make sure that you have a balance of ACE in your new activities (e.g., not all chores, or all things on your own).

Have a look at what you've asked yourself to do. How do you feel when looking at it? If you have a sense of optimism, an 'I can do that' kind of feeling, you've got it right. If you feel heavy, overwhelmed or demotivated, you're asking too much of yourself and you need to break it down more.

Keep reviewing your diary each week as you work on making changes.

We can think about our examples earlier to illustrate how to use these ideas.

What could Jenny do, and are there any particular risks for Jenny as she starts to try to improve things?

Jenny is still working, but much of the structure that she had to her week has fallen away. She is going out less and has less contact with other people. For Jenny, many of the things she used to do are potentially still available, so she can build gently back up, reconnecting with the previous activities. She has lots of thoughts about her own limitations, so it is important for her to make sure that she sets goals for herself that she will achieve; otherwise, she will make her sense of limitation worse.

Conrad has some slightly different challenges. He has a real gap in his day-to-day life as a result of no longer running his own company. He also needs to work on finding a new job or venture. What could he do?

Conrad seems stuck in a repetitive situation, and his first task will be to do something different, to get out of the rut. Much of what Conrad starts to do will have to be new activities. He will need to do things that he wasn't doing before but that fulfil a similar need – that give him a sense of achievement, connection and enjoyment. He will also have to work to reduce his exaggerated perception that he cannot work by building his confidence gradually over time. He will have to think about what this might involve for him, starting to do a little work to support somebody else – volunteering or a part-time job, perhaps, or starting a small project without too much pressure that he can build himself up with. He could also consider, as he starts to move out of the sadness trap, whether he wants to return to how things were before or whether he might want to do things a bit differently. There is more about this process in Chapter 7 on happiness.

After Kwame's wife left, he stopped seeing his friends and talking to his family as much. He had less to do because he used to do so much with his wife, and he stopped doing things around the house. He continued to work. What do you think Kwame should focus on when he is starting to do more?

Kwame is still working, so he has some structure and routine and is doing something that will help with a sense of achievement. He does not seem to be doing enough, though, and has few activities that are connected or enjoyable. He has both family and friends whom he can reconnect with, which will be important to help him get out of the sadness trap. He could pick one person out of all of these to have a little more contact with in the next few days. The untidiness of his house is an obstacle here, and he could set himself one small task to do each day to improve it. Kwame could also think about things that he might start to enjoy. These might be things he does on his own or with somebody else, things he used to do or new things that he tries out. It is important for him to start small so that he is likely to succeed. Tidying one kitchen worktop and messaging one friend in one day, for example, shouldn't feel too overwhelming but would give him the sense that he'd made a start. This will help him to feel that he is doing something positive for himself, which will challenge his sense of his own limitation and help him build confidence that he can do things that will help him get out of the sadness trap.

Reducing thoughts of limitation: challenging thoughts

Remember that sadness is always associated with limitation. Accepting a loss means also accepting that we cannot do anything to change it. We all have limitations, and there are always things outside of our control. However, the sadness trap highlights how loss and limitation can be magnified by how our minds work when we feel sad. Starting to do more is a powerful way to challenge some of these thoughts, as we are less limited than we were before we started to do more. But sometimes we can find ourselves stuck with thoughts about our own limitations that are more difficult to manage.

Conrad is having thoughts that he wouldn't be able to manage work and that he doesn't have much to offer. These thoughts are magnifications of the limitations he has experienced, and they get in the way of his efforts to reduce his withdrawal and to do more (e.g., in relation to work and socialising). Conrad's thoughts ("I've lost everything") magnify his losses and are likely to get in the way of his efforts to bring about change.

One important way out of the sadness trap is to counter this magnification of thoughts. The process outlined here is another common intervention in CBT known as thought challenging. Lots of studies have shown it to help with a variety of difficulties.[14]

Identifying thoughts

The first task is to notice the thoughts. Most of the time, we go around with an internal stream of thoughts running through our minds that we don't usually stop to question very much. These thoughts are usually helpful and allow us to think and make sense of things around us. The thoughts Conrad is having, though, are less helpful and unlikely to be entirely accurate. We need to identify the thoughts that are most common and that are most linked with the sadness trap. These are likely to be those about our limitations; they will often start with 'I' and might be linked to particular situations: "I'll never be able to do this" or "I won't have anything to say".

Once we have identified the most emotive thoughts, we can start to do something with them. There are three main ways of challenging our thoughts. The first way is to see what kind of thinking pattern we are using that might be magnifying our limitations; the second way is to examine the evidence for the thought; and the third and final way is to examine the helpfulness of thinking in this way. We'll cover each in turn.

Negative thinking styles

We think in different ways when we are sad, and particularly when we are stuck in the sadness trap. In fact, there are particular types of thinking styles that we are more likely to engage in, which are outlined in Table 2.1. Identifying the two or three most characteristic thinking styles of our own can help us to identify when we are thinking in ways that are likely to be inaccurate and feed the sadness trap.

Table 2.1 Ten types of negative thinking styles[15]

Thinking style	Description	Example
All-or-nothing thinking	Everything is seen in terms of two extremes (all or nothing). All-or-nothing thinking can often be expressed as "either . . . or".	Either I can do things perfectly or I'm rubbish at them. People either like me or they hate me.
Overgeneralisation	A single event is taken to represent a repeating pattern.	"I always get low grades." (after being given a single low grade) "Nobody will ever want to be with me." (after a rejection from a potential partner)

(Continued)

Table 2.1 (Continued)

Thinking style	Description	Example
Mental filter	A small aspect of something receives a large proportion of the attention, and the perception is filtered as a result.	"I look awful in this dress." (after nine people say something positive but one questions the neckline, and this comment receives all of the attention)
Discounting the positive	Positive experiences are discounted through being attributed to chance, to the nicety of the person who might have made a positive comment or through moving the goal posts.	"I was just lucky the right questions came up." "They're just saying that because they like me." "It wasn't that difficult really."
Jumping to conclusions	Thoughts are interpreted as facts in the absence of any evidence to support the conclusion. This can also include mind-reading and being sure about the future.	"They're thinking that I'm stupid." "They're obviously laughing at me." "Something is bound to go wrong today."
Magnification	The importance of problems is magnified and the importance of the things that are going well is minimised, leading to a disproportionate interpretation.	"I'll never get over this difficulty." "Everything is absolutely terrible."
Emotional reasoning	Emotions are used as if they represent truths about the world.	"I feel hopeless, so my problems must be unsolvable." "I feel miserable, everything in my life must be awful."

Thinking style	Description	Example
Shoulds, musts and oughts	Statements including the words should, must or ought tend to indicate a refusal to accept things as they are. They indicate a lecturing style of thought process in which criticism is never far away. Directed towards ourselves, we can feel bossed about and rebellious. Directed towards others, they can make us feel angry and frustrated.	"I should have more friends." "I ought to have a partner by now." "I should have a better job." "I must please everybody." "They shouldn't behave like that"
Labelling / name calling	Rather than describing the event or behaviour, we describe the character trait of the person who engaged in the behaviour.	"I'm utterly useless" rather than "that was a bad mistake". "I'm worthless" rather than "they didn't notice me". "I'm careless" rather than "I forgot to do that".
Personalisation and blame	A tendency to personalise and blame rather than consider the different factors in a situation. Like many of these thinking errors, personalisation and blame can be directed towards the self or towards others.	"I'm such a bad player, that's why we lost the match." "The world has it in for me." "Everything would be fine if it weren't for him"

Challenging thoughts

Once we have identified the main thinking styles we use, highlighting when we are using them can take much of the sting out of the content. Saying to ourselves, "I'm jumping to conclusions again," takes out some of the heat and allows us to do something different. It is important to think what you might say to yourself when you notice yourself using these patterns.

Conrad might say to himself, "I'm blaming myself for everything again" when he finds himself dwelling on losing his business, or "I'm more than just my job" when he finds himself overgeneralising. Having a phrase that makes sense to us and captures the essence of our thinking styles can help to make sure we use it in the moment.

Kwame had found himself thinking that he would never get over his wife leaving and that he could not cope on his own. What kind of negative thinking styles was he using?

Kwame may be overgeneralising. He looks at the pile of washing up and takes this to mean that he is not coping. He may also be discounting the positive, because he is still managing to go to work and to pay the bills. Finally, he could be labelling or blaming himself unduly, calling himself lazy and dwelling on what might be wrong with him. Kwame might put all this together and try to remember not to give himself such a hard time.

Another way of challenging our thoughts is to examine them in terms of accuracy. As we said, being stuck in the sadness trap makes us think differently; we are more likely to focus on other difficult times in our lives and predict negative outcomes in the future. We often forget information that is inconsistent with how we feel or with the current focus of our thoughts. Our ways of thinking magnify our limitations, and we forget that we didn't think this way when we didn't feel so sad.

We can counter this process by getting a more balanced view of the situation, looking at the evidence for and against particular thoughts. We start with the evidence for, because this is uppermost in our minds and demands our attention, and once we've captured this, we can look for alternative views and perspectives. Conrad's thought that he doesn't have much to offer – if he were to organise an event with his friends, for example – is one he could examine further. He could first look for all the evidence that this was true, what things were consistent with the idea that he didn't have much to offer his friends. Then he could look for evidence that this was not true – the information that was inconsistent with this idea.

Conrad: "I don't have much to offer my friends."

Evidence for	Evidence against
I can't talk about my work anymore	We never really talk about each other's work anyway
I haven't been doing much for the past few weeks	Some of the most enjoyable times we've had have been playing silly games
I don't have as much energy as I used to	They've all sent me messages asking to do things recently
	I've supported them through difficult times, when they've felt down

In the table that Conrad creates, the column to the left (evidence in support of that way of thinking) is much easier than the one on the right (evidence against). Exercise 2.6 has some questions you can ask yourself to try to complete the right-hand column, the evidence against.

Thoughts are important in helping us to make sense of the world. Many of the thoughts we have in the sadness trap, we have because we are trying to do things differently. For example, thoughts about our own limitations are in some ways attempts to make us change and work harder to do more and get out of our stuck situation. Thinking about how helpful these thoughts are in motivating us can help to challenge them. If we think of a sports coach and the kinds of things that a good and bad coach might do to motivate us, this can help. For example, think about the impact on our performance if the coach called us "useless" and said, "you'll never amount to anything", versus a coach who said, "that wasn't a great time, perhaps you could try working on . . . and . . . and give it another go". We don't have to be positive when things are not going well, but different ways of framing things can make a big difference to how helpful our thoughts can be.

Exercise 2.6   Countering the magnification of limitation

Thinking styles

What kind of thinking style am I using?
Which are the thinking styles that I tend to use at these times?
Do I have a phrase to remind myself of?

Accuracy

What are all the alternative ways of viewing this situation?
Is there information that doesn't support my conclusion?
Would other people agree with my conclusion?
If someone else was in this situation, what would I say to them?

Helpfulness

Am I trying to motivate myself and doing the opposite?
Am I being mean to myself?
What is the impact of thinking this way?
Is there something I can do about this?

New thoughts

Once we have done some work on challenging the thoughts going through our minds, we can come up with new thoughts that might be more accurate or more helpful. These new thoughts should be more linked with the situation, will probably have some more detail in them, and might even point us in a useful direction.

What could Kwame say to himself following the process of noticing his thoughts and challenging them? What about Jenny?

Kwame might think to himself that he has found it difficult to get over the loss of his marriage, but he has managed to continue working and stay in his house. He could think about himself more positively as he does a little more around the house and reconnects with his family. Maybe he might think, "I struggled to begin with, but I am doing the right things to make an improvement", or "Things are more difficult for me right now because of how I'm feeling, but I am trying to make things better", or perhaps "It will be difficult for me without my wife, but I will get there in the end".

Jenny might start to challenge the thoughts she has with details like, "It's okay if I'm a bit quieter when I go out with my friends" or "I can build my confidence back in time".

Magnification can be reduced by challenging thoughts and replacing them with more balanced, realistic thoughts

Recognising shame and guilt

Some of the thoughts you might identify when doing work on magnification in the sadness trap might also cause other emotions. Using these thoughts to identify other emotions you might struggle with can be really helpful.

The most extreme thoughts about limitation are statements about our whole identity in all situations, like "I'm useless", "I'm worthless", "I'm powerless" or "I'm hopeless". These kinds of thoughts will lead to high levels of sadness but will also lead to high levels of shame. Shame is caused by a perception of ourselves as flawed or inadequate, and these thoughts highlight this perception. If you have picked out thinking styles like labelling/name calling and personalisation/blame, then you may well be experiencing high levels of shame. To understand the impact of these thoughts and what to do about them, it is best to read Chapter 6 on shame alongside this one.

It is also common to experience high levels of guilt alongside sadness. Guilt is caused by a perception that we have done or not done something that has fallen short of what we should have done. High levels of guilt are linked with rigid or excessively high standards. If you have picked out shoulds, musts and oughts, all-or-nothing thinking or personalisation and blame as some of your thinking styles, then you may be experiencing high levels of guilt. In this case, you could read Chapter 5 on guilt alongside this one.

Summary

Sadness is an important emotion that helps us to live fulfilled and happy lives. It holds communities together, gives us space to reevaluate our lives at times of difficulty, and encourages deeper bonds between us. There are a number of ways of responding to sadness that can ensure it remains a helpful and important emotion. When we get stuck in the sadness trap, this is the result of excessive withdrawal, which can result in a magnification and multiplication of loss and limitation and send us into a difficult spiral. There are two main ways out of the sadness trap – the first focusing on doing more and the second on challenging thoughts, particularly those about our limitations. These are evidence-based CBT interventions that should move us back into a healthier relationship with sadness.

Notes

1 Many of these ideas come from the work of Stein and Levine and their theory of emotional understanding. They worked hard to differentiate between

the aspects of different emotions that enable their distinction, and they tested many of their ideas in samples of children with a fair degree of success. A good paper that outlines their ideas in more detail is Stein and Levine (1987).

2 For an interesting discussion on the differences between sadness across cultures, see Barr-Zisowitz (2000).

3 The stages of grief is a really helpful theory developed by Kübler-Ross and Kessler (2005). The five stages are denial, anger, bargaining, depression and acceptance. Other subsequent models have included other stages like 'pain and guilt' or reconstruction. The problem with stage theories is that they tend to be interpreted in a prescriptive fashion and people are 'expected' to follow this course. This can have negative implications for those who take a different route, do them backwards, or skip bits out altogether (Stroebe et al., 2017). This book holds the principle that there is no 'right' way to feel, no 'shoulds' with emotions. But if we feel a particular way, it is possible to understand the cause and the function of this emotion and consider how best to respond.

4 Scherer and Wallbott (1994)

5 For more information on the 'positive' aspects of sadness, see Barr-Zisowitz (2000).

6 For further discussion on this idea across cultures, see Barr-Zisowitz (2000).

7 For a thorough exploration of the different processing styles associated with different emotions, see Isbell et al. (2013). For more information about how our emotion links with our expectation of our own success, see for example: Kavanagh and Bower (1985).

8 For a thorough examination of crying in humans, see Vingerhoets (2013). An experimental study that demonstrates the impact of seeing tears on the ability to recognise sadness can be found in Balsters et al. (2013).

9 The idea that the experiences termed depression are primarily caused and maintain by withdrawal is supported by a whole variety of authors including Leventhal (2008), who outlines an equation that corresponds with the sadness trap in this chapter.

10 The fact that most people who receive a diagnosis of depression have usually experienced a life event that would make them sad is well known (e.g., Kendler et al., 1999).

11 The strategies here of focusing on doing more and thought challenging are consistent with the evidence base for CBT for depression. The main interventions are behavioural activation and cognitive therapy, which focus on these two aspects of the difficulties (e.g., Barth, 2013).

12 Behavioural activation is an intervention based on behavioural science that links our behaviour to our emotion. The sadness trap comes from an overuse of withdrawal, and so reducing the withdrawal and doing more is an important part of getting out of it. Behavioural activation has been shown to be helpful for people who have received a diagnosis of depression (e.g., Richards et al., 2017).

13 Frude provides this elegant structure that allows us to think about what activities are important from a positive psychology perspective (Frude, 2014).

14 CBT, which includes work on thought challenging, has been shown to be effective for those given a diagnosis of depression in a variety of studies.

One paper, which brought together the results of nearly 200 studies and over 15,000 participants, found that CBT and behavioural activation were both better than control conditions (Barth et al., 2013).

15 This table is adapted from Burns (1999).

References

Balsters, M.J., Krahmer, E.J., Swerts, M.G. and Vingerhoets, A.J., 2013. Emotional tears facilitate the recognition of sadness and the perceived need for social support. *Evolutionary Psychology*, 11(1), pp. 148–158.

Barr-Zisowitz, C., 2000. Sadness. Is there such a thing? In M. Lewis and J.M. Haviland-Jones (eds.), *Handbook of emotions*. New York: The Guilford Press, pp. 607–622.

Barth, J., Munder, T., Gerger, H., Nüesch, E., Trelle, S., Znoj, H., Jüni, P. and Cuijpers, P., 2013. Comparative efficacy of seven psychotherapeutic interventions for patients with depression: A network meta-analysis. *PLoS Medicine*, 10(5), p. e1001454.

Burns, D., 1999. *The feeling good handbook* (Revised edn). New York: Penguin.

Frude, N., 2014. Positive therapy. In R. Nelson-Jones (ed.), *Theory and practice of counselling and therapy*. London: Sage, pp. 69–93.

Isbell, L.M., Lair, E.C. and Rovenpor, D.R., 2013. Affect-as-information about processing styles: A cognitive malleability approach. *Social and Personality Psychology Compass*, 7(2), pp. 93–114.

Kavanagh, D.J. and Bower, G.H., 1985. Mood and self-efficacy: Impact of joy and sadness on perceived capabilities. *Cognitive Therapy and Research*, 9(5), pp. 507–525.

Kendler, K.S., Karkowski, L.M. and Prescott, C.A., 1999. Causal relationship between stressful life events and the onset of major depression. *American Journal of Psychiatry*, 156(6), pp. 837–841.

Kübler-Ross, E. and Kessler, D., 2005. *On grief and grieving: Finding the meaning of grief through the five stages of loss*. New York, NY: Simon and Schuster.

Leventhal, A.M., 2008. Sadness, depression, and avoidance behavior. *Behavior Modification*, 32(6), pp. 759–779.

Richards, D.A., Rhodes, S., Ekers, D., McMillan, D., Taylor, R.S., Byford, S., Barrett, B., Finning, K., Ganguli, P., Warren, F. and Farrand, P., 2017. Cost and outcome of behavioural activation (COBRA): A randomised controlled trial of behavioural activation versus cognitive-behavioural therapy for depression. *Health Technology Assessment*, 21(46), pp. 1–366.

Scherer, K.R. and Wallbott, H.G., 1994. Evidence for universality and cultural variation of differential emotion response patterning. *Journal of Personality and Social Psychology*, 66(2), p. 310.

Stein, N.L. and Levine, L.J., 1987. Thinking about feelings: The development and organization of emotional knowledge. *Aptitude, Learning, and Instruction*, 3, pp. 165–197.

Stroebe, M., Schut, H. and Boerner, K., 2017. Cautioning health-care professionals: Bereaved persons are misguided through the stages of grief. *OMEGA-Journal of Death and Dying*, 74(4), pp. 455–473.

Vingerhoets, A., 2013. *Why only humans weep: Unravelling the mysteries of tears*. Oxford: Oxford University Press.

Chapter 3

Anger

Anger is a common emotion that energises our bodies and makes us feel hot and tense. It is unpleasant and is not usually thought of as a useful emotion. It often receives labels like 'toxic', and many social scientists have written about anger as if it were more of a hindrance than a help. Some have suggested that anger is responsible for all the violence in the world, and it would be best to get rid of it.

These negative views of anger in our society have led to real problems in helping us all to understand and respond to our own anger. What are helpful and healthy ways of responding to anger? How do we know if we have problems with anger? There are relatively few mental health diagnoses that relate specifically to anger, and those that do tend to be more extreme (for example, bipolar disorder or borderline personality disorder). There are also fewer ideas about what can help, and less research into what works and when, in comparison to other emotions.

This chapter explores anger as a human emotion like any of the other emotions in this book. It starts with what makes us angry and how our minds and bodies respond when we're angry. It looks at the function of anger and the times when it is helpful, useful and important in our lives. It considers how we can tolerate anger and respond in ways that are helpful, protective and respectful.

The chapter moves on to look at what can happen when there are difficulties with anger. These difficulties are not an inevitable response to anger itself but can be understood as problematic ways of responding to anger that set up vicious cycles outlined in the anger trap. Being stuck in the anger trap can lead to intense, frequent experiences of anger, alongside explosive and harmful behaviours that have an extremely negative impact on individuals and those around them. Links are also made between anger and other emotions, shame in particular. The anger trap

DOI: 10.4324/9781003138112-4

is used to work through a number of different ways of getting out of the trap.

Understanding and accepting anger

Anger is like all the other emotions in this book. It is a response to particular situations around us, and it produces a response in our minds, bodies, behaviours and facial expressions. These responses serve a particular purpose and are usually helpful. This next section will help you to think about your own experience of anger and hopefully challenge some of those negative opinions you might hold about anger, so you can better understand and accept it.

Exercise 3.1 Feeling angry

Think about a recent time when you felt angry; make sure it was anger, rather than a less intense experience like irritation or frustration.

How would you describe the experience?
What did you notice/were you most aware of?
What made you feel angry?
How did you respond/what did you do?
What happened afterwards?

What causes anger?

Exercise 3.1 asked why you were angry. If you picked an intense feeling of anger, it was probably easy to remember the reason you were angry, and it is likely that it was somebody else. Usually, anger is caused by someone else's behaviour. When we describe what made us angry, we usually have quite a lot to say, and we usually focus on what the other person did, or did not do that we think they should have done. So what does this mean about anger and what tends to prompt it?

When we feel angry, it is usually because somebody has done something we perceive to be unjust, rude, hurtful or mean.[1] This behaviour of the other person (or people) has the potential to have a negative impact on us or on something or somebody important to us. In this way, we can understand the other person's behaviour as a threat: an interpersonal threat. Somebody is doing or saying something that represents a threat to us or our way of life.

Anger is caused by a perceived interpersonal threat

Have a think about your example in Exercise 3.1. How would you define the threat? There are lots of potential interpersonal threats around us. The most obvious are physical threats. If somebody threatens us with violence – for example, pushes or hits us – this is a very clear interpersonal threat. Equally, if somebody does this to somebody we care about, this is an interpersonal threat. Other threats might be to our possessions; people can attempt to take things that belong to us or treat our possessions badly. Other interpersonal threats might come from people getting in the way or preventing us from gaining things that we want or goals that we are working towards. In each of these cases, it shouldn't be too difficult to define the interpersonal threat.

More subtle kinds of threats come from our perception of others' behaviour towards us; they threaten our sense of identity, respect or importance. These kinds of threats can be identified from thoughts like "He's treating me badly", "She's completely ignoring me" or "They are laughing at me". These are threats to our sense of self. Sometimes it is this perception of threat that lies behind many of the times when anger appears disproportionate to the situation. For example, if you are really angry at somebody for not clearing up after themselves, it may be because you have taken it as a sign that they don't respect you. If you are furious because your friend never repaid the money you lent them, it's probably not because you desperately need the small sum of money back but rather because you have taken this as a sign that they are not considering you and are taking advantage of you. The word 'dissing' is shortened from 'disrespecting', which captures this sense of threat from others. These kinds of perceived threats relate to another emotion – shame. Being treated disrespectfully, laughed at, ignored or taken advantage of, or being treated as inferior, are all threats of being shamed or humiliated. This can lead to intense feelings of anger and is covered more later in this chapter and in Chapter 6 on shame.

Being treated badly, disrespected or laughed at are all interpersonal threats that can lead to anger and also to shame

A common cause of anger in today's society is driving, leading to the term 'road rage'. It appears that driving is an activity particularly likely to produce anger.[2] Driving is unique as it involves contact with lots of other people, all at a distance. When we're driving, there are many things people can do that we might perceive as interpersonal threats. If we are clear about where we're going, other drivers slowing us down is already a potential threat, and just the presence of other vehicles on the road might make us feel angry. If there is somebody travelling particularly slowly, then they are threatening our ability to get where we're going. Other driving behaviours, like overtaking, changing lanes, pulling out, letting in or not, jumping queues and so on, can all be interpreted as interpersonal threats. They can be threats to our ability to get where we're going, and they can also be perceived as being rude or disrespectful. When we're driving, we are very aware of the behaviour of other road users, but we have no other information about them, often treating the individual as if they *were* their vehicle. This results in a clearer sense in our own mind of their fault and also much less communication between us, so they may be completely oblivious of our frustration, or we might not see their apology.[3]

It is possible that, in your example in Exercise 3.1, you found yourself angry in a situation that did not involve somebody else. If so, this was probably a less intense feeling, a feeling of frustration perhaps. The word 'frustration' doubles to define both the emotion and its cause. To be frustrated is to be prevented in the progress or achievement of something, and it results in a feeling of frustration. In these kinds of situations, there is still some kind of threat – we cannot get or do what we want or need to do – but instead of another person getting in the way, it is an object, a situation or our own abilities.

If we feel more intense anger in response to these situations, it is usually because we personalise the object or get angry with ourselves. Computer equipment is a good example of this kind of situation – when it doesn't work, or it deletes lots of our work, we have a tendency to personalise it and treat it as if it were another individual who is deliberately getting in our way. Shouting at a computer screen or threatening to throw it out of the window are examples of this kind of behaviour that many of us may relate to.

The only other factor that has been linked with anger is physical discomfort. Sometimes we can find ourselves feeling angry because we are in pain, because we are tired or because we are hungry.[4] The recently-defined idea of feeling 'hangry' captures the anger we feel when we are hungry.[5] Sleep deprivation has also been linked with increased anger.[6]

These conditions might produce anger on their own, or we might find that they increase our baseline feeling so we are quicker to anger in response to interpersonal threat.

Anger can be increased by pain, hunger and tiredness

What happens when we're angry?

Anger has a significant impact on many parts of our lives, our bodies, the way we think and how we feel. The next section looks in more detail at these changes.

Feelings

Most of us experience anger fairly often. It can last for minutes, hours or days, but it usually dissipates fairly quickly, although not as quickly as fear. Anger is usually felt as a 'hot' emotion, described in ways like 'my blood was boiling', 'he was being hot-headed' or 'we had a heated discussion'. For most of us, anger is unpleasant.

Like all emotions, anger can be experienced to varying degrees. What kinds of words did you use in Exercise 3.1 to describe your anger? Words that you may have used in increasing intensity include tetchy, annoyed, irritated, frustrated, cross, angry, outraged, furious, seething, irate, livid, apoplectic and incandescent. There are also lots of colourful expressions that can capture anger, like 'seeing red', 'losing my rag', 'going bananas', 'hitting the roof', 'going ballistic' and 'losing the plot'.

Bodily responses

Anger has a dramatic impact on the body that is very similar to the impact of fear. Our heart rate increases, our breathing deepens and our muscles tense. Our senses are sharpened (vision, hearing, touch, etc.) and our attention is narrowed to focus on the threat – in this case, whatever has made us feel angry. This can feel like 'tunnel vision', particularly at more intense levels of anger.

This reaction is produced by the 'fight-or-flight' sympathetic nervous system and controlled by adrenaline in the same way as it is for fear, although anger takes longer to dissipate than fear.[7]

Facial expression

Anger is an emotion that tends to be outwardly expressed and is often obvious on our faces. We lower our eyebrows and wrinkle our foreheads to produce a frown. This makes our eyes look more narrow and penetrating, producing a glare or scowl. As we tend to focus our attention on whatever has made us angry, we tend to focus this glower onto somebody else, which is a powerful communication. It is thought that our innate expression of anger is a baring of the teeth that animals often display. Humans suppress this and instead show a tightly closed mouth as a signal of restrained anger.[8]

Thoughts

When we're angry, we often experience lots of thoughts. In Exercise 3.1, you probably wrote a lot about why you were angry, which is one focus of thoughts. We focus on how the other person could dare to do such a thing, or how on earth they did not think about the impact that it would have on us.

The other focus of our thoughts is the future and what we'd like to do about it: thoughts of revenge, attacking others and destruction.[9] Sometimes these thoughts can develop into fantasies of action, and we can find ourselves imagining getting our own back. Sometimes these can become extreme, and we can indulge in violent or even murderous daydreams. There is more on this in the next section.

When we're angry, it can be difficult to move our attention away from the threat – the incident that has made us angry – and to concentrate on other things. We can find ourselves focusing all our attention on what the other person did to us and imagining how we might get our own back. This focus can lead to an intensifying of the anger.

With increasing intensity of anger, we can find it more and more difficult to think rationally, and when we are intensely angry, we are often irrational and impulsive.

Behaviours

Anger is an emotion we want to express outwardly; we want to approach others when we are angry. Our facial expression when we're angry is a powerful signal of this desire to approach; we hold others' gaze and might move our whole body so as to face them or even move towards them. An increased volume of our voices or the stress given to our words can communicate our anger and displeasure. More intense verbal behaviours in response to anger might include shouting and screaming, as well as swearing and cursing. The majority of profanities tend to be short and contain hard consonants, lending themselves to being used in anger. These behaviours might be experienced by others as verbal aggression.

Other behavioural responses to anger include physical behaviours. More subtle behaviours include a hardening, pulling up or widening of the body or a change in stance to appear bigger or more threatening. We may clench our fists, or our breathing may become louder. We might bang objects, slam doors or throw things. At their most intense, behavioural responses to anger include punching, kicking, hitting, throwing things and all-out physical violence. Spitting and throwing shoes, in some cultures, can combine this aggressive display of anger with a sense of contempt.

There will be times where we will engage in behaviours such as these, but at other times they will play around in our minds instead as fantasies of action. We might spend our time imagining what it would be like to do these things – to humiliate others with our sharp tongues or to beat somebody in a fight.

There is a powerful urge to express anger in these ways, and it can feel as though we have relatively little control over our anger. Sometimes, we might feel that anger takes hold of us, and we say and do things that we would never do when we are calmer. It is interesting to note that the expressions we commonly use to describe high levels of anger highlight a sense of 'madness' or loss of control. The link between anger and control is important in terms of the function of anger.

Having said that, though, it is important to note that anger and aggression are not the same. Anger is an emotion that is prompted by the perception of an interpersonal threat. Aggression is a behaviour directed towards others.

We can be angry without acting aggressively
We can act aggressively without feeling angry

Anger and the brain

The Introduction showed how the brain is made up of three parts: reptilian, mammalian and rational. Anger functions in the same way as fear to protect us from threat, and so it is a quick, instinctive and primitive response driven by the reptilian brain.

Similar to fear, it is the reptilian brain's role in driving anger that can result in some of the irrationality and impulsivity in anger. The slow, decision-making rational brain that can take account of long-term consequences and the feelings of others, for example, can be knocked offline by intense anger driven by the reptilian brain. This means that we may do and say things when we are angry that we wouldn't do when we are calm.

What is the function of anger?

Many of us have a perception that anger is a damaging emotion, that it serves no useful function and instead is 'toxic', 'harmful' and more of a liability than an asset. Many authors have written accounts of anger from the perspective that it is responsible for much of the terror, hatred and harm in the world.[10] But if anger were such a harmful emotion, why do humans experience it – what could its function be?

In Exercise 3.1, think about your experience of anger. What did you do when you felt angry, and what happened afterwards? Was it useful? Did it help? If not, have you ever had a positive outcome from feeling angry? In one study of hundreds of people from the United States and Russia, the majority of people reported a positive outcome from their experience of anger.[11] So what is the function of anger, and when is it useful?

Anger is an emotional response to a perceived threat, the perception that we are being mistreated, undermined, betrayed, used, disappointed or hurt by others. Our bodies respond to this perception of threat by gearing us up for action, increasing our heart rate and breathing and tensing our muscles. Our senses are sharpened, and our attention is focused on the threat. Our face displays our anger towards the person who has made us angry, and we want to approach them.

The result is that anger gears our body up to counter the threat; we threaten the person we believe to be threatening us. Anger does this by making us appear bigger and stronger – our eyes appearing more menacing, our voice more assertive – and we are more likely to approach the other person with more confidence and energy than we otherwise would.

Anger between two people, in this context, can lead to an escalation in threat until the point where one party has managed to intimidate the others into feeling fear, at which point the other retreats (flight response to threat). This is a similar process to that seen in other mammals where, for example, two individuals will size each other up, walking backwards and forwards, before deciding whether to engage in battle. During this time, they vocalise their dominance and parade their physical prowess, the aim being to intimidate the other party into backing down so that the individual can have whatever they are considering battling over.

Anger functions to protect us from the threats posed by others. It does this by gearing us up to pose a counterthreat. The desired result is that we protect ourselves from other people who are threatening to take something from us, take advantage of us or treat us with disrespect.

Anger can help to get our own way, gain possessions, power, autonomy or respect

Anger helps us to look after our interests. Have a think about your experience of anger you write in Exercise 3.1 and other experiences you may have had. Are there occasions where anger has helped you to protect your interests? Got you what you wanted? Stopped other people taking advantage? Maintained others' respect for you?

Most of the time, anger is experienced and expressed at fairly low intensities; annoyance and irritation are expressed and heard by the other person, which leads to resolution. For example, many of the upsets we cause others, the times when we make others angry, are not intentional, and so when we perceive another's anger, we quickly apologise, with the result that we have effectively backed down and the situation is resolved.

However, there are occasions where anger is experienced and expressed much more intensely, in ways that might be described as 'losing it' or 'going bananas'. This is because, as anger increases in intensity, there is increased irrationality. With increasing irrationality comes increasing unpredictability, and unpredictability is threatening in somebody who is hostile. This means that as our anger intensifies, we become more unpredictable and so more threatening to those around us. As a result, we are more likely to win the argument, battle or standoff. In this context, even the irrationality and impulsivity of anger serves a function – it serves to protect our interests, at least in the short term.

This increasing irrationality, combined with the narrowing of attention that comes with intense anger, illustrates how the object of anger might shift over time. Initially, the prompt to anger might have been something in the environment – a threatened loss of a possession or object. With increasing anger, however, the threat can become more significant – a perceived threat to respect, esteem or power. In this way, with increasing anger, the threat can become increasingly personal and increasingly intense, and the aim of defeating the other person overrides the desire to obtain or protect the object.[12] This links with the threat of shame or humiliation – feeling humiliated as a result of backing down, for example – covered earlier and also covered in the anger trap, later in this chapter.

Anger, then, functions to protect us from threats posed by those around us. These might be threats of loss of things that are important to us or threats to our image, self-esteem or self-respect. Anger helps us to respond to these perceived threats by gearing up our bodies in the 'fight' response, to allow us to counter the initial threat and get the other person to back down. Whilst physical violence is arguably used less in today's society than it might have been in the past,[13] expressing discontent, indignation or anger through tone of voice, body posture or verbal threats and complaints remains a powerful way in which we can protect ourselves from the harm others may otherwise do to us, or those who are important to us.

Anger does not inevitably lead to disrespect, aggression and violence but is instead an emotion that can enable us to protect ourselves against the threats of others. In fact, the desire to avoid other people's anger often leads to many of those behaviours that we consider respectful and decent – for example, apologising to others and using polite language like 'please' and 'thank you' to demonstrate that we understand and appreciate the impact we have on those around us. Anger, as an individual and societal response to interpersonal threat, can help to maintain the values and rights of citizens.

There are times, however, where the expression of anger becomes unhelpful, hurtful and harmful, and in these cases, we can consider that we have become stuck in the anger trap. Details of how this works and what can be done about it are discussed later in the chapter.

Tolerating anger and using helpful responses when we're angry

When we feel angry, the best way to respond is to act, to do something. This next section will outline some ideas to help us do this. It will start with how we can respond when we have a little time but will also cover what to do when we're stuck in the moment and don't have the time or space to follow this process. Exercise 3.2 puts these ideas together to help you apply them when you need them.

Define the threat

When we're angry, we need to identify what has caused the anger. Asking the question "What is the threat?" can help clarify in our minds what the issue is.

The perceived threat is usually somebody else and what they have done or said. Initially, we may think of lots of things that the other person has said, or we may be able to think of things throughout the day that have built up. Usually, though, there will be one main issue – either the most significant thing or lots of situations we have perceived in the same way. Then we need to ask what it is about what they have done or said that we have interpreted as a threat. Are they threatening us physically? Are they threatening to take something important or get in the way of something we want? Are we interpreting their behaviour to mean something about how they view us?

Working through our experience to arrive at a statement that sums up the threat can help clarify things in our minds and counter some of the fog and clouded thinking we experience when we're angry. We should arrive at some kind of statement that represents the threat we perceive in the situation. Examples include: "They're going to hurt me", "They're going to stop me . . . ", "They're ignoring me", "They're treating me like I'm inferior" or "They're not looking after my child like they should". Each of these brief statements captures what it is about the situation that has made us feel angry.

This process can take some time. Sometimes we'll have time and other times we won't, and we might have to go through this process after we've been angry and acted on it. This can be a really helpful process, though, because there are likely to be patterns to our anger and it can help us the next time, when the threat may well be similar.

Check the threat

Once we've identified the threat in this way, we can consider whether we're accurately perceiving the situation. When we're angry, the reptilian brain is activated, and we may be misinterpreting or exaggerating the threat. Giving ourselves some time to allow the anger to reduce and using the control we can have over our bodies to help with this can be really useful. We can slow our breathing, relax our muscles and move our attention away from the threat. Remember that even though anger is primarily a response to an interpersonal threat, it can be made worse by physical discomfort including hunger, tiredness and pain. Having something to eat, 'sleeping on it' or managing pain might all be very basic but powerful ways of giving us some time to consider.

Talking to others about our experience is also a useful way of checking the threat. The process of identifying the threat will help us communicate more clearly with others, giving them a sense of what happened and how we have interpreted it, and this will allow them to help us consider whether we have things the right way around.

One occasion when many adults may find themselves misinterpreting the situation is in relation to children. Much of children's behaviour is carried out without much regard for others; they can push boundaries, repeatedly ignore instructions and generally be quite self-absorbed. But this is how children are: their brains work differently from those of adults, and they are not capable of determining the impact of their behaviour on others in the same way that adults are. They are also unlikely to be grateful to their parents for being their parents. Adults' tendency to forget that children are children is nicely highlighted by the phrase 'the little adult assumption', where we accidentally assume that children are more capable than they really are.[14] This is a particularly important part of checking the threat – have we attributed to children the ability to manipulate, disrespect or devalue when they are just being children?

Resolve the threat

Once we have identified the threat and checked the threat, we need to try to resolve the threat.

This will usually involve responding in ways that are consistent with the feeling – approaching and confronting the person who is threatening us. Anger provides the motivation and energy we need to follow through with things we might otherwise avoid and encourages us to confront others when they threaten us. Anger is also perceived by other people, and showing and displaying anger can be helpful in letting others know that we are serious. There are a number of things we can do to make sure it goes as well as possible. Exercise 3.2 can support you to use these ideas in practice.

Think about somebody you've come across recently who has used anger well to get themselves heard or taken seriously. In all likelihood, they used just a little bit. They were obviously angry, but they probably didn't shout or throw things or rant. A little bit of anger goes a long way. A firmer tone of voice, a stronger body position and a clearer statement are often powerful displays that we're angry. Too much anger can be unhelpful, as it can make it more difficult for us to express ourselves, and other people can stop taking us seriously if they perceive us as 'too angry'. Using too much anger to try to resolve situations might be a sign of being stuck in the anger trap, as outlined in the next section.

We know what the threat is, which helps clarify what we want to say. We want to stick with our perception of the situation and express the link between what the person did and how we perceived their behaviour: "I felt . . . when you . . . ". Examples include "I felt angry because I thought you had ignored me", "I was cross because you didn't seem to value my contribution" or "I was furious when you broke . . . because it was really important to me". Communicating in this way is much more likely to be heard than labelling others' behaviour. Labelling others' behaviour is more likely to be experienced as attacking than sticking with what we perceived the threat to be. Imagine how you would respond to "I was cross when you didn't acknowledge me" compared with "You ignored me again!"

When we're angry, it is tempting to provide other examples of situations where people have made us angry, or where we feel they have treated us badly. It is only possible to resolve one issue at a time, so if we bring up lots of different issues, the other person is more likely to experience it as an attack and it is likely to escalate. If we can experience some kind of resolution from an issue in this way, we can apply this to other situations that might also be making us angry at a different time.

We also need to focus our minds on this situation: what would a resolution be like? What are we hoping for from this confrontation? Do we want the person to apologise? Do we want something returned or compensation? What are our expectations of the other person? Having some ideas about where we might want to end up can keep us oriented to the discussion. If we're going to manage this, we also need to listen to the response. Being clear in our communication can lead to clear responses. We need to take time to listen.

As the intensity of anger increases, we are more likely to get taken over by the reptilian brain, experience tunnel vision and find that the aim has become to 'win' rather than our longer-term objectives. If things are getting too hot, if it is becoming difficult to do all of the things outlined earlier, then pause and come back to it. Just saying "I need a minute" or "I'll be back soon" can be enough to allow us to calm again before continuing. This is much better than ending up feeling too angry and doing or saying something we might later regret. Remember that the ability to think rationally decreases with the increasing intensity of anger, so we need to be prepared to do this sooner rather than later, as it will become more and more difficult as anger builds.

Exercise 3.2 Responding to anger

These questions and reminders should help you to respond to anger.

Define the threat

I'm angry, and it's important to identify what I'm perceiving as a threat.

Who am I angry with?
What has this person done or said that has made me angry?
How am I interpreting this behaviour?

THE THREAT IS _____

Check the threat

Am I perceiving this threat accurately enough? Have I misinterpreted or exaggerated something?

Is there any other way to view this situation?
Am I viewing something as deliberate that probably wasn't?
Can I check this out with someone?
Am I making a 'little adult assumption'?

Resolve the threat

I need to approach the person and confront them about this. Remember:

NOT TOO HOT – a little anger goes a long way
Stick to my perception
Keep it brief
Stick to this topic: we can only discuss one thing at a time
Remember to listen, too
Be clear about what I want
Give myself space if I need to

Helping others with anger

What is the most common phrase used by others when we're angry?

"CALM DOWN"

This is one of the worst things you can say to an angry person: it doesn't tend to help much. Why do you think this is? Think about a time when somebody said this to you – what was the tone of their voice? How did you interpret it? Anger is a response to an interpersonal threat; we perceive that somebody is treating us badly. In this context, being told to calm down is like dismissing our concerns, being told that what we perceive as important doesn't matter.

When we're talking with angry people, we want them to know that we take their concerns seriously and we want to know what is going on. If they are so angry that they can't do this, then we can use the ideas about calming the body to direct them to do things that are likely to calm them down. For example, we can take them somewhere quieter, invite them to sit down, get them a drink to gently move their focus of attention away from the threat and encourage them to take a breath. Using our own bodies to model a slightly less energised or activated state can also help, using a calmer tone of voice and being more relaxed in our posture. These should be only a little calmer, or it will appear that we are missing the point and our calmness will become irritating in itself. All of this is done in preparation for us to listen, and this should be clear.

Then, we want to give them time and space to explain what is going on. To begin with, we can let them talk, but over time, as they calm, we can begin to interrupt to clarify and support them to work through their anger. The process will then follow that detailed previously and outlined in Exercise 3.2: define the threat, check the threat and resolve the threat.

Anger trap: problems with anger

This section looks at the problems we might experience with anger. There are relatively few diagnoses that relate specifically to anger, although depression is a commonly used label, and there is a newer diagnosis of 'intermittent explosive disorder', although this focuses exclusively on behaviour and the experience of anger is not a part of the disorder.[15] Even though there are few diagnostic labels specifically for problems

with anger, difficulties with anger are commonly reported in the general population and are common reasons for seeking help.[16]

Interventions for problems with anger include antidepressants and anger management classes, but the evidence in support of these treatments is not particularly strong. This is particularly problematic for anger management classes, which are often recommended in these situations.[17] Some of the reasons why anger management might not be enough will be explained in this section, along with some ideas about a more comprehensive approach.

The most common response to anger is outward expression. When we are threatened, we respond by countering the threat and trying to protect our interests. Often, this can be useful and serves to help us to live alongside others with mutual respect and care. At other times, though, our responses to anger can result in increased conflict, disrespect, hurt and harm and can lead to the breakdown of relationships and isolation.

The anger trap shows the processes that lead to this situation. The central aspect is a sense of overestimated threat and two separate vicious cycles around each side. The next section explains how the trap fits together.

Two examples will illustrate the processes:

> Connor has recently been suspended from college. This followed a number of incidents of aggression in the classroom and elsewhere on college grounds, towards both teachers and other students. Connor has found education difficult since primary school and says that the teachers pick on him. He has been offered extra tuition on multiple occasions but tends to avoid it because he does not want his peers to know that he finds things difficult. Much of his aggression occurs when he is put on the spot in class or when he feels stupid. Outside

the classroom, other students are scared of Connor because of his unpredictability, and they have labelled him as 'mad' and 'nuts'. He has become the person to wind up and fight.

Nicola's mother was a critical woman who was highly stressed and quick to anger in her early life. Nicola remembered fearing her mother and feeling that she could never do anything right. She had been able to get on with life okay, but she started to find herself struggling more with anger when she married and had a young family. She has a stressful job where she feels that she picks up everybody else's slack and feels devalued and taken advantage of. Nicola has become more irritable at home and has been shouting at her children when they don't do as she asks. When her children are asleep, Nicola feels terrible for shouting at them and worries that they will be scared of her like she was her own mother. Her husband has told her that her behaviour is unacceptable and that he will leave her if it continues. Nicola has worked hard to try to restrain herself, but despite some periods of success. something always seems to get to her in the end and she finds herself losing it again.

Overestimated threat

In these examples, both Nicola and Connor are perceiving high levels of threat from others. Connor is expecting his teachers and his peers to make fun of him when he doesn't know things; we could label the threat as "They'll treat me like I'm stupid" or "They'll laugh at me". Nicola appears to be experiencing her colleagues as disrespectful and devaluing; she might have statements like "They'll think I'm useless" or "They'll take advantage of me". Importantly, Nicola is also viewing the behaviour of her children as disrespectful, deliberate or a personal slight (see earlier section on checking the threat).

Both Nicola and Connor are experiencing a sense of overestimated threat. Nicola has a good reason to overestimate the threat. She has had experiences in her early life of being criticised and bullied by others, so it made sense to expect this. In later life, though, at work or at home, Nicola is anticipating more threats from others than are likely to be there.

Connor probably has a reason to overestimate the threat too. It may be that in his earlier life he experienced abuse, violence or humiliation. Equally, he may still be experiencing this at home, and for young people like Connor it can be particularly difficult to open up about these experiences, given their expectations of how others will respond.

Most people in the anger trap will have had experiences that lead them to overestimate threat. Examples include bullying at school, a violent household in childhood, intensely critical teachers or parents or experiences of conflict either as a civilian or a member of the armed forces or emergency services. These kinds of experiences will also link with shame, which is caused by a focus on ourselves as inadequate, defective or bad. Nicola and Connor have both had early experiences where other people made them feel ashamed, so they overestimate the degree to which others will do this in the future.

Early life experiences can lead to overestimations of threat

Threats from others tend to be overestimated in two ways. The first is frequency, where more people, more often, are perceived as being disrespectful, rude or threatening. The second is intensity, where the degree of disrespect, rudeness or threat is perceived as greater or more significant. In the anger trap, there will be more frequent and greater intensities of anger as a result of this overestimation of threat.

Explode

The perception of a threat from another – a threat of disrespect, harm or a slight – causes a feeling of anger. This anger is likely to be particularly intense if it links with an experience of shame, of feeling inadequate, defective or bad, as one of the responses to shame is to angrily defend against it (see Chapter 6). The most common way of expressing anger is through approaching others and expressing it. In the anger trap, because of the tendency to overestimate threat, anger tends to be expressed more often and more intensely.

Frequent and intense expressions of anger, sometimes resulting in hurting others, can be the most obviously problematic part of the anger trap. Both Nicola and Connor experience this difficulty with expressing anger. There is often a sense that anger comes out of nowhere, that it is immediately very intense and that there is little control over its expression. As a result, anger is experienced as an explosion by the individual and those around them. Sometimes, it might even feel good – threatening others can make us feel powerful and dominant and is a relief after feeling threatened and small. In many ways, this is the function of anger – expressing anger in this way is the natural response. For Connor, the feeling of being picked on by peers or teachers will be temporarily relieved when he is fighting or throwing furniture around the classroom; he will be the one in control, the one with power. For Nicola, after a day of feeling devalued and unimportant at work, she will briefly feel that she is the powerful one at home.

However, there are other consequences of expressing anger in this way. Expressing anger around others can lead to an escalation and a real increase in the threat. This is Connor's experience – expecting threat from others and behaving as such leads to a real increase in conflict and tension. Connor is approached by others who are expecting or hoping for conflict, and they do exactly as he expects as a result – laugh and him and tell him he's stupid, which ignites his anger. The second consequence usually follows afterwards, where the behaviour prompted by the anger (e.g., verbal or physical aggression) is judged negatively by the individual or those around them. This results in an increase in potential threat – being judged or criticised by others. Connor is devalued by others, both peers and teachers, because of his behaviour. Where the overestimated threat links directly to a perception that others are humiliating and shaming, expressing anger in explosive ways can result in further shame and humiliation.[18]

Nicola labels herself 'a useless mother' for shouting at her children, and her husband is also threatening to leave her as a result of her behaviour. These both represent real and significant threats and are likely to fuel the anger trap.

So a tendency to overestimate threat can lead to increased anger. Increased anger can lead to increased expression of anger, which can lead to increased conflict and increased judgement by self and others, which leads to more threat, feeding the trap.

Bottle-up

Both Nicola and Connor do other things when they feel angry; they don't always respond in an explosive manner. Both of them work hard to try to 'keep a lid on things', to 'keep calm' and to avoid conflict with others. This is particularly true following a big blowout, when they tell themselves they'll never do that again and work really hard to try to make sure they don't get into another fight or have another argument with the children.

This is the other side of the anger trap – the bottling-up side. On this side, the feelings of anger in response to the perceived threat are suppressed, ignored or pushed away. When this is successful, both Nicola and Connor might feel they have achieved something; they have avoided the highly problematic and distressing experiences that come from expressing anger. However, the issue that prompted the anger in the first place remains unresolved, and so whilst they have not acted on the anger, the feeling is still there. For Nicola, when she bottles up her anger, puts her head down and keeps going, she is left with the sense that her colleagues and her children are taking advantage of her. Connor is left with the sense that people are laughing at him and treating him like's he's stupid, and he's not doing anything about it. In both cases, the function of anger, which is to protect from others, has not been enacted, so the individual is exposed to being taken advantage of, used or mistreated by others. Some of this will be their overestimation of threat, but some of it may also be accurate – bottling up anger can lead to others taking advantage.

Over time, bottled-up anger builds, to the point at which it can no longer be tolerated and is expressed in an explosive manner.

Summary of the anger trap

The anger trap consists of two interlinking vicious cycles: an exploding response to anger and a bottling up of the anger. In the anger trap, both responses are used and there is a switching between them that keeps everything stuck. Nicola's and Connor's anger traps show how it works for them.

These two parts are fundamental to the anger trap, and they help explain why some approaches to anger management often don't work. Anger management classes based on assumptions about anger being toxic, problematic or harmful will work predominantly on the explode side of the trap. This can lead people to judge themselves even more harshly for their anger and explosive behaviour and can push them to work even harder to bottle everything up. Any benefit in the short term will not be possible to sustain in the longer term.

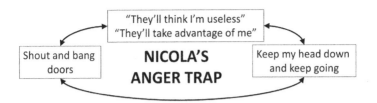

The anger trap highlights that, like in the other traps described in this book, it is the response to the emotion that is the problematic element, not the emotion itself. This means that changing the way in which we respond to anger can help us move out of the trap. Have a go at drawing your own anger trap (Exercise 3.3), which will help you think about the kinds of things you could do to get out of it, covered next.

Exercise 3.3   Draw your own anger trap

If you think you might be stuck in the anger trap, have a go at drawing your own. Take a moment to think of three times fairly recently where you felt angry. Write down a couple of words to help you remember those times (e.g., at the supermarket, kids' homework).

1. _____

2. _____

3. _____

Start with the threats from others first. Write down the kinds of thoughts that you had in these situations. There are likely to be lots of different thoughts, but try to focus them down into what the threat was – what did it mean to you that the other person was doing or saying that? Examples might include "He's treating me like trash", "They're ignoring me on purpose" or "They'll laugh at me".

Next, think about the kinds of things you do if you go around to the explode side. What do you do if you act on your anger?

> Then think about the longer-term consequences of these actions. What do you think of yourself afterwards? What do others do or say afterwards?
>
> Now think about what you do when you don't act on your anger.
>
> What are the longer-term consequences of doing this? How do you feel? How do others treat you?

Getting out of the anger trap

The anger trap illustrates what happens when we get tangled up with anger. It shows us that even though anger problems might be most obvious at the points of explosion, responding by bottling up is equally problematic. This means that getting out of the anger trap takes more than just a focus on what happens when we explode. We cannot work to try to remain neutral and calm all the time and 'just walk away' or 'calm down'. Instead, getting out of the trap involves experiencing tolerable levels of anger and responding differently. This should allow a reduction in problematic responses to anger and a reevaluation of the levels of threat. To do this, there are a number of steps that can be helpful. First is reducing the threats to try to reduce the heat and give more space to try other things. Second is responding differently to manageable levels of anger, which can break the two cycles of the anger trap and allow a reevaluation of the threat.

> **Getting out of the anger trap involves tolerating anger and responding differently**

Reducing threat

The anger trap highlights the importance of perceived threat from others. It is this perceived threat that leads to a feeling of anger in the first place. Both Connor and Nicola have good reasons to overestimate the threat from others. Being stuck in the anger trap also increases the threats they experience from others, so they experience anger more frequently and intensely than they would otherwise.

One of the most practical ways to begin work on getting out of the anger trap is to think about ways to reduce the perception of threat from others. There are likely to be some patterns to the perception of threat and the experience of anger. Particular situations, times of day, or individuals may make us angrier than others.

Nicola, for example, may well find that getting the children ready for school in the morning is a particularly difficult time, or that bathtime and bedtime are when she feels particularly angry because she perceives she is being ignored. Connor might find that particular lessons, teachers or peers are likely to make him feel angry because he perceives these situations as threatening.

First steps out of the anger trap involve avoiding or escaping from situations particularly likely to lead to high levels of anger

Once the patterns where anger is most problematic have been identified, it is possible to make some practical changes to reduce the level of threat. These are avoidance and escape.

Avoidance

The most anger-inducing situations can initially be simply avoided. If Nicola often finds herself shouting at her children before they go to bed, then it might make sense, on a temporary basis, for somebody else to take responsibility for putting the children to bed. Being angry and shouting at bedtime is not likely to be particularly helpful, and avoiding this outcome may allow the situation to calm and for Nicola and her children to enjoy other time together. For Connor, it might make sense, as he returns to school, to start off in lessons that are less likely to feel threatening and make him feel angry, so that he has more chance of being at school in a calmer state. Equally, he could avoid particular peers who might be more likely to lead to a perception of threat.

Escape

Another practical option is to devise a plan to leave situations that are likely to lead to a trip around the anger trap. For example, Nicola could be involved at bedtime, but if she starts to feel irritated or annoyed, she could have a plan to say or do something so that somebody else could take over before things escalate. Connor might have a plan where he can leave situations with some kind of signal and go to a particular place in school if things feel as though they are escalating. These will usually need planning in advance, so that others know what is going on and know not to pursue or hamper these efforts to leave.

Both avoidance and escape on their own are too close to the bottling-up side of the trap and are unlikely to be sustainable in the longer term. However, both are useful short-term strategies to allow situations to calm, give a sense of control and allow time and space for other changes.

Responding differently to anger: bodily responses

The significant impact of anger on the body was highlighted earlier in the chapter. Anger results in increased heart rate, deeper breathing and tense muscles. Our senses are sharpened, and our attention is narrowed to focus on the threat. In the anger trap, this is likely to be activated quickly and intensely under the control of the reptilian brain, and it becomes more difficult to use the rational brain to think logically. To get out of the anger trap, it is important that there is some kind of different response to anger, and starting with a different bodily response can allow the rational brain more time to think.

The body's response to anger is controlled by the reptilian brain and so happens almost automatically. However, there are three areas of the system that we can override: breathing, muscle tension and the direction of attention. In anger, relatively small changes to the body can have significant positive impacts on our ability to think and do things differently. This is a similar process to fear, and there is further information about this in Chapter 1.

Breathing

One of the classic pieces of advice when we're angry is to take a breath. It can be frustrating when this advice is offered alone, as clearly it is not enough. However, adjusting our breathing and using this moment to pause can disrupt our usual automatic responses enough to allow us to think and do other things differently. It is the out-breath in particular that can calm and reduce the intensity of anger a little.

Muscle tension

When we are angry, our muscles tense, ready for fighting. Commonly, it is our hands and faces where there is particular tension. By consciously letting go of some of the tension in our bodies, particularly in our hands and faces, we can reduce the intensity of anger. This can be combined with a longer out-breath to help reduce the tension. Relaxing the tension in our hands and faces can have the added benefit of reducing how angry we appear to others, which can also have a positive impact on the situation.

Focus of attention

When we are angry, our attention is narrowed and directed towards the person who has made us angry (the threat). If we can reduce this narrowing of attention, even just a little, by noticing our breath and our muscles and perhaps trying to take in a little of what is around us, we can reduce the 'tunnel vision' often experienced in extreme anger and give the rational brain a better chance to function. The ability to redirect our attention can be practiced, and Exercise 1.4 outlines one way to do this; other ways are to use mindfulness or meditation.

Responding differently to anger: reevaluating threat

The purpose of these adjustments to our bodily sensations is not to get rid of the anger and carry on regardless ('bottling up') but to reduce the intensity of anger so we can better tolerate it. This allows the rational brain a chance to think, and then to make decisions to respond in a different way.

Not responding immediately or with such intense anger can give a different experience of situations, which can allow a reevaluation of threat. Nicola's example highlights this process.

> Nicola decided to stay out of the way when the children were leaving the house in the morning, as this was a difficult time, and she made the decision to stand back or leave whenever she noticed herself getting heated. After a couple of weeks of this and becoming more aware of how her body felt at these times, she started to remain in the situation but take a couple of deeper breaths and let some of the tension go in her body as she watched her husband encourage the children to get ready. She reminded herself that they were children and noticed that as her husband broke the tasks down into smaller chunks, they seemed more able to do them. Witnessing this repeatedly helped Nicola to see that they did not deliberately play up or make life difficult (most of the time) but needed more help than she'd thought they did. When she viewed their behaviour in this way, it caused her less anger, and she was better able to support them.

In this example, Nicola tries to reduce the intensity of her anger so she can remain in the situation and not go around either side of the trap. As a result, she can experience the situation differently and reevaluate her interpretation of it. She has not 'controlled' or 'managed' her anger; she has tolerated it to allow a reevaluation of its cause.

Nicola was overestimating the threat in these kinds of situations. For Connor, though, tolerating the anger and not really getting involved is going to be a difficult task because he is so stuck in the trap, and those around him are used to him responding in particular ways.

Responding differently to anger: assertiveness

In the anger trap, there are two types of response, both of which keep the trap going: explode and bottle-up. A different way of responding to anger is assertiveness.

Assertiveness is a term that dates back to the 1950s, and it received lots of research and attention around this time. Whilst the term is used less commonly today, the ideas remain in many forms and are included in many CBT treatment manuals.[19] Assertiveness can be defined as the ability to:

- Say "no"
- Ask for favours or make requests
- Express feelings
- Initiate, continue and terminate general conversations[20]

In this way, an assertive response to anger finds the middle ground between exploding and bottling up. It is the position where it is possible to express anger, frustration or discontent in a manner that is more likely to result in a positive outcome.

> **Assertiveness allows the expression of discontent without exploding or bottling up**

Saying "no"

Saying "no" is often considered the main feature of assertiveness, but its importance is often overstated and misunderstood. Saying "no" is not important in itself; it is the result of a prioritisation of our own needs and wants. Learning to say "no" begins with learning to prioritise ourselves and our time. Nicola's example highlights the process:

> Nicola made the decision to assert herself more at work. She began by thinking about what the most important aspects of her job were, what she was employed to do and where her skills were best used. She discussed this with her manager to make sure they were in agreement. When her colleagues asked her to help, Nicola started to make small changes. She didn't say "yes" straight away but said she could help when she had finished what she was working on; or, when this was too difficult, she made it known that she was busy on other things. Nicola found that people responded fine to these actions, and she began to say that she did not have the time to do things when she was confident that they did not fit with her role. Over time, her colleagues seemed to value her work more and were more appreciative when she did help them. Nicola built her confidence at work and surprised herself one day by declining to help her mother, which was something she could never have imagined doing.

In Nicola's example, we can see that prioritising herself leads to a different way of responding when she experiences interpersonal threats (e.g., thinking she was being taken advantage of). When she was asked to do something that would take her time away from her own work, previously Nicola went around the bottle-up side of the anger trap. She may previously have only experienced a low level of anger, resentment or annoyance, but over time, this built up. By being more assertive, this anger does not build up, and others interact with her differently, noticing her work and respecting and valuing her more. This results in fewer experiences of interpersonal threat and less time in the anger trap.

> **Saying "no" is the result of
> prioritising our own needs and wants**

Making requests

Asking other people to do things and asking for help can be difficult. We first have to accept that we cannot do it on our own and share this admission with others. Then we have to take the risk that others might say "no". These situations can feel as though they are inviting interpersonal threats – judgement from others, for example. Equally, they can help test the perception of threat, finding out whether others will help us. Connor's situation is a good example:

> Connor's experiences led him to expect that others would not support him or would even ridicule him if he asked for help. This left him trying to manage things on his own, with the result that he found education very difficult. During Connor's reintroduction to college, he was put in a small group. He made an effort to ask for help, starting small – asking for extra paper, and then another copy of the questions – and over time, he started to ask for little bits of help with the work. He found that the teacher helped him, and the other students didn't really take much notice. Connor started to feel that he was progressing in his education and was less likely to feel stupid when he did not understand something. He plucked up the courage to ask this teacher for help around break times, when others were winding him up, and they came up with a plan for how he could respond.

Through making requests of others, Connor is able to respond differently when he does not know something or cannot do something on his own. Rather than silently trying to continue or getting frustrated because he can't do it, he is able to ask for help and experience others responding positively.

Clarity is important when asking for help. Requests should be brief and clear; instructions that contain lots of irrelevant material or background are confusing. Politeness is also important, demonstrating respect for the person who is being addressed. Polite requests often start "Could you please . . . ", "I wonder if you could . . . " or "I would be very grateful if you would . . . ". It is important, though, not to confuse politeness with apologising. Apologising for requests undermines the request and the person requesting it and is not so likely to produce good results. Examples of apologies include "I'm very sorry to have to ask you but . . . " and "I know it's a pain, but could you . . . ". Gratitude for requests undertaken is also important and a way of demonstrating respect to others, which is then likely to be reciprocated.

Expressing feelings

This book is all about the importance of feelings in our daily lives. Our feelings drive many of our needs, wants and desires, and being able to understand, tolerate and express these feelings allows for positive interactions with others. Each chapter of this book highlights the importance of different emotions for us as individuals and for our social lives.

In learning to be assertive rather than explosive or bottling up, we need to express how we feel in ways that are likely to be heard. It usually involves brief, clear statements expressed from an 'I' point of view: "I feel sad/angry/happy/scared, etc. when . . . ", which stick to a single situation. It involves the expression of all feelings, not just anger. Being open about how we feel deepens our relationships with other people and enables greater trust and understanding. This can reduce interpersonal threats and assumptions that can lead to overestimating interpersonal threat. Nicola's example about expressing feelings highlights its importance:

> Nicola had been working on a project at work for some time. She'd invested lots of her time and energy into it and was pleased with its progress. One day, she heard from a colleague that her manager was thinking about giving this project to somebody else, and she was disappointed and angry. She took a few minutes, and then went to see her manager and calmly but firmly expressed her disappointment and anger. She explained what she had been doing, where she had got to and what she had planned to do next. Nicola's manager responded with respect to the work she had done, her commitment to the project and her confidence in approaching her, and she gave Nicola more time to see it through. She also appeared to notice her more in meetings and asked for her contribution more regularly.

In this example, we can see that Nicola expressed herself from her own point of view, focusing on what she had been doing, what she had planned and how she felt about the proposal to give the project to somebody else. She stuck to the situation at hand and did not attack the manager or the colleague to whom the project might have been given. She received a positive response in relation to that project and to her confidence in approaching the manager.

Initiating, continuing and terminating conversations

The ability to converse with others is an important part of assertiveness, and it is an opportunity to talk to others without experiencing threats.

Having a conversation about plans for the weekend, the weather or the news (perhaps not politics!) allows people to be in each other's company in a neutral space and to build trust. For people like Nicola and Connor who expect to experience others as threatening, having neutral everyday conversations can help to reduce this sense of threat. It is something that can be practiced by slightly lengthening all conversations – in corridors, in shops or on the phone – to include a little bit of chatter. This allows for practicing conversational skills and provides an experience of being in the company of others in a calm, neutral emotional state.

Summary: getting out of the anger trap

All of the ideas outlined in this section are designed to support different responses to anger. To get out of the trap, anger can be tolerated but responded to differently. The initial steps are to reduce the heat of situations, avoiding and escaping situations that are particularly likely to produce high levels of anger. This allows for tolerable levels of anger to be experienced and for alternatives to the bottle-up and explode cycles to be practiced. Responding in different ways to manageable levels of anger means that the perception of interpersonal threat can be both tested and reduced. Over time, greater levels of respect and harmony should build, and anger will continue to be experienced but at lower levels and responded to in ways that are more likely to be helpful than harmful.

Summary

Anger is an important emotion. It is not always bad or toxic. It is a response to a perceived interpersonal threat, and it can help us to stand up for what is important, for ourselves and those around us. It energises us to approach and confront people where we need to and most of the time, it has a positive outcome. Getting stuck in the anger trap, however, can be extremely distressing and can have serious consequences for everybody involved. The anger trap highlights the two cycles of response to anger – 'bottle up' and 'explode' – and shows how learning to better manage feelings of anger can allow different responses that communicate the feeling and prevent both bottling up and exploding. Over time, this can lead to a different experience of the world and a reduction in the experience and perception of interpersonal threat.

Notes

1 A survey of college students found that the most common cause of anger was a sense of being "misled, betrayed, used, disappointed, hurt by others, or treated unjustly" (Izard, 1991, p. 235). Other authors have also highlighted the role of others in anger, describing it as "developing in response to unwanted, and sometimes unexpected, aversive interpersonal behaviour" (Kassinove & Tafrate, 2002, p. 31).
2 Parkinson (2001) and Deffenbacher et al. (2016).
3 A study examining the underlying reasons for increased anger on the road found that anger on the road appeared less mixed with other emotions than in other situations. Anger on the road was also linked with purer appraisals of the other person's fault, was more likely to be caused by communication difficulties and was slower to be noticed by the person causing the anger (Parkinson, 2001).
4 Berkowitz (1990)
5 MacCormack and Lindquist (2019)
6 Krizan and Hisler (2019) had 142 people take part in a study in which half were intentionally deprived of sleep and the other half were allowed to sleep normally. Both groups were then exposed to loud, irritating noises. The study found that across individuals and across different situations, those deprived of sleep were significantly angrier than those who had slept normally. This supports the idea that loss of sleep causes increases in anger.
7 Scherer and Wallbott (1994)
8 Izard (1991)
9 A survey of college students found that most of the thoughts following an incident prompting anger were about revenge (Izard, 1991).
10 Tucker-Ladd's (1996) introduction to his chapter on anger includes the phrase "anger may do more harm than any other emotion" and goes on to describe two problems with anger, "how to prevent or control your own anger and how to handle someone aggressing against you". By the second page there is reference to Hitler, Stalin, genocide and murder. Nowhere in the chapter is anything positive or functional attributed to anger as a human emotion.
11 Kassinove et al. (1997)
12 This shift from a blocked goal in the environment to a personal slight is described by Lewis as the difference between anger and rage (Lewis, 1993).
13 Pinker (2012)
14 This phrase comes from a guide to support parents with the discipline of young children (Phelan, 2016).
15 Intermittent explosive disorder was first introduced to the DSM-IV and remains in the DSM-V, and it describes 'aggressive outbursts' that are disproportionate to the situation and cause distress and impairment to functioning (APA, 2013).
16 A 2015 study in the United States found that almost 8% of a community sample of 34,000 people reported experiencing 'inappropriate, intense, or poorly controlled anger' (Okuda et al., 2015). Another study found that around half of those presenting for help with mental health problems experienced problems with anger (Posternak & Zimmerman, 2002). Finally, a study of

clinicians found that they reported working with anger problems as often as fear and anxiety problems, although they also reported more confusion and less confidence working with these difficulties (Lachmund et al., 2005).

17 One study found evidence for cognitive behavioural interventions but comments on the lack of evidence relating to the far more common anger management class (Lee & DiGiuseppe, 2017).

18 This is the 'shame-rage' spiral highlighted by Scheff (1987).

19 Speed et al. (2018).

20 These four parts of assertiveness are taken straight from a very short paper written by Lazarus in 1973. His note aims to distinguish between assertiveness and hostility and highlight the four separate skills required in assertiveness, highlighted here. The paper also includes a personal story about buying shirts from a man who was surly and unhelpful. Rather than attacking him, reporting him to the manager or leaving the store, Lazarus reports saying that he appeared to be having a bad day and asking what was wrong. This led to a productive conversation and benefit for both parties.

References

APA, 2013. *Diagnostic and statistical manual of mental disorders* (5th edn.). Washington, DC: Author.

Berkowitz, L., 1990. On the formation and regulation of anger and aggression: A cognitive-neoassociationistic analysis. *American Psychologist*, 45(4), p. 494.

Deffenbacher, J.L., Stephens, A.N. and Sullman, M.J., 2016. Driving anger as a psychological construct: Twenty years of research using the Driving Anger Scale. *Transportation Research Part F: Traffic Psychology and Behaviour*, 42, pp. 236–247.

Izard, C.E., 1991. *The psychology of emotions*. New York: Plenum Press.

Kassinove, H., Sukhodolsky, D.G., Tsytsarev, S.V. and Solovyova, S., 1997. Self-reported anger episodes in Russia and America. *Journal of Social Behavior and Personality*, 12(2), pp. 301–324.

Kassinove, H. and Tafrate, R.C., 2002. *Anger management: The complete treatment guidebook for practitioners*. Atascadero, CA: Impact Publishers.

Krizan, Z. and Hisler, G., 2019. Sleepy anger: Restricted sleep amplifies angry feelings. *Journal of Experimental Psychology: General*, 148(7), p. 1239.

Lachmund, E., DiGiuseppe, R. and Fuller, J.R., 2005. Clinicians' diagnosis of a case with anger problems. *Journal of Psychiatric Research*, 39(4), pp. 439–447.

Lazarus, A.A., 1973. On assertive behavior: A brief note. *Behavior Therapy*, 4(5), pp. 697–699.

Lee, A.H. and DiGiuseppe, R., 2017. Anger and aggression treatments: A review of meta-analyses. *Current Opinion in Psychology*, 19, pp. 65–74.

Lewis, M., 1993. The development of anger and range. In R.A. Glick and S.P. Roose (eds.), *Rage, power, and aggression*. New Haven, CT: Yale University Press, pp. 148–168.

MacCormack, J.K. and Lindquist, K.A., 2019. Feeling hangry? When hunger is conceptualized as emotion. *Emotion*, 19(2), p. 301.

Okuda, M., Picazo, J., Olfson, M., Hasin, D.S., Liu, S.M., Bernardi, S. and Blanco, C., 2015. Prevalence and correlates of anger in the community: Results from a national survey. *CNS Spectrums*, 20(2), p. 130.

Parkinson, B., 2001. Anger on and off the road. *British Journal of Psychology*, 92(3), pp. 507–526.

Phelan, T., 2016. *1–2–3 Magic: 3-Step discipline for calm, effective, and happy parenting*. Naperville, IL: Sourcebooks.

Pinker, S., 2012. *The better angels of our nature: Why violence has declined*. London: Penguin Group.

Posternak, M.A. and Zimmerman, M., 2002. Anger and aggression in psychiatric outpatients. *The Journal of Clinical Psychiatry*, 63(8), pp. 665–672.

Scheff, T.J., 1987. The shame-rage spiral: A case study of an interminable quarrel. In H.B. Lewis (ed.), *The role of shame in symptom formation*. Hillsdale, NJ: Erlbaum, pp. 109–149.

Scherer, K.R. and Wallbott, H.G., 1994. Evidence for universality and cultural variation of differential emotion response patterning. *Journal of Personality and Social Psychology*, 66(2), p. 310.

Speed, B.C., Goldstein, B.L. and Goldfried, M.R., 2018. Assertiveness training: A forgotten evidence-based treatment. *Clinical Psychology: Science and Practice*, 25(1), p. e12216.

Tucker-Ladd, C., 1996. *Psychological self-help*. Springfield, IL: Clay Tucker-Ladd.

Chapter 4

Disgust

Disgust is an aversion or repugnance from something that can be caused by a whole variety of experiences, ranging from poor hygiene, small creatures, lesions and rotting food to unacceptable behaviour like cheating, lying or taking advantage. In each case, it produces a similar response – a desire to keep away.

In this chapter, we'll explore the functions of disgust in each of these areas, and we'll cover how we can tolerate disgust and helpfully respond.

Disgust, like all emotions, can be linked with problems, and there are two types of difficulties commonly seen with disgust. The first is when it is combined with fear, usually in relation to fears of small animals, blood, contamination or food. For these difficulties, we'll illustrate how disgust can be incorporated into the fear trap. The other types of difficulties involve disgust in a social context, where disgust is often seen alongside anger and shame (e.g., self-disgust), and this is covered towards the end of the chapter.

Exercise 4.1   Feeling disgusted

Think about a recent time when you felt disgusted.

How would you describe the experience?
What did you notice/were you most aware of?
What made you feel disgusted?
How did you respond/what did you do?
What happened afterwards?

DOI: 10.4324/9781003138112-5

Understanding and accepting disgust

To begin with, we'll explore the causes of disgust, its impact on the five elements of emotion and its function. Have a look at Exercise 4.1 to see how much you know about disgust already.

What causes disgust?

There are a number of different potential causes of disgust that you might have identified in Exercise 4.1. Most causes of disgust fall under one of these six broad categories[1]:

Poor hygiene
Displays or evidence of unhygienic behaviour, like people sniffing, picking their nose, smelling, or dirty tissues and unflushed toilets
Small creatures
Like maggots, slugs, worms, cockroaches, rats, spiders and teeming insects
Sexual behaviour
Promiscuity, prostitution, unusual sexual behaviour
Atypical appearance
People who are deformed in some way, or particularly fat or thin, wheezing or moving oddly
Lesion disgust
Cuts, sores, weeping wounds
Food
Rotting or decomposing food

There are other, more unusual causes of disgust for some people – for example, clusters of holes like those in honeycomb, on sponges or on strawberries.[2]

Even though these six categories of disgust are often considered the most obvious causes of disgust, we can also be disgusted when others' behaviour falls short of society's standards. When people lie, steal, cheat, take advantage or treat others poorly, this can cause feelings of disgust.[3] This form of disgust requires more complex judgements to assess behaviour against a perceived standard.

What happens when we feel disgusted?

What did you notice about disgust in relation to the five elements of emotion in Exercise 4.1? Like all emotions, disgust arises out of changes in all five elements, but some are more noticeable than others.

Feelings

We feel disgust quite often, but it's usually quite brief and not usually very intense. There is no particular felt temperature.[4]

Some common words used to describe the feeling of disgust include dislike, aversion, revulsion, repugnance, distaste, abhorrence and repellence. Where the cause of the disgust is somebody else – because of their hygiene, their appearance or their behaviour – it can be called contempt: a looking down from a superior position on others.

Bodily responses

Disgust has a unique impact on the body, causing an increase in salivation and an intense feeling of nausea and revulsion. Sometimes this can be so extreme that it triggers vomiting.[5] Disgust is linked with activation of the parasympathetic (brake) nervous systems, and there is also a decrease in heart rate that seems unique to disgust.[6] This is linked to fainting in response to blood or needles. Disgust also has a narrowing effect on attention, focusing our attention on the cause of our disgust.[7]

Facial expression

Disgust has a unique facial expression. We move our top lip upwards and wrinkle our nose to block the nostrils. We often open our mouths, and we may stick out our tongues. We have developed this facial expression so that deliberately sticking out our tongues is used to signal distaste and rejection.[8]

Thoughts/interpretations

We do not have many conscious thoughts when we're disgusted. Our thoughts tend to be labels of the emotion or whatever has made us feel the emotion, like "yuck" or "gross".

Our interpretations of situations, however, are very important in disgust. This is illustrated by the fact that some foods, for example, make us feel disgusted even when we've never tasted them – it's the idea of a bad taste or offensive substance that causes disgust.[9] Advertisements sell us products to kill germs and clean dirt that we cannot see; they give us the idea that things are dirty, and we then feel the need to clean them. Two judgements in particular have significant impact on disgust: contagion and similarity.

Contagion is the idea that things that have come into contact with disgusting things become disgusting themselves. People who are disgusted by particular foods will often not eat other food if it has come into contact with it. For example, somebody who dislikes tomatoes may refuse to eat a salad even after the tomatoes have been removed. Another example comes from debates about reusing treated wastewater in countries with frequent water shortages (e.g., Australia). Despite the availability of technology to ensure safety, and the potential disastrous impact of insufficient water, the public remain largely opposed to these ideas primarily because of disgust. The role of contagion in this situation is highlighted by phrases like 'toilet to tap'.[10] Some bizarre examples of contagion come from experimental studies that showed that people were more disgusted by a juice after it came into contact with a dead, sterilised cockroach. The same researchers found that a used, freshly laundered sweater was considered much more disgusting if it had previously been worn by somebody convicted of murder.[11]

Similarity is the process in which things that look like other disgusting things become disgusting themselves. Tapioca topped the 'most hated' school dinners list in 2003, something probably linked to its common nickname 'frogspawn'. Other nicknames included 'worms' for spaghetti and 'bullets' for peas.[12] Oysters also come near the top of many people's most disgusting foods, often being likened to snot. Experimenters have demonstrated this effect by showing that we are much more likely to feel disgust and not want to eat a chocolate bar if it has been shaped to look like faeces rather than a disc.[13]

Disgust is often based on interpretations of similarity or contagion

Behaviours

Most of our responses to disgust involve creating distance between ourselves and the cause of disgust. This is a different response to fear: we don't run away from disgusting things; we just give them a wide berth.

Where the disgust is caused by an offensive substance, we might spit it out, screw up our faces to try to avoid smelling it and move away. Where the disgust is caused by other people, in whatever form, we would tend to avoid and stay away from them. This avoidance of others and keeping our distance can also be called contempt or shunning.

What is the function of disgust?

As omnivores, humans can eat a whole variety of different things, but we run the risk of eating things that are toxic or failing to get a sufficiently balanced diet. This has been called the 'omnivore's dilemma', where we experience a tension between competing goals to eat new foods and to avoid poisons and harmful foods.[14] Disgust is the protective side of this tension, guarding against potential pathogens like bacteria, viruses, fungi and parasites. The Disgusting Food Museum in Sweden highlights this tension between prized foods and disgusting ones (like baby-mouse wine and pickled sheep's eyes).[15] If we have come into contact with a potentially harmful substance, we will get rid of it, spit it out or even be sick. We will then avoid any future substance that is similar to that one, and we will avoid anything that has come into contact with it – all of which should help protect us from illness and disease.

Avoiding people with poor hygiene or who appear atypical in some way can also help us to avoid those who might be harbouring bacteria or germs. Disgust of others can also help prevent sexual activity that is likely to make us ill or is unlikely to lead to healthy offspring. Disgust, for example, can prevent sexual contact with inappropriate partners – for example, those much older or younger than ourselves or those too genetically close – and it can ensure that we pick the most suitable partners that are most likely to be compatible.[16]

Disgust that is caused by others' behaviour falling short of society's standards is extremely powerful and results in people being avoided and shunned by others. This type of disgust is often combined with a sense of moral superiority and can be called contempt. The experience for those on the receiving end is extremely unpleasant, and this is covered in more detail in Chapter 6 on shame. Consequences like this are powerful motivators to uphold society's standards and to behave in ways that are socially acceptable.

Self-disgust results in self-condemnation that can result in disgust and shame. This is covered in more detail later in this chapter and in Chapter 6.

Disgust protects us from pathogens, supports appropriate sexual contact and protects society's standards

Tolerating disgust and using helpful responses when we're disgusted

The most powerful response to disgust is to move away and to keep ourselves at a distance from whatever has made us feel disgusted. In many situations, this is entirely possible, and we can live much of our lives keeping away from disgusting things.

Like all emotions, this is not our only choice – we can choose to tolerate the emotion and continue with what we need to do. Can you think of something that made you feel disgusted where you tolerated the feeling and continued anyway? Many professions require this ability, including plumbers, rubbish collectors and health professionals. Equally, parents and pet owners have to develop their tolerance to regularly deal with bodily fluids and faeces.

Adjusting attentional focus, contagion and similarity

When we are increasing our tolerance of disgust, there are subtle changes we can make to how we are interpreting situations that can make it less difficult. Remember that disgust is caused by a sense of contagion and similarity. Both contagion and similarity are based on a particular way of interpreting or seeing a situation.

Contagion is usually linked to the past – where something has been before it is now or who used it before us – and so a focus on this aspect of the situation will likely increase the disgust felt. If we lie in a hotel room bed and think about all the people who have laid there before us, and the things they might have got up to, our sense of disgust would increase and make our stay unpleasant. If we focus on how the room and the bed are now and on what we're doing, the disgust will reduce, and we can enjoy our stay.

Similarity between objects or situations will be enhanced by a focus on the similar properties of the object or person. For example, if we are eating tapioca and we keep thinking about how similar it looks to frogspawn and have an image of frogspawn in our minds, this will make the tapioca disgusting. The newest craze for tapioca is 'bubble tea', in which the balls of tapioca are instead labelled 'bubbles', which makes it much less disgusting and – in many people's opinion – quite delicious. Noticing the imagery that's in our minds when we feel disgusted can be particularly helpful if we need to tolerate a feeling of disgust, as this will highlight different aspects of the situation and increase or reduce the feeling of disgust.

You can practice this going through your daily life. If you are cooking, you can focus on some of the more disgusting attributes of the food you're making – for example, the consistency of egg white, the sliminess of raw meat or the smell of particular ingredients. Allow your mind to focus on the disgusting qualities of these foods and to link them with other similarly disgusting things. Then move your focus away from these aspects of the foods and back to aspects of the cooking you prefer, like the smell of spices or the taste of a sauce. You should notice changes in your levels of disgust, particularly in your stomach.

So if you're feeling disgusted – by a substance, a person's characteristics or their behaviour – then think about what you're focusing on. Are contagion and similarity getting carried away and making you feel more disgusted than you need to be? Can you focus on other aspects of the situation to reduce the disgust?

Problems with disgust

Disgust is a predominantly helpful emotion that serves to protect us from potential illness and disease, to help produce healthy offspring and to uphold society's standards. There are times, however, when disgust can lead to difficulties. This rarely happens on its own, but in combination with difficulties with other emotions.

Disgust can combine with fear to produce high levels of avoidance and escape of particular situations that then get in the way of life. This is commonly seen in fears of small creatures and of blood injury and injection (phobias) as well as contamination (obsessive-compulsive disorder). Disgust in social situations can combine with anger or shame to cause significant difficulties in relationships with other people – problems which can be given labels as wide as depression, bipolar disorder or personality disorder.

We'll cover disgust and fear first, and then disgust, anger and shame.

Disgust and fear

For some examples of the fear trap, the driving force behind many of the behaviours is not fear alone, but disgust too. Spiders and insects, for

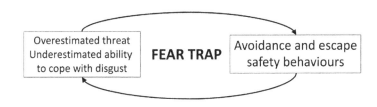

example, often cause disgust as well as fear. Blood also causes a disgust reaction, and fears of contamination are linked with high levels of disgust. Selective eating is also covered.

For each of these issues, both fear and disgust drive the fear trap. As we've seen, disgust drives very similar behaviours to fear – avoidance and escape – so these remain the same. Disgust is not associated with particular thoughts, but it is usually the perceived ability to cope with the disgust that is problematic. So the fear trap has an added dimension, as shown.

Given that the behaviours in the trap are the same whether there is just fear or fear combined with disgust, the way out of the trap remains the same too. Reducing the avoidance, escape and safety behaviours will enable the reptilian brain to reassess the threat and reduce the fear. Equally, with more experience of the object, the disgust response reduces too. It is important to note that disgust will probably take longer to reduce than the fear.[17]

> **Reducing avoidance, escape and safety behaviours reduces disgust in the same way as fear**

To illustrate these ideas, we'll look at small creatures, blood and contamination in turn. We'll also cover problems with selective eating.

Disgust and small creature fears

Many fears of small creatures are also accompanied by disgust. Spiders are the classic example, but the same is true of creatures like mice, rats, locusts, cockroaches and so on. Here is an example:

Desmond had been fearful of spiders his whole life, and he could remember his grandmother being particularly fearful of them too – checking cupboards and larders for spiders before she took things

"Spiders will harm me" "I can't cope with the disgust of spiders"	**DESMOND'S FEAR TRAP**	Check for spiders Avoid places where spiders might be

out. Desmond said he knew that the spiders he'd come across were harmless, but when he was near a spider, he was terrified. He also said that he shuddered when he thought of their legs and thought he'd be sick if their hairy legs touched his skin. As a result, Desmond had spent many years avoiding spiders, asking others to remove them from rooms, checking rooms before he entered and avoiding holidays in countries that had big spiders.

Desmond's example highlights the fear and the disgust that he experiences in response to spiders. These two emotions drive similar behaviours – avoidance and escape – which keep him overestimating the threat of spiders. He has the sense that he'll be sick if he has a spider on him, which suggests fears about how he'll manage the disgust he feels. Desmond could still use the fear trap to understand his difficulties, as shown in his fear trap, but we could add in the threat about disgust.

Desmond can follow the same process with his fear trap as outlined in Chapter 1 on fear. He needs to reduce his avoidance, escape and safety behaviours to help his reptilian brain to learn firstly that spiders are not as dangerous as it thinks they are, and secondly that he can cope better with disgust than he thinks. Disgust, like fear, also reduces with continued experience, so if Desmond can look at pictures or watch videos of spiders and maybe go closer to them, or even hold spiders that people have found for him, he will find that he is less scared of them and also that he finds them less disgusting, although the latter may take longer.

Blood injury and injection fears

A common issue with fears of blood and injections is that of fainting. Fainting is caused by a sudden drop in heart rate and reduction in blood pressure. Many people will be scared of fainting on sight of blood, and this represents their underestimation of ability to cope with the situation.

Fainting is entirely possible, particularly if it has happened before, but it is possible to reduce its likelihood using applied tension.[18] Applied tension involves increasing muscle tension throughout the body at the first sign of any reduction in blood pressure. This increases the blood pressure and counteracts the decrease in blood pressure that can occur as part of disgust, thus reducing the likelihood of fainting. It is a simple process that involves tensing all the muscles in the body, starting from the feet, lower legs and torso all the way up through the arms and to the neck and head.

Using applied tension alongside the usual processes of reducing avoidance, escape and safety behaviours allows the reptilian brain to learn that it is overestimating the threat. It also builds confidence in the ability to cope with disgust and fainting.

Contamination

The final area where disgust and fear combine is in contamination fears (sometimes labelled 'contamination obsessive compulsive disorder').

> Shirley had always been a clean and tidy person, but she had become increasingly concerned about cleanliness since her mother became ill. She had frequent thoughts that she or a member of her family would get ill, and these thoughts would scare her. She also regularly experienced a horrible feeling on her hands and all over her body when she had the sense that she was dirty. She would clean and clean until this feeling reduced, but it always seemed to come back fairly soon afterwards, and if somebody came in to where she was from outside, she'd have the sense that there was dirt trailing behind them. Shirley had stopped going out as much as a result of these experiences and the idea that she'd have to spend ages cleaning herself and the house if she went out, so it seemed easier just to stay home.

Shirley is fearful about getting ill, but linked to this is the sense of disgust she feels when things are dirty. Both the fear and the disgust drive the behaviours of overcleaning and avoidance. This is illustrated in her fear trap.

Shirley has to do the same things to get out of the fear trap – reduce the avoidance, escape and safety behaviours to allow her reptilian brain to learn that she is overestimating the threat and to help her learn that she can cope with things she might perceive to be dirty. As we've said earlier, she will find that her levels of fear reduce more quickly than her levels of disgust will, but she will learn that she can tolerate the disgust better than she thinks and the disgust will also reduce over time.

Selective eating

The other area where there are problems with disgust is with food and eating habits. Many children go through phases of fussy or selective eating – not liking fish, greens, eggs or mushrooms, for example. Most of the time this doesn't matter because they like enough other foods, and as they grow, they continue to experiment with different tastes. Sometimes, though, these selective eating habits can persist beyond childhood, and older children and adults can find that their eating habits are so selective that it gets in the way of their lives either socially – because they can't eat out or share food with friends – or because they don't get sufficient nutrients.[19]

The main issue here is the same as those outlined earlier. There are overestimations of threat associated with food – for example, around choking or vomiting – and there is an underestimation of ability to tolerate disgust. Avoidance is the main behaviour that keeps this going; foods that are considered threatening or disgusting are avoided, so the reptilian brain keeps overestimating the threat of these foods and underestimating the ability to tolerate disgust.

The way out of the fear trap is always the same. Using the circles (Chapter 1) to slowly introduce new foods and experiment with different textures, smells and tastes increases the tolerance of both fear and disgust. Over time, this will reduce the overestimation of threat and increase the confidence in the ability to tolerate disgust. In the longer term, the fear and disgust associated with these foods will reduce (disgust might take longer than fear).[20]

Disgust, anger and shame

The areas we've covered so far mainly focus on disgust linked with objects and creatures. Disgust caused by other people can lead to different problems.

High levels of disgust relating to others are likely to result from a perception that other people are treating us or people we care about in 'disgusting' ways. Our most likely response to this is anger. So if we are experiencing problematic levels of disgust in relation to others, we are most likely stuck in the anger trap. The behaviour we perceive as disgusting represents the threat and the trap follows from here. See Chapter 3 for a full outline of anger and the anger trap.

As we've said, disgust results in avoidance and keeping distance from those perceived as disgusting. If others avoid us or shun us as a result of what they perceive to be disgusting, this will cause us to feel shame. We might also perceive ourselves – or aspects of ourselves – as disgusting (self-disgust), which is likely to result from a perception that we are inadequate, defective or bad. This, too, causes shame. For a fuller understanding of shame and the shame trap, please see Chapter 6.

Summary

Disgust has often been described as the most primitive of emotions, one that is evolutionarily most closely linked to its purpose. Disgust still serves this important function of protecting us from potential pathogens, and therefore from disease and illness. It makes us spit out and maybe expel offensive substances and avoid potential dangers in the future. It is often linked with fear in situations where it becomes unhelpful, and this chapter has shown how minor adaptations can be made to the fear trap to account for it.

Disgust can also be caused by a sense that we or others have fallen short of society's expectations. It is a more complex emotion in these arenas, being linked with anger, shame and contempt and serving to protect society's standards. Problems with disgust in this area can lead to significant difficulties with anger and shame, which are covered in more detail in other chapters.

Notes

1 These categories come from a paper that aimed to put together a whole variety of potential types of pathogen disgust under headings. The six categories outlined here best explained the data (Curtis & de Barra, 2018).
2 Over recent years, more has been written about individuals who are disgusted by particular patterns of holes, like those on a sponge or soap bubbles. The research has focused on it as a disorder, 'trypophobia' (e.g., Kupfer & Le, 2018), but it appears that these kind of stimuli cause disgust in a potentially significant proportion of the population.
3 Tybur et al. (2013)
4 Scherer and Wallbott (1994)
5 Rozin et al. (2008)
6 The physiological impact of disgust is less clear than that of other emotions, but these conclusions are drawn from the available research (Cisler et al., 2009).
7 Gable and Harmon-Jones (2010)
8 Izard (1991)
9 Woody and Teachman (2000)
10 Duong and Saphores (2015)
11 Rozin et al. (1986)
12 BBC Good Food (2003)
13 These ingenious experiments were conducted by Rozin et al. (1986).
14 Haidt et al. (1997)
15 The Disgusting Food Museum is in Malmö, Sweden, and they have exhibits of bull's penis, maggot cheese, pickled sheep's eyes and baby-mouse wine. These exhibits highlight the fine line between new and unusual foods and disgust.
16 From an evolutionary point of view, disgust is thought to help with three issues: avoiding disease, avoiding inappropriate sexual contact and communication and coordinating condemnation with others (Tybur et al., 2013).
17 Mason and Richardson (2012).
18 Öst et al. (1991)
19 This has been given the strange diagnosis "Avoidant and Restrictive Food Intake Disorder", or ARFID, when it results in weight loss, nutritional deficiency or interference with functioning. It refers to either concern about the sensory characteristics of food (disgust) or aversive consequences of eating (fear).
20 There are not many evidence-based interventions for this diagnostic classification yet. However, there are trials into CBT based on the principles outlined in this chapter and in Chapter 1 on fear (Thomas et al., 2018).

References

BBC Good Food, 2003. Tapioca tops BBC good food magazine's 'most hated' school dinners survey. Available at: www.bbc.co.uk/pressoffice/bbcworldwide/worldwidestories/pressreleases/2003/08_august/school_dinners.shtml (accessed 16/04/2021).

Cisler, J.M., Olatunji, B.O. and Lohr, J.M., 2009. Disgust, fear, and the anxiety disorders: A critical review. *Clinical Psychology Review*, 29(1), pp. 34–46.

Curtis, V. and de Barra, M., 2018. The structure and function of pathogen disgust. *Philosophical Transactions of the Royal Society B: Biological Sciences*, 373(1751), p. 20170208.

Duong, K. and Saphores, J.D.M., 2015. Obstacles to wastewater reuse: An overview. *Wiley Interdisciplinary Reviews: Water*, 2(3), pp. 199–214.

Gable, P. and Harmon-Jones, E., 2010. The blues broaden, but the nasty narrows: Attentional consequences of negative affects low and high in motivational intensity. *Psychological Science*, 21(2), pp. 211–215.

Haidt, J., Rozin, P., McCauley, C. and Imada, S., 1997. Body, psyche, and culture: The relationship between disgust and morality. *Psychology and Developing Societies*, 9(1), pp. 107–131.

Izard, C.E., 1991. *The psychology of emotions*. New York: Plenum Press.

Kupfer, T.R. and Le, A.T., 2018. Disgusting clusters: Trypophobia as an overgeneralised disease avoidance response. *Cognition and Emotion*, 32(4), pp. 729–741.

Mason, E.C. and Richardson, R., 2012. Treating disgust in anxiety disorders. *Clinical Psychology: Science and Practice*, 19(2), pp. 180–194.

Öst, L.G., Fellenius, J. and Sterner, U., 1991. Applied tension, exposure in vivo, and tension-only in the treatment of blood phobia. *Behaviour Research and Therapy*, 29(6), pp. 561–574.

Rozin, P., Haidt, J. and McCauley, C.R., 2008. Disgust. In M. Lewis, J.M. Haviland-Jones, and L.F. Barrett (eds.), *Handbook of emotions* (3rd edn). New York: Guilford Press, pp. 757–776.

Rozin, P., Millman, L. and Nemeroff, C., 1986. Operation of the laws of sympathetic magic in disgust and other domains. *Journal of Personality and Social Psychology*, 50(4), p. 703.

Scherer, K.R. and Wallbott, H.G., 1994. Evidence for universality and cultural variation of differential emotion response patterning. *Journal of Personality and Social Psychology*, 66(2), p. 310.

Thomas, J.J., Wons, O. and Eddy, K., 2018. Cognitive-behavioral treatment of avoidant/restrictive food intake disorder. *Current Opinion in Psychiatry*, 31(6), p. 425.

Tybur, J.M., Lieberman, D., Kurzban, R. and DeScioli, P., 2013. Disgust: Evolved function and structure. *Psychological Review*, 120(1), p. 65.

Woody, S.R. and Teachman, B.A., 2000. Intersection of disgust and fear: Normative and pathological views. *Clinical Psychology: Science and Practice*, 7(3), pp. 291–311.

Chapter 5

Guilt

Guilt is caused by a perception that we've done something wrong. While it is not as intense as some of the other emotions covered in this book, it lingers and has a powerful impact on the ways in which we think, often leading to a preoccupation with the event we feel guilty about and what we can do about it.

Guilt is one of the social emotions, and it is important in maintaining positive and trusting relationships with those around us. It does this by encouraging us to behave well to avoid the feelings of guilt that come when we don't and to rectify any mistakes we might make. Alongside other emotions like disgust (Chapter 4) and shame (Chapter 6), guilt plays a role in holding communities and people together.

Sometimes, though, we can become plagued by guilt that it is difficult to shake. This can lead to a preoccupation with the past, going over and over things in our minds, or a sense of being overwhelmed with tasks and responsibility. Problems with guilt do not usually occur on their own; they commonly occur alongside fear and sadness. This has perhaps led to a diagnostic focus on these other emotions, and problems with guilt are often bundled in with diagnoses like depression, obsessive-compulsive disorder and post-traumatic stress disorder.

The guilt trap shows how guilt can trap us in the past, dwelling on things and trying to fix or repair things that we cannot possibly fix. It outlines the two main ways in which guilt can become problematic and how these can be tackled.

Understanding and accepting guilt

Guilt has an impact on our thoughts, feelings and behaviours. However, it has less impact on our facial expressions and bodies, and there are important differences in the situations that cause guilt. Exercise 5.1

DOI: 10.4324/9781003138112-6

will help you to start thinking about what guilt is, and the next section explores it in more detail.

Exercise 5.1   Feeling guilty

Think about a recent time when you felt guilty. You may also have felt other feelings, like sadness or fear, but focus on the feeling of guilt.

How would you describe the experience?
What did you notice/were you most aware of?
What made you feel guilty?
How did you respond/what did you do?
What happened afterwards?

What causes guilt?

Exercise 5.1 asks you to remember a time when you felt guilty and to think about what made you feel this way. Your description probably starts with "I . . . ", and that is because guilt is linked not with an external event but with our own behaviour – a sense that we have done something wrong. This may be something we've done that we shouldn't have done, or it may be something we should have done but haven't.

Guilt comes from a belief that we've done something wrong

Guilt is a more complicated emotion than the ones outlined so far in this book. For us to feel guilt, we have to have a sense of morality, a set of standards or values we believe we should live up to. We feel guilty when we sense a shortfall between our own behaviour and these standards or values.[1] Because of this complexity in the emotion, young children are thought not to experience guilt; it emerges later than other emotions, beginning around 18–24 months of age.

Have a think about your example in Exercise 5.1. What were the standards or values in this situation that you felt you did not live up to? The standard is probably easiest to express as "I should . . . " or "I must . . . ". Each of us has many standards like these that we develop during our lives. They may be shared with our parents or wider families, with our friends, with our generation, with our culture or with our religion. These standards and values are important and have a significant impact on many of the decisions we make throughout the course of our lives. Exercise 5.2 helps you to consider some of the standards and values that are particularly important to you.

There are some values that are shared across cultures. Most cultures have values and standards relating to harming and killing other people and certain sexual behaviours (e.g., incest). Beyond this, though, the values that are important to different individuals and different cultures can vary widely. Eating animal products or consuming alcohol, for example, can violate standards in some cultures and be encouraged in others. Because of this variability in standards and values, the kinds of situations that make each one of us feel guilty are very different.

You will probably feel quite comfortable with most of the values and standards you write in Exercise 5.2. They will help you to live your live in the way in which you want to and – for the most part – in harmony with those around you. There may be times, though, where the standards you set for yourself are too extreme or inflexible. This might lead you have problems with guilt or with what you do to try to avoid this guilt, which is covered later in this chapter.

Exercise 5.2   Standards and values

Which aspects of life are particularly important to you? Some broad areas to consider are outlined next. Try to define what is important for you in each area and what your value or standard is. Some might be phrased as "I would like to be . . . "; others might be closer to "I should . . . ", "I ought . . . " or "I must . . . ".

- Work/education/achievement
- Health/fitness/diet/appearance
- Politeness/community/other people
- Family (including parenting)
- Religion

Are there particular things that you repeatedly have a go at yourself for?

Are there things that you particularly notice about others, or have a go at others for?

What standards or values do you think other people would say were important to you?

Some of these areas will be more important than others, so when you have something in relation to each one, pick the top few that are most important for you.

What happens when we feel guilty?

Guilt has a significant impact on the five parts of emotions outlined in the Introduction. However, its impact in some areas is much more subtle, with the result that it can be harder to detect by others than the emotions covered so far in this book.

Feelings

We tend to experience guilt fairly frequently. It feels less intense than emotions like fear and anger, but it tends to linger, often for several hours or all day. It is an unpleasant emotion and, like other emotions, it can be experienced at different levels of intensity. There aren't many words that describe guilt, but others include regret and remorse.

Bodily responses

Guilt doesn't have a particular impact on the body; there are no distinct physiological changes associated with guilt. Sometimes people experience a 'lump in the throat', but even this is more common in sadness than in guilt.[2]

Facial expression

Similar to the bodily response, guilt is difficult to detect on the face. There are few characteristic facial expressions associated with guilt, which links with the difficulty of detecting the culprits of wrongdoing, even when the guilty one is too young to actively disguise or hide their facial expression. Guilt may result in our holding our heads a little lower and averting our gaze.[3]

Thoughts

Guilt hangs heavy in the mind. It results in a great deal of thought that is focused around two areas. The first is on the event that brought about the feelings of guilt. We find ourselves dwelling on what we have done or not done, wondering "why?" and "what if?" The second focus is what to do about it. We rehearse and play through scenarios in our minds about how we could tell people about what we've done and how we can apologise or make amends for our behaviour.[4] We might also think about the possible outcomes of each of these, which bring other emotions – for example, sadness at our imagined losses or fear about others' imagined anger. These thoughts can go over and over in our minds, distracting us from other things and making it difficult to sleep or to relax.

Behaviours

Our immediate reaction to a feeling of guilt is a desire to withdraw. The crowd of thoughts and ideas in our minds and the unpleasant feeling of guilt make us want to retreat and to spend time thinking. There is also often a reluctance to engage and share our wrongdoing with others and an urge to want to keep it to ourselves, at least until we have thought about some way of making amends. This process is similar, although usually less intense, than that seen in sadness.

We also want to make amends, to repair what has been damaged by our action or inaction. We may be able to undo the situation, or we might have to do something else to atone for it. We may need to own up to our conduct, to explain ourselves to the person we believe we have wronged or perhaps to somebody in authority – for example, a legal or religious authority or a moral leader like a parent or grandparent.

> **Guilt makes us dwell on what happened**
> **and think about how to make amends**

Guilt and the brain

Guilt is an emotion that requires more rational brain actions than the emotions covered so far in this book. It is not a primitive response to an external threat; it is an assessment of our own behaviour as not in line with our standards or values. The brain has not been taken over, and we are likely to find ourselves engaging in lots of thought and planning to make amends for our perceived wrongdoing. Problems with guilt can be caused by biases and problems in the way that we process information in our rational brains, which is covered later in this chapter.

What is the function of guilt?

Guilt is an important emotion in the social lives of humans. It is sometimes called a social emotion or a moral emotion. Its primary function is to encourage us to behave morally in the context of our society, to form and maintain positive trusting relationships with those around us.

Because guilt arises from our own behaviour, we usually have a choice about whether or not to feel guilty. The easiest way for us to avoid feeling guilty is not to do things that are outside our standards and morals. If we behave in line with our standards and values, we will avoid the unpleasant feeling of guilt and have good relationships with others, which leads to a mostly positive and caring society.[5] If we do act in ways not in line with our standards and morals, the unpleasant feeling of guilt is most effectively reduced by making amends. Owning up, apologising and rectifying the wrong in some way is the behaviour most likely to result in a reduction in guilt. Doing this is also helpful in repairing relationships and maintaining trust and positivity between people.

> **Guilt helps us to form and maintain positive, trusting relationships with those around us**

Tolerating guilt and using helpful responses when we feel guilty

Guilt follows from perceived wrongdoing – a belief that our behaviour has fallen short of our standards.

When we feel guilty, we can ask two questions: "What have I done?" and "What can I do now?"

What have I done?

Firstly, we need to clarify in our minds what we have done wrong: what did we do or not do that we perceive as falling short? Do we know what we should have done or how we would have liked to have acted?

If we are clear that we are right to feel guilty – that we have done something wrong – then we can continue. However, when guilt is produced by biases or distortions in the way we think, we can address these using the ideas covered in the section on problems with guilt.

Dwelling on why we feel guilty once we have answered this question is unlikely to be particularly helpful. Once this is clear in our minds, we should move fairly quickly on to the next question.

What can I do now?

Sometimes there will be a variety of different options following an event that produced guilt. When we feel guilty, we can be drawn inwards to dwell and think and go backwards and forwards between different options. To try to reduce this tendency, it can help to take a more active approach to thinking about what we can do now, as outlined in Exercise 5.3.

Guilt is a consuming emotion that will linger and hang around. The most effective way to respond to it is to make amends; it is not possible to think our way out of guilt. The faster we act, the better it is likely to be for all concerned.[6]

> **The most effective response to guilt is to make amends with as little delay as possible**

Exercise 5.3   Responding to guilt

When we feel guilty, we can ask two questions: "What have I done?" and "What can I do now?"

What have I done?

First, I need to be clear on what I have done wrong:

What do I feel guilty about?
What do I think I should have done/not done?
Do others agree that I have done wrong?

What can I do now?

I need to quickly move on to what I'm going to do about it. Action is the most effective response to guilt, and going over and over it is unlikely to help.

Is there anything I can do?
Whom do I need to own up to? Anybody else?
What are ALL the options, no matter how silly?
Which is the best next step of these options and why?
Do I need somebody else's view or some help with this process?

NOW DO IT!

Helping others with guilt

When others feel guilt, the process is generally quite similar to when we feel guilty. The two questions are the same: "What have you done?" and "What can you do about it?" and the process needs to involve action rather than just thought. When others are feeling guilty, we may have a greater role in supporting them to assess the rationality of their conclusions (see next section). Otherwise, our role is to support them to take action and reduce time spent dwelling.

Guilt trap: problems with guilt

Like all emotions in this book, guilt is predominantly helpful, but there are times when guilt can have a negative impact on our lives. These fall into two broad categories: problems with extreme or restrictive standards and problems with misinterpretations of events. These kinds of problems might be given labels like depression or post-traumatic stress disorder.

As the chapter has outlined so far, the experience of guilt is directly linked with how we interpret our behaviour in comparison to a set of standards or values. If we experience problems with guilt – excessive guilt or guilt that dominates our lives – then there will be some kind of overestimation of responsibility. This overestimation of responsibility leads to feelings of guilt that encourage us to withdraw from others, dwell on the events we feel responsible for and to work hard to

try to make amends. The problem is that these behaviours can prevent us from reevaluating our levels of responsibility. This is shown in the guilt trap.

Guilt is the result of two related processes: the standards we hold for ourselves and our interpretation of our behaviour against these standards. Overestimations of responsibility can arise from problems in these two areas. Problems with extreme or restrictive standards tend to lead to problems with frequent and ongoing experiences of guilt in daily life that serve to maintain unhelpful behaviours. Problems with misinterpretation of situations tend to lead to problems of guilt that are associated with a smaller number of significant life events that feel difficult to move on from. Because the overestimation of responsibility arises for a different reason in each case, the situations are explored in turn.

Extreme or restrictive standards

One common reason for getting stuck in the guilt trap is standards that are too extreme or restrictive. These standards lead to excessive levels of responsibility in lots of different situations. This example highlights the problem:

> Eileen worked part time and had a young family. She was busy all the time, taking on extra responsibilities at work, and looking after her children and the house. She rarely stopped, rarely went out and despite her husband's encouragement to sit down and relax, continued to be busy from morning until night. Eileen said that she 'just has to be doing something'. When she tried to sit down and relax with her husband or her children, she felt guilty and had lots of thoughts about all of the things that need doing, and she said to herself, "It's easier just to get on with it."

Eileen is working extremely hard all the time. She is so busy that it is having a negative impact on her and on her relationships with her husband and children. She is keeping busy to avoid the guilt that she feels when she relaxes. This implies that relaxing or having time for herself is somehow not in line with the standards and values that Eileen has for herself. She may have a standard like "I must always be productive" or "If something needs doing then I should do it". These are examples of standards that are too extreme and give her too much responsibility. Eileen can either work really hard to try to reach them, making herself exhausted and preventing her from enjoying her life, or she can try to relax and then find herself dwelling. Both of these options result in Eileen being distant and disconnected from those around her and have a negative impact on her life. This is shown in Eileen's guilt trap.

Eileen is working hard to try to live up to her high standards, but some of the time she might find that she gives up and stops trying. In this case, she would feel guilt but would also likely feel sadness (Chapter 2) and maybe shame (Chapter 6) as well.

Extreme standards lead to overestimations of responsibility, intense guilt, dwelling and working too hard

In this example, we can see that Eileen is holding herself to these standards. On other occasions, it might be other people that hold these high standards. For example, if other people are disappointed or angry whenever a mistake is made, this invites a standard of never making any mistakes. If other people are upset if they're not put first or their feelings aren't considered, then the standard is that they should always be put first. This is commonly known as 'guilt-tripping' and involves using guilt to try to get others to act in accordance with their own wishes and desires.

Questioning standards

The standards we hold are often ideas we live by but have never put into words. During this chapter, you may have started to be clearer about what some of your standards are. Identifying the most problematic standards and putting them into words can help you start to think about how useful they are.[7] Exercise 5.4 has some ideas about how to identify the standards that might be problematic.

Exercise 5.4   Finding extreme standards

Exploring your standards and values can be a helpful process, to get out of your own head and take a wider view. It can be helpful to do this with somebody else. It can also help to start with those aspects of your life that are most difficult and think about the standards that apply there.

Look at the language of your standards and values in Exercise 5.2. Extreme standards will be more restrictive, and the language will indicate this. Standards that are written "I should . . . ", "I must . . . " or "I should always/never . . . " are more likely to be extreme.

To try to find your extreme standards, have a go at pushing what you have written to make it more extreme and see if you still agree with it.

- If you have "I should always try my best", would you also agree with "Only 100% effort is enough"?
- If you have "I should be a good parent", would you also agree with "My children should never be unhappy"?
- If you have "I should help those around me", would you also agree with "I must always put others before me"?

Turn your standards upside down to see if they get more extreme:

- "I should always do well" might become "I must never make any mistakes"
- "I should always help others" might become "I must never let anybody down or upset people"

> **Think about how you behave. Do you behave 'as if' a more extreme version of your standard is true even if, when you write it down, you know it's too much?**
>
> - "I know I can't be the best at everything I do, but I behave as if I should be"
> - "I know everybody won't always like me, but I act as if I'm trying to be liked by everybody"

Once you have identified the extreme standards, you can start to explore them. You can think about where they come from, how well they work and whether you might want to change them. Exercise 5.5 can help with this process.

When you have an idea about the aspects of these standards that may be problematic, you can think about what alternative, slightly less-extreme standards might be like. The important changes to make are those that give you a little less responsibility, that accept that you don't have control over everything and that some aspects of life are outside your control. The new standards should give you a little more flexibility and take the pressure off.

The last stage of the process is to link these new standards back to what you'll do and how you might behave if you were to act in line with these standards. Initially, it is likely that you will find an increase in feelings of guilt because you are not following your usual standards, but over time these feelings should reduce and as you start to feel more comfortable with new, more flexible standards, the guilt should ease.

What changes could Eileen make to her standards?

She could start by examining what they are and considering how helpful they are and whether they work. For the less helpful standards, like those outlined previously, she could adjust them and change her expectations of herself to allow more flexibility and reduce the feelings of guilt she experiences:

Eileen and her husband talked one evening about how busy she was and why she continued to do so much, even when it wasn't necessary or didn't need to be done at that point. Eileen found herself talking about what life was like when she was growing up and how her mother was so busy all of the time. She could see that her standards came from these early experiences. Eileen also remembered feeling sad that she did not get to do more fun things with her mother. Eileen then spoke to her mother about these memories. This helped Eileen to question these standards about always being busy and to adjust them so that they took account of the importance of spending time with her children. Initially, she had to be quite strict with herself, and she set aside some time each evening to spend with her children and her husband. Over time, she became more comfortable with leaving things undone and prioritising other things as her standards became more flexible.

Exercise 5.5   Questioning extreme standards

Now that you've identified your extreme standards, you can question and maybe change them:

Where did these standards come from?

Are there other people in your life who share these standards?
Are there people in your life who benefit from you having these standards?
Did you have experiences in your early life that led you to have these standards?

How helpful are these standards?

What are the benefits of these standards?
What are their downsides?
Are there times when they really don't work?
Do they work well for the other people in your life who share them?

What about alternatives?

Do you know other people who don't have these standards?
What kind of standards do they have?
How do they approach things?

> **How could you adjust your standard to make it more flexible?**
>
> Are there modifications to make to it?
> Are there times when you might want to prioritise something else?
> Are there times when this standard doesn't apply?
>
> **What would you do differently with this new standard?**
>
> What will you ask yourself to do differently?
> How will you remember?
> How will you stick to it?

Misinterpreting the situation

Other problems with guilt relate to particular moments or events that are difficult to move on from. This is usually because of an overestimation of responsibility for a particular event – a misinterpretation of the situation. Hiroshi's example highlights this kind of problem with guilt:

> Hiroshi was driving his brother (Shen) home one night and swerved to avoid an animal. He lost control of the car and they hit a tree. Both were okay, but Shen was left with significant back pain and difficulty walking. Shen didn't blame Hiroshi for the accident and had adjusted his life to manage these difficulties, feeling quite positive about the improvements he was making through physiotherapy. In fact, Shen had other things on his mind because he was going through a separation, which was far more painful. Hiroshi, however, continued to blame himself for the accident, thinking about it most days, particularly when he saw his brother's injuries. In fact, Hiroshi blamed himself for Shen's separation and indeed any issues at all that his brother had, thinking that none of this would have happened but for the accident. He dwelled on what had happened and what he could have done differently. Hiroshi felt terrible when things went well for him, or even when his children did well at things, as it somehow felt wrong.

Hiroshi's experience of guilt relates to a specific, significant situation. He feels guilty about the accident, feeling that he shouldn't have

crashed and that he should have done something differently to avoid it. He knows his brother doesn't blame him and he knows he didn't do it on purpose, but in his head the accident is entirely his fault, and everything afterwards is linked to it. Guilt is doing what guilt does: making Hiroshi preoccupied with the situation and with trying to do something to repair it or make amends. The problem for Hiroshi is that there is nothing he can do to repair or fix it now. As a result, Hiroshi is stuck in the past in a pit of guilt that he cannot get out of. This is shown in Hiroshi's guilt trap.

Hiroshi's experience illustrates how problems with guilt can follow from an interpretation of events that overestimates the level of responsibility.[8] As the driver, he had some responsibility for the accident, but he doesn't have responsibility for everything since this point and doesn't have responsibility for his brother's separation. Because of this overestimation of responsibility, Hiroshi has started to hold himself back as a result of being stuck in the guilt trap. If his feelings were even more intense, he might start to actively put himself down or punish himself to try to fix the situation and reduce the guilt he feels.[9]

Overestimating our level of responsibility is quite common after experiencing difficult situations. It often follows a significant event that was unexpected or unusual and is therefore difficult to make sense of. Sometimes it might be called 'survivor's guilt'. Examples include events like accidents, disasters, attacks or acts of war, illnesses or anything that results in a significant change to life or circumstances. One possible way of making sense of these kinds of events is to blame ourselves – to feel responsible. Often, this kind of guilt comes from a sense of responsibility for an action that is partly or entirely outside of our control.

> **Overestimating responsibility for a difficult event can lead into the guilt trap**

Events that happen during childhood are particularly likely to be misinterpreted in this way, as in this example:

> Cleo's parents had always seemed to get along fine, until one day they told her that they were going to separate. Cleo's father moved out, and Cleo and her mother carried on quite similarly to how they had before. When Cleo went to visit her father and found him living in a small place on his own that wasn't very nice, Cleo felt guilty that he didn't have nice things and that he was all on his own. She thought about him often and about what it was like before. She called him every day and went to stay with him even though she didn't like it there, and she kept asking her mother to have him around for dinner and on the weekend.

In this example, Cleo feels guilty because she can continue to live quite comfortably while her father seems to be worse off. Guilt does what it does, and Cleo thinks a lot about the separation and tries to think of things she can do to make it better. Cleo feels guilty because she believes at some level that she has done, or has not done, something that resulted in this situation. But of course, Cleo, as a child, is not responsible for her parents' separation, and she cannot bring them back together or improve her father's living conditions. This is shown in Cleo's guilt trap.

If the guilt trap is driven by an overestimation of responsibility that comes from a misinterpretation of situation, the only way to move forward is to explore the situation and the way in which it is being interpreted.

Exploring the interpretation of situations

As humans, our rational brains are designed to pick out patterns from the world, to try to make sense of what is going on and then to predict the future. If we know that tomorrow will be fairly similar to today, we can plan and organise on this basis. This process is what helps us to have a sense of influence and control over what happens to us and the world around us. The problem comes when things happen to us that are outside of our control, that are random or unexpected. Our tendency to feel in control and that we have an influence means that we take more responsibility for these events than we should. The alternative is to feel completely out of control and unable to influence anything.

The challenge, following these difficult experiences, is to incorporate the unexpected, unusual and random into our ways of seeing ourselves so that we can have a sense that usually we can control things, but sometimes we can't. The way we do this is to think and talk through the situation to make sense of it, to allow our rational brains access to the information and to work through it.

But our natural inclination following a difficult situation is to try not to think or talk about it. It was difficult, distressing, perhaps terrifying or horrifying, and we don't want to feel this pain and distress again. We might also be concerned about distressing other people. The problem is that by not thinking through exactly what happened and talking it through with others, we cannot make sense of the experience. It remains something unexpected, out of the ordinary, something that we could and should have done something about. This interpretation of the situation gives us responsibility for it and makes us feel guilty. Guilt makes us preoccupied with the events and what we can do about them, and it has a dramatic impact on how we behave as a result. We think a lot about the event, but this starts from a misinterpretation of the event, so it can go around and around in our minds – keeping us stuck in the guilt trap.

The way to move on from this kind of experience of guilt is to talk and think about the event from the beginning and to remember what happened: what we saw, heard, smelt and felt. We start with what actually happened – rather than starting with our misinterpretation of what happened – and we think through the event rather than thinking around it. This can allow new perspectives, new ideas and different ways of seeing the event that can, over time, allow us to examine our interpretation of the event and reduce our feelings of guilt.[10] These examples can illustrate the process:

> One evening, the day before Hiroshi and his family were due to visit his brother, Hiroshi happened to say to his wife that perhaps they shouldn't mention that they were thinking of moving to a new house. His wife was confused about why, which started a conversation in which Hiroshi told her how he felt about the accident. She thought

he had gotten over this, and she told him that Shen's relationship had been strained long before the accident. Having not talked about the accident much at all, Hiroshi started to talk more about it and eventually talked to his brother about it. Shen said that the accident had actually made him realise how unsupported he'd felt in his relationship and that he thought it was best for him that they separate. He also said that he'd missed spending time with Hiroshi, particularly now that he was on his own, and he asked if they could do a bit more together; he also asked for help moving out. Hiroshi started to see that there were things he could do to help his brother; he found that Shen didn't dwell on the accident nearly as much as he did, and he started to feel less guilty and allow the accident to fade into the past.

When Cleo left her father's home one day and looked back through the window, she saw him sitting on his own, looking very sad. She immediately started to cry, and her mother asked her what was wrong. When Cleo told her, Cleo's mother then let her father know how she was feeling. Cleo's mother explained that the separation had nothing to do with Cleo and that both her parents still loved her. Later that day, Cleo spoke to her father, and he explained that it was his choice to move out and that it had nothing to do with her. He also said that he was looking for somewhere to live more long term that was nicer than where he was now. He asked her if she would like to help him next time he went looking. Cleo and her parents continued to talk about the situation when it came up, and she started to feel less guilty and closer to both her parents.

In these examples, Hiroshi's and Cleo's misinterpretations of the situation are understandable. Their reluctance to talk about the situations is also understandable; they don't want to feel the hurt and the pain, or for those around them to feel it either. But by keeping it to themselves, they remain stuck with an interpretation of the situation that is not shared by others around them, and they dwell on the past and feel as though they have to do something to make it better. By talking and sharing with other people, they get different perspectives, people challenge their interpretations and over time, the guilt can lessen.

Sometimes these kinds of significant events in our lives and a reluctance to talk about them can leave the memories of these events 'unprocessed', with the result that they have a significantly greater impact on our daily lives than they otherwise would. These kinds of memories can leave us feeling not only guilty but also scared, ashamed and sad.

Chapter 1 on fear has a section on traumatic memories and the differences between processed and unprocessed memories, and there are chapters on the other emotions too.

If you feel that there is one particular event – or a few significant events – that you are struggling with in this way, Exercise 5.6 has some questions you can ask yourself to think about what to do from here.

Exercise 5.6   Exploring the interpretation of events

If you're stuck thinking about events from the past, trying to make things better that you know you can't really make better, you might need to think a little more about the events themselves. Here are some questions you could ask yourself to help with this process:

Who could I talk to? Are there people:

Who I like to talk to or who are helpful to talk to?
Who were/are involved too that it could be helpful to talk to?
Who talk to me about it already, that I could say a little more to?
Who are completely separate that I could talk to?
Who've been through a similar experience?

How could I talk to them? Would I like:

To have a big heart-to-heart conversation?
To say just a little more about how I experienced the event, then build up over time?
To talk a little when we're doing something else, so it doesn't feel like too much?
To ask about how they experienced it first?

Do I need to seek a professional person to talk to?

Does this feel too big to talk about to the people I already know?
Is everyone around me struggling too much with it for me to talk to them about it?
Do I feel that I'm going to be overwhelmed by talking about it without professional help?
Have I asked those around me for their view?

Summary

Guilt is different from other emotions in this book in that it is prompted by our own action. It is a response to the sense that our behaviour is not in line with the standards we set for ourselves and helps to maintain morality and good relationships with those around us. Getting stuck in the guilt trap comes from an overestimation of responsibility, which is the result of one of two processes: extreme or rigid standards or a misinterpretation of specific situations. The ways out of the guilt trap are different depending on which of these processes led into the trap, and they involve either an exploration of standards or an exploration of the situation.

Notes

1 These ideas were outlined by Ausubel (1955), who identified three psychological conditions necessary to feel guilt: 1. Acceptance of moral values; 2. Sense of obligation to abide by these moral values; and 3. Ability to perceive discrepancies between behaviour and values.
2 Scherer and Wallbott (1994)
3 Izard (1991)
4 Izard (1991)
5 Research supports the idea that individuals who are more likely to interpret ambiguous events in line with guilt – so-called 'guilt-proneness' – do engage in behaviours that could be considered more moral. For example, guilt-prone individuals were less likely to engage in aggressive or criminal behaviour and less likely to have problems with substances and risky sexual behaviour (Stuewig & Tangney, 2007).
6 Izard (1991)
7 The ideas in this section are important components of CBT. These kinds of standards are often labelled rules for living or dysfunctional assumptions and date back to Beck's Cognitive Therapy for Depression (1979).
8 This idea that problems with guilt can arise where there is exaggerated or distorted responsibility for events is highlighted by Zahn-Waxler and Robinson (1995).
9 O'Connor et al. (1999).
10 This is the kind of approach taken in many different approaches to trauma, including trauma-focused CBT and eye movement desensitisation reprocessing (EMDR). A recent review found strong evidence for CBT in the treatment of trauma (Roberts et al., 2019).

References

Ausubel, D.P., 1955. Relationships between shame and guilt in the socializing process. *Psychological Review*, 62(5), p. 378.
Beck, A.T. ed., 1979. *Cognitive therapy of depression*. New York, NY: Guilford Press.

Izard, C.E., 1991. *The psychology of emotions*. New York, NY: Plenum Press.

O'Connor, L.E., Berry, J.W. and Weiss, J., 1999. Interpersonal guilt, shame, and psychological problems. *Journal of Social and Clinical Psychology*, 18(2), pp. 181–203.

Roberts, N.P., Kitchiner, N.J., Kenardy, J., Lewis, C.E. and Bisson, J.I., 2019. Early psychological intervention following recent trauma: A systematic review and meta-analysis. *European Journal of Psychotraumatology*, 10(1), p. 1695486.

Scherer, K.R. and Wallbott, H.G., 1994. Evidence for universality and cultural variation of differential emotion response patterning. *Journal of Personality and Social Psychology*, 66(2), p. 310.

Stuewig, J. and Tangney, J.P., 2007. Shame and guilt in antisocial and risky behaviors. *The Self-Conscious Emotions: Theory and Research*, pp. 371–388.

Zahn-Waxler, C. and Robinson, J., 1995. Empathy and guilt: Early origins of feelings of responsibility. In J.P. Tangney and K.W. Fischer (eds.), *Self-conscious emotions: The psychology of shame, guilt, embarrassment, and pride*. New York, NY: Guilford Press, pp. 143–173.

Chapter 6

Shame

Shame is an unpleasant emotion that we feel when we perceive ourselves to be inadequate or defective. It is caused by failure, dislike, exclusion and exposure and is particularly uncomfortable in front of other people. When we feel shame – or less-intense embarrassment – our attention is entirely focused on that aspect of ourselves we perceive as inadequate or defective. This results in a cycle of self-focus that disrupts everything, making it difficult to think clearly, talk or act.

Most people will struggle to think about any positive function of shame, but like the other emotions in this book, it is actually a mostly helpful, healthy emotion. It is a powerful motivator of many of our most valued attributes, including competence and conscience.

In this chapter, we'll expand our understanding and acceptance of shame, looking at its causes and its function. We'll also explore its impact on us, particularly its ability to make us feel inept and unsure about what to do. We'll look at how we can tolerate it and respond in helpful ways.

The shame trap illustrates what happens when we have difficulties with shame. This will highlight underlying issues for many people who may have received diagnoses like depression, bipolar disorder and personality disorder. The potential overlaps with other emotions like sadness and anger are also explained. The chapter ends with ideas about how to get out of the shame trap and begin to lead more fulfilling, healthy lives.

Exercise 6.1   Feeling ashamed

Think about a recent time when you felt ashamed. It might have been an intense feeling of humiliation or disgrace, or a lesser feeling of embarrassment.

DOI: 10.4324/9781003138112-7

How would you describe the experience?
What did you notice/were you most aware of?
What made you feel ashamed?
How did you respond/what did you do?
What happened afterwards?

Understanding and accepting shame

Have a look at Exercise 6.1 to explore what you know about shame. It is perhaps the most misunderstood of the seven emotions. Shame is thought of as extremely painful, overwhelming and awful. Many of us believe that we hardly ever feel shame, but it is probably more common than we think. It has a reputation as the underlying factor behind many of society's problems, as a plague and something to get rid of and something that is altogether unhelpful.[1] But shame has a function just like the other emotions in this book. It is a powerful emotion with a powerful function, and human society would scarcely function without it.

What causes shame?

Shame can be caused by a whole variety of different situations. The four most common causes are failure, being disliked, being exposed and being excluded. When we fail at things, we can feel clumsy, inept, incompetent or stupid. This is often more intense when we fail in front of other people. It is also possible to feel shame after an event – for example, after we give a presentation, go on a date or perform in front of people. The feedback that we get from others after the event – however long afterwards – can make us feel shame. Feeling not liked by others or not valued or respected can also cause shame, which is why relationship breakups are often so difficult. Another common cause of shame is feeling exposed: having something private about us suddenly shown to others. This might be our bodies, like finding that we were seen when getting changed or that our clothing did not cover us in the way we thought. It could also be a behaviour or characteristic that was previously hidden and is suddenly exposed, like something that we enjoy or value being highlighted as different or unusual. It can be 'as though something we were hiding from everyone is suddenly under a burning light in public view'.[2] Feeling left out is also a common cause of shame – for example, finding out that people have met up without inviting us or that somebody else has taken our place for something.

Shame is caused by failure, being disliked, exposed or excluded

Shame, like guilt, is a 'social emotion' that is brought about through our interactions with other people. To feel shame, we need an understanding of the standards we believe we should live up to and an ability to compare ourselves against these standards. Believing that we have fallen short of how we think we ought to be can result in shame. Unlike guilt, though, the experience of shame relates to a perception of ourselves as globally inadequate or defective. We haven't *done* something bad; we *are* bad.

Shame results from a global evaluation of ourselves as inadequate or defective

This is not to say that every experience of shame encompasses everything about us. For example, we can feel shame about our abilities in one area but not another. Following a bad day at work, we might evaluate ourselves as 'a bad member of staff', which would make us feel shame but might not impact too much on our perception of ourselves as a good friend. It is still a global evaluation – it is we that are bad, rather than that we just had a bad day – but it doesn't encompass our whole identity. Depending on how important to our overall identity work was, this would be a more or less intense feeling. Sometimes, shame can apply to our entire sense of identity – for example, if we viewed ourselves as 'a bad person'.

Shame is an intense emotion – an extremely uncomfortable, painful feeling. Embarrassment is less intense and tends to be caused by inadequacies or defects that are perceived as less 'serious', that are less about the core aspects of ourselves and that have fewer moral consequences. Situations that are embarrassing rather than shaming are also more tolerable and survivable and can be more easily laughed off or made light of. There's disagreement about whether shame and embarrassment are different intensities of the same emotion or different emotions altogether.[3] For the purposes of this book, we'll proceed on the basis that there is enough similarity between the two to consider them together.

Embarrassment is less intense than shame, caused by defects that are less serious

Unlike guilt, shame is not always caused by our own behaviour. Shame involves the (usually sudden) focus of attention on an aspect of ourselves that we consider inadequate. This might be something we've done, but it could equally be the way we look or the way we are. Other people have the power to focus attention like this, pointing out ears that stick out, an underdeveloped physique or a certain behaviour and laughing, teasing and mocking. Even though shame might be prompted by others, the experience is internal:

> "shame is felt as an inner torment, a sickness of the soul. It does not matter whether the humiliated one has been shamed by derisive laughter, or whether he mocks himself. In either event he feels himself naked, defeated, alienated, lacking in dignity and worth."[4]

In Exercise 6.1, you were asked to think about a time when you felt ashamed. Did you do it? Of all the exercises in this book, this is probably the one you were most likely to skip. We commonly try to avoid feeling shame, and just thinking about these times in our lives can bring back the feelings, so you may have avoided it altogether. Alternatively, you may have thought that you don't feel shame, that it's not a common emotion for you. If you have a think about all those different causes of shame – failure, exposure, dislike and exclusion – and the fact that it doesn't have to be your entire being but can be focused on a particular role, probably you feel shame more often than you think. If you think about a time when one of those things happened – when something didn't go as well as you wanted, when somebody saw something you'd rather they didn't, when someone gave you less-than-positive feedback or excluded you – are there more occasions when you felt shame?

Another way to think about shame is to consider its opposite, pride. Pride also gets negative press in popular culture, described as 'coming before a fall' or the same as arrogance or conceit. But pride is caused by a focus of attention on something we've accomplished or something we value about ourselves. Pride is more intense when the focus of attention is shared by others. Pride is something we seek. We might put ourselves in the spotlight to get it, give a speech, give a presentation, write a book, perform of tell a joke – all of which allow us the potential for pride. But things can't always go right, and shame is what happens when it goes wrong.

What happens when we feel ashamed?

Shame has a major impact on the five elements of emotions outlined in the Introduction. It is a powerful experience and extremely unpleasant.

Feelings

Shame is an extremely painful, uncomfortable feeling. It is quite sudden and feels hot, illustrated by the expression 'burning with shame'.[5] This also relates to the experience of blushing that can accompany shame and embarrassment (covered more later).

There are a variety of different words to describe shame at varying intensities. Examples include humbled, embarrassed, shamefaced, demeaned, humiliated, disgraced and mortified. The intensity of the experience is illustrated by the power of these words.

Bodily responses

We feel shame in our bodies: an increase in heart rate, a sudden burst of adrenalin. These experiences are caused by the activation of the sympathetic nervous system (the accelerator), like in fear and anger.[6] In shame, though, our attention is sharply focused on ourselves, not on anything outside us. We are entirely focused on that aspect of ourselves we perceive as inadequate or defective. Like feedback between a microphone and a speaker, we are caught up in an all-consuming circle of self-focus that disrupts everything, making it extremely difficult to think clearly, to talk or to act; it's like we're stuck in a 'torment of self-consciousness'.[7]

> **Shame catches us in a circle of self-focus**
> **that makes it difficult to think clearly, talk or act**

Facial expression

Feeling ashamed, we look away from people and look down, as captured by the expressions 'hiding our faces', 'hanging our heads' and 'not being able to look people in the eye'. Sometimes we might smile – not at but away from people.

Blushing is a powerful indicator of shame and embarrassment that is prompted by the autonomic nervous system, and we cannot control it.[8] It is restricted to the face, neck and sometimes upper chest. Adults are less likely to blush than children and adolescents, which may be due to learning to control the response, to a raising of the blushing threshold or perhaps to an increased ability to avoid or escape shaming or embarrassing situations.[9]

Thoughts

When we feel shame, we are sharply aware of ourselves not meeting some standard we believe we should meet. The meaning we place behind this is that it says something about us as a person. Our entire focus is on that aspect of ourselves we see as bad, defective, useless or incompetent. As noted earlier, we haven't *done* something wrong; we *are* wrong. There are four main areas in which we might evaluate ourselves in this way: failure, dislike, exposure and exclusion. Exercise 6.2 helps you to identify the thoughts you might have about yourself when you feel ashamed in these four main areas.

Because we are so focused on viewing ourselves in this way, our thinking becomes muddled and confused. As Darwin said, we can "lose our presence of mind and utter inappropriate remarks".[10] In the scenario you remembered in Exercise 6.1, do you remember this – a sense that you couldn't think straight, didn't know what to say, perhaps said something stupid or exactly the wrong thing?

Exercise 6.2 What do you sometimes think of yourself?

Have a look through these examples and see what you think of yourself when you feel embarrassed or ashamed. Are there particular phrases that run through your mind? Circle the ones that fit best or add your own to help identify your thoughts. Are you more likely to feel embarrassed or ashamed in one area rather than another?

Failure:

I'm so clumsy
I'm an idiot
I'm not good enough
I'm incompetent
I'm useless

Dislike:

I am uninteresting
Nobody likes me (I'm unlikable/unlovable)
I'm a horrible person

Exposure:

I'm unattractive
My . . . is too . . . (e.g., nose too wonky, buttocks too big, etc.)
I'm ugly
I looked like an ass

Exclusion:

I'm to blame
I'm a bad person
I'm unimportant
I'm undeserving

Behaviours

Shame is a horrible feeling, and our overwhelming desire is to get rid of it. What do you remember doing when you felt shame? Whilst it is felt most intensely in the moment, it lingers afterwards and can be difficult to shake off. There are three behaviours associated with shame: protect, defend and repair.[11]

One of the most common behaviours when feeling shame is to try to *protect* ourselves from further shame. We might do this by withdrawing, getting out of the situation, hiding and never going back. We want 'the ground to swallow us up' and to go into ourselves. When we do this, our bodies literally get smaller – we shrink into ourselves and hide away. We might avoid the company of others, push people away and desperately try not to think about it. We might go to bed and try to escape from the whole world. When we do this, it can be really hard to get back out again, and we may end up avoiding places, people or activities that remind us of this time.

Another possible reaction is to *defend* ourselves.[12] We redirect the attention from ourselves onto someone else – either the person or people we believe to have shamed us or a convenient scapegoat. This is often done in an aggressive or hostile way and usually results in shaming somebody else. The result is that we 'pull others down with us', trying to regain some sense of self-respect.

The final reaction to shame is to *repair* whatever made us feel ashamed. If the shame was caused by a sense of ourselves as incompetent, then working to improve our competence and have another go is a way of repairing our self-image. For example, if we gave a presentation and came away feeling that it was a disaster, then doing another presentation to try to do a better job would repair our self-image. In fact, most people are much more likely to want to do another presentation if it goes badly than if it goes fine.[13] If we feel ashamed because we believe we are disliked, we might work hard to make ourselves more likeable – to approach others more and be more friendly and interested in other people. If we feel ashamed because we have been excluded, we might think about our character and our values and we might apologise, make amends and work harder to behave more in line with society's standards or to be more ethical. Of course, not all situations can be repaired, but there are often things we can do to improve our own image and our image in the eyes of others.

Three reactions to shame are protect, defend and repair

What is the function of shame?

We feel shame when some aspect of ourselves does not meet the standards we perceive society to hold. We are lacking in some way: lacking in attractiveness, decorum, competence, character or morals. Shame is an extremely unpleasant emotion, and we want to avoid it. The best way to do this is to make sure we're not lacking, that we live up to our own and society's expectations.

Societies around the world have a structure of laws and people whose job it is to enforce these laws. Day to day, though, what stops you from breaking these laws? What keeps you behaving in line with society's expectations? Most likely it's not the rule of law and subsequent penalty; it's what your mother would think, what your children would say, how your friends would react and how you'd feel about yourself. All of these are examples of the shame you'd feel if you did things that weren't in line with your own and society's standards. Avoiding shame is a powerful force that motivates us all to uphold social and cultural standards.

The force of shame in upholding society's standards is evident in the language used to describe the feeling. For example, the word 'disgrace' involves taking away grace – favour, regard, goodwill or gratitude – from somebody because they have let their community down. 'Mortify' literally means 'to put to death' because of some serious offence against society.

When we do something wrong or make a mistake, demonstrating our shame – for example, through blushing – shows we are aware that we have behaved in a way that is not acceptable. People who blush when they have done something unacceptable are viewed less negatively than people who don't.[14]

When we feel shame, we are highly motivated to do something about it and will often work to repair our self-identity. Depending on the cause of the shame, this will be different in different situations. If we have failed, the actions to repair this would be things like working hard, practicing and asking people for help. This helps build a sense of skill and ability to avoid future occasions when we feel inept or incompetent. If something about us has been exposed, we may work to improve our image or character to counter this, and this might lead to making more of an effort with other people to try to rectify our mistakes, make amends and apologise. If we have been disliked or excluded, this might make us work harder to make others like us, to be more amenable or make more effort.

So shame makes us want to be better people.[15] We can avoid shame by being good citizens and by upholding society's standards. If we feel shame, we are highly motivated to make amends and to improve ourselves. Did you respond in this way to your example in Exercise 6.1? Can you recall times when shame has made you try to better yourself? Perhaps shame might not be such a negative, harmful emotion after all.

Shame makes us want to be better people

Shame and the brain

Shame, like guilt, requires the ability to understand the world in complex ways, to assess ourselves against some perceived standard and to understand that we've come up short. As a result, some of the brain activity between shame and guilt is similar. However, shame is also a much more energising emotion and also activates the reptilian brain threat system, resulting in the protect and defend responses to shame.[16] This reptilian brain activation means that some of the helpful responses to shame are similar to those in fear and anger, particularly around attentional focus.

Tolerating shame and using helpful responses

Shame comes from feeling or being in the spotlight. If we are going to be noticed, to be seen by others, then sometimes we will feel shame, because we can't always get everything right. If we are going to compete in sporting events, play music in front of an audience, speak in public, go to job interviews, dance in front of others, have sex, talk in groups of friends or even walk down the street in daylight, we will, at certain points in our lives, feel shame. Things will go wrong, whether it's forgetting our lines, playing wrong notes, saying stupid things, tripping over our own feet or farting at the wrong time. Shame is not a feeling we can avoid and it is not a feeling that separates us from other people; it is a part of being human. In fact, feeling shame becomes more likely as we work hard for things we might value, like becoming well known and respected or leading others. If we achieve a high level of success, we can have the spotlight shone on us for reasons we might want (and we may sometimes feel pride), but this also increases the risk of the spotlight catching something we'd prefer it didn't.

Trying to avoid shame and embarrassment would stop us doing all sorts of things that we might value. Instead, we need to learn to tolerate shame and embarrassment, to give us the time and space to respond in more helpful ways.

Tolerating shame

One American course on shame starts with 'three quick things about shame', which are: we all have it, we're all afraid to talk about it and the less we talk about it, the more we have it.[17] We noted at the beginning of this chapter that all of us probably feel shame more often than we think and that we tend to avoid it, to try to protect ourselves from what we perceive to be its harmful nature. But shame is a part of being human, an emotion like all others that we have to accept if we're going to live fulfilling and healthy lives.

To get better at tolerating shame, we have to notice it, know when we're feeling it and put words to it. All of the material in the first part of this chapter is useful here, noticing the causes of the emotion and the impact this has on the five elements of emotions. The exercises earlier in this chapter can help. For example, you could try to complete Exercise 6.1 once a week to keep track of times when you feel ashamed or embarrassed. Alternatively, you could use Exercise 6.2 to try to notice when you're thinking in particular ways about yourself (e.g., "I'm thinking I'm an idiot again", "I'm feeling unattractive" or "I feel like those people are putting me down"). These kinds of exercises should help you to tolerate shame, particularly at lower intensities.

Starting to talk about the times when we feel ashamed or embarrassed can be really helpful too. Starting with everyday moments of failure, exclusion, exposure or dislike increases the tolerance to shame but also allows a gradual reevaluation of the perceived causes. It can also prompt others to talk about their experiences of these emotions, increasing the sense that they're normal, often helpful experiences. Remember to choose wisely who to talk to: people who are likely to respond with empathy, understanding and humour and by sharing their own experiences.

Other ways to increase our tolerance of shame are to deliberately push ourselves to do things that might make us feel uncomfortable. These kinds of activities will be different for different people but can involve a whole range of options that challenge us to do things that might result in embarrassment and shame. Sometimes it might be something small, like the way we move our bodies or being louder and more expressive when we talk. At other times, it might be more specific – a bit like a dare – to wear different clothes, go to events we'd normally avoid or do activities that challenge us. At the more extreme end are activities known as shame-attacking exercises, which involve challenging ourselves to do things that would cause higher levels of shame. Examples might include:

- Talking about yourself positively to others
- Approaching and talking to somebody you don't know
- Singing a song while walking down the street
- Asking for food that isn't on the menu
- Asking somebody for feedback about something you've done[18]

The point of these kinds of activities is to demonstrate to ourselves that we can tolerate shame and that we can tolerate other people's funny looks or disapproval. It also commonly demonstrates that other people are not nearly as interested in us as we might imagine. Different things will be embarrassing or shaming for different people, and there is a whole load of possible activities that might help achieve this. It is important that they are silly rather than scary or mean and poke fun at ourselves rather than others. And often the result is just that: things that we were ashamed of actually turn out to be fun, enjoyable and liberating.

Gently protect and defend using attentional focus

Our natural response to shame and embarrassment is to protect ourselves by leaving and avoiding the situation or angrily defending ourselves by shaming somebody else. Both of these are extreme responses that reduce the shame in the short term but often don't work very well in the longer term (see shame traps). Once we can better tolerate embarrassment and shame, we can use protect and defend much more subtly and to greater effect by redirecting our own attention and/or directing other people's attention.

Direct our own attention

Shame completely consumes our attention with the aspect of ourselves we perceive to be inadequate or flawed. Being caught in this loop of self-focus interferes with our thinking and our behaviour, and we can find that situations get even worse as a result. One way to protect ourselves and reduce the impact of embarrassment and shame is to direct our attention away from ourselves.

We covered attentional focus in Chapter 1 on fear, to reduce the focus on threat. The process is very similar in shame, where we move the attention away from ourselves and focus it outwards. Exercise 1.5 in Chapter 1 will help you to practice moving your attention around. Over time, we are looking to be more aware of where we are focusing our attention and to have a greater influence over what we focus on. The aim is to be able to focus our attention on what we're doing rather than on how others might be perceiving us. If we're giving a presentation, we want to focus on what we're saying and getting our point across rather than on how we think we're coming across to the audience. In a social situation, we want to be concentrating on the conversation we're having rather than on our perceived inadequacies as we talk. If we're walking down the road, we want to be focusing on what we're doing and where we're going rather than on how we imagine others might be seeing us. If we can get better at this process, then we'll still make mistakes and still feel some shame or embarrassment, but we can reduce its intensity and move on from it more quickly.

As an example, can you think about a time when you were talking to somebody – perhaps in a slightly pressured situation or when you were nervous – and your voice went funny (like you ran out of breath or felt you needed to swallow) or you forgot a word? When we notice things like this, there is a pull of our attention towards ourselves – caused by embarrassment and shame – and thoughts like "I look like an idiot" or "They're noticing I'm struggling". At this point, if our attention moves all the way back to ourselves, it becomes even more difficult to speak or to find the right word because we get caught in the cycle of self-focus. If we can push our attention back out, looking at the people we're talking to and concentrating on what we're saying, we can get through this moment and carry on. We'll still feel aware of our mistake and perhaps still feel embarrassed or even ashamed, but we have prevented the situation from getting worse.

> ## Focusing our attention outwards on what we're doing can reduce shame and embarrassment

This shifting of attention away from perceived flaws and inadequacies is particularly important in social situations where there are fears about performance and it overlaps with fears of social situations, covered in Chapter 1 on fear (where there is an example).

Direct others' attention

Sometimes it's not just our own attention but that of other people that's focused on us when we feel shame or embarrassment. Sometimes this is accidental, and sometimes other people do it deliberately. In these cases, there are things that we can do that direct other people's attention away from us and onto other things.

Our first option is to change the subject, moving on to shift the focus of attention and stop it from dwelling too long on whatever has made us feel ashamed. It won't stop it from happening, but it will shorten the experience and give something else to focus on. The key to this is to make sure that you close down the previous conversation and start up a new one without stopping. So if somebody brings up something that you're embarrassed or ashamed about, you can give a brief response and move onto the next topic: "Yes, that was a bit of a disaster, but yesterday went much better, thanks" or "I thought you might have heard about that. How is your day going?" Closing down the conversation and opening up a new one all at once moves the attention away from us and on to something else, discouraging a focus on things we'd rather not have a focus on. Sometimes we can anticipate these kinds of situations and even prepare something to say in advance — for example, if we're returning to a situation after a significant event or a period of absence or if people repeatedly highlight things about us.

If these kinds of strategies don't work, then we are likely in the company of somebody who is more aggressively focusing on things we don't want to focus on. There are ways to respond to this without being attacking, like "that's a bit harsh", "ouch!", "what's up with you today?" or "that's mean/unhelpful". Done calmly, these kinds of statements will move the focus of attention back to the person who made us feel this way but without us feeling ashamed of our own behaviour afterwards. Alternatively, we can go for a simple request to the person to stop: "please don't do that" or "I've had enough now".

A final option is to laugh along or laugh at ourselves to try to turn shame into embarrassment and reduce its intensity. As long as we feel in control of this process and it is not cruel, this can help us to embrace the feelings and move on through them. One area of society that highlights this process is comedy. Comedians show us some of the best examples of ineptitude, getting things wrong and being exposed. They show themselves tripping over things, saying things that they shouldn't say and being useless or incapable in all sorts of situations. Usually, we laugh with them, not at them, and we laugh not just because it's funny but also with relief that it's not just us that messes up. As we said at the beginning of this section, shame is a normal part of human existence and something all of us feel. We don't need to feel ashamed of feeling shame, and accepting it and laughing about it is a powerful way to lighten it.

> **Shifting others' attention away**
> **gives us back control in social situations**

All of these ideas are ways of moving the attention away from us and giving us back a sense of control. They all require some ability to think on our feet but don't require huge intellectual gymnastics. They can be usefully combined with the previous section, where we work to make sure that our attention isn't entirely consumed with ourselves.

Leave it or repair it

Once we've got through the moment that made us feel ashamed, sometimes it just dissipates, and we can move on. At other times it hangs around, and we find that it keeps popping into our heads, bringing that unpleasant feeling.

Shame focuses our attention on the aspect of ourselves we perceive to be inadequate. This means that we can find ourselves discounting important things about ourselves because they are outside our attentional focus. One of the most important things we can do – if embarrassment or shame lingers after the event – is to question ourselves. We need to assess the reality of our perception that we've failed, been exposed, disliked or excluded.

To do this, we have to tolerate the feeling, think about the experience and try to clarify exactly how we're evaluating ourselves to determine if it's fair. Exercise 6.2 helped you to identify the common ways in which you might see yourself when you feel ashamed. Exercise 6.3 helps you to start to question this evaluation of yourself. Sometimes, our questioning will lead us to reevaluate ourselves so that we no longer feel ashamed and can move on without needing to make any other changes. For example, we might feel shame when getting some negative feedback immediately following an event. Later on, we might be better able to put this in context with all the positive feedback we also got and take a more balanced position. This might mean that we are okay with how things went and no longer need to think about it. Sometimes, though, we will conclude that there is something about us that is lacking and that we do need to do something about it.

Most of our helpful responses to shame come from repairing whatever it is that has made us feel shame. The main factor that determines our response is how possible we believe it is to repair the situation.[19] If we think it is possible or likely that we will repair our self-image, then we are much more likely to attempt it. This makes sense: if we feel shame and our efforts to repair it are unlikely to succeed, then we are needlessly risking further shame. If we are likely to succeed, then we can rid ourselves of the feeling and replace it with a feeling of relief, satisfaction, happiness or pride.

> **We are most likely to try to repair
> when we think we have a good chance of success**

Responding in helpful ways to shame involves thinking about what we can do about it. To do this, we need to be clear about what aspect of ourselves is lacking – what has caused us to feel ashamed. It might be a failure, dislike, exposure or exclusion. We have to tolerate the feeling of embarrassment or shame to do this; we have to sit in it and think about it rather than pushing it away, which is the first challenge.

Next, we have to think about our options in terms of doing something about it. Sometimes there are quite clear answers to what we have to do to repair the situation. For failures, we might have another try, practice more or gradually build up our confidence at particular things. For situations where we've felt exposed or other people have excluded or disliked us, we might be able to apologise, make amends or explain. On other occasions, the options will not be so clear, and we are left with much longer-term ideas like "next time that happens I'll . . . " or "in the future I'll make sure that . . . ". These kinds of reparations are also helpful and effective in alleviating the shame and in improving ourselves and our relationships. Sometimes these kinds of experiences orient us towards the future but don't involve particular actions. Exercise 6.3 provides some ideas about how you can respond to shame, including both questioning your evaluation of yourself and considering how to repair it. Some examples outline how we can respond helpfully to shame:

> Emily was the maid of honour at her best friend's wedding. She had helped her friend prepare for everything and the wedding had gone very well. At the wedding reception, she'd stood up to give a speech but was overwhelmed by everybody looking at her and how formal it all felt, and she became flustered. She forgot what she wanted to say, tripped over her words and cut it short, feeling embarrassed afterwards. Nobody else was as bothered by it as Emily was, but she found it difficult to move on from and a part of her wanted to leave. One of her friends suggested that she say a few words to introduce the first dance. Emily calmed herself down, changed her clothing so she was more comfortable, took a few notes to give herself confidence and had another go in the less formal situation of the dance. It went much better, and the bride gave her a hug afterwards. She felt much happier for the rest of the evening and really enjoyed herself.

In this example, Emily felt the pull to hide away and to protect herself from embarrassment. Instead, she talked with people and came up with the idea of having another go, doing things to give herself a better chance of doing it well. As a result, Emily was still embarrassed about the first speech but felt she had recovered from the experience and could get on with her evening.

> Jack was walking in his local area one day when he saw an unusually dressed woman being taunted by a group of young people.

She wasn't being hurt, but she looked uncomfortable to Jack. He turned the other way and walked on by, being afraid to intervene. Jack found himself thinking about this for the rest of the day, feeling terrible that he hadn't done anything. He didn't mention it to anybody, and nobody had seen him, but he felt ashamed of what he saw as his cowardice. He couldn't do anything about it now, but he vowed to himself that the next time he saw somebody in need, he'd make sure he offered his help immediately rather than dithering about it. Some months later, he saw somebody get knocked off their moped and quickly rang for help as other people rushed over to the rider. Jack was proud that he'd responded quickly on this occasion rather than hoping that somebody else would do it, and it built his confidence in himself that he was a decent person who would step up when required.

In this example, it was not possible for Jack to repair the situation, and he had to manage with an uncomfortable feeling for a long time. But this feeling did ensure that he responded in a different manner on the following occasion and urged him to be a better citizen.

It is important to note that the most helpful ways out of shame involve tolerating the feeling to allow us to think about it and then taking some risks, often by putting ourselves back in the spotlight. Having another go when we failed or going to see the people in front of whom we felt embarrassed or ashamed risks further shame, but it also offers the opportunity to feel better and maybe even to feel pride and a sense of achievement. We can see this process in both of these examples.

Exercise 6.3   Responding to shame

When we feel ashamed, there are things to consider. The first is whether we're accurate in our evaluation of ourselves and the second is what, if anything, we can do to repair it.

Questioning my evaluation of myself

Embarrassment and shame will focus my mind on myself in a negative way. When I'm feeling calmer, I can think about the situation in more detail. These questions can pull my attention out a bit so I can get a clearer, fairer evaluation of myself:

What am I thinking of myself as a result of this situation?
Is there any other way to view this situation?
Would others really view me in this way?
Has anybody said anything to me about this situation, and could I ask what they think?
What would I think of somebody else in this situation?
Is there a bigger picture?
Am I focusing on this situation when there are others that show me in a different light?
Even if this was true of me then, is it true of me now?

What can I do now?

The most helpful response to embarrassment or shame that results from a sense of myself as genuinely lacking in some way is to repair it, to do something about it. I am much more likely to do this if it feels manageable and realistic than if it feels really difficult or impossible.

What is it that's lacking about me?
What do I wish I could do, was better at or did more often?
How would I like to improve myself?
What would I prefer that others saw in me or saw me doing?
What are ALL the options, no matter how silly?
Which of these feel manageable and realistic?
Which is the best next step of these options and why?
Do I need somebody else's view or some help with this process?

Helping others with shame

Helping others with shame involves the same principles as it does for us, with the added dimension of the relationship with have with them. One of the most powerful things we can do is give others an experience of being able to talk through what they feel, how they're thinking about themselves and the situations they're in and not shame them ourselves, talking instead with compassion and understanding. We don't need to jump in to defend them or disagree with their perception of themselves, but we can gently guide them through the questions in Exercise 6.3 to question and explore the experience and give it some direction. A gentle, warm, compassionate stance in any conversation about shame or embarrassment will provide other people with a very different experience and allow them to better tolerate the feelings and do something helpful with them.

Shame trap: problems with shame

Shame is an emotion that encourages us to improve our abilities, skills, character or standing in society. When we cannot repair whatever has made us feel shame, though, we can find ourselves stuck in intense, horrible experiences of shame that dominate much of our lives. These kinds of experiences are likely to be the underlying issue for many people who receive diagnoses like depression, bipolar disorder and personality disorder.

An excessively negative self-image leads to intense feelings of shame that drive desperate attempts to protect, defend and repair. Problems arise when these attempts to get rid of the shame are excessive and tend to fuel rather than reduce the negative self-image. The shame trap highlights the links between these elements.

Some examples will show how it works.

> Sarah had never felt particularly successful. Her parents had a bitter and prolonged divorce that disrupted her schooling, leaving her trailing her friends in terms of success and achievement. She'd drifted through a number of jobs that were not particularly challenging or fulfilling for her. Being laid off from one of these positions

| "I'm useless"
"I'll never amount
to anything" | **SARAH'S
SHAME TRAP** | Avoid challenging myself
Give up at first risk of failure
Avoid others so I don't have
to talk about it |

left her with no income and she moved back to live with her mother, becoming isolated from her friends and reluctant to speak to people in case they asked her what she was doing. She had applied for jobs and got interviews but pulled out of them, thinking that she wouldn't be able to perform the role. She spent most of her time in her room, comparing herself with others and having thoughts about how useless she was and how she would never amount to anything.

Sarah has a sense of herself as useless and that she'll never amount to anything, which is an excessively negative global self-image resulting in high levels of shame. This emotion focuses Sarah's attention, and she dwells on those aspects of herself she views as inadequate. She desperately tries to protect herself from further experiences of shame, avoiding doing things she might fail at like jobs that are too taxing and interviews. This stops her from doing things that will make her feel more capable. Sarah is also avoiding situations where she might talk to people about those aspects of herself that she is ashamed of. As a result, she won't have experiences where people don't view her as useless or where they share their own difficulties, making her feel less useless and more like everybody else. This is illustrated in her shame trap.

Sarah's experience might also result in other emotions like sadness, and her withdrawal might be the result of both shame and sadness (Chapter 2). She would benefit from understanding both emotions and might even find that she is in both traps, but she will find that the ways forward will be similar for both.

Here is another example:

José always struggled with his weight. Both his parents were on the larger side, and he'd been teased at school as a result of his weight. In many areas of his life, he has progressed well – having a stable

job, a nice flat and some close friends – but he has felt increasingly out of control of his weight. He avoids looking in the mirror because he thinks he's fat and disgusting, and he always wears dark, baggy clothes to try to cover up. José joined a gym on a few occasions, but he couldn't bear to go because he thought people would view him negatively. He has also tried dieting but has never managed to stick to it for more than a few days. These failures made José feel even worse, so he has been reluctant to try again.

José is also trying really hard to protect himself from shame. He believes himself to be physically disgusting as a result of his size, which makes him feel embarrassed and ashamed. These emotions focus his attention on this aspect of himself and he tries to protect himself from the feeling by avoiding thinking about it, avoiding looking at himself and avoiding situations where aspects of his body might be revealed. Because José can't bear to think about his size and weight, it makes it very difficult for him to formulate a plan to do anything about it, and his attempts quickly fail because he cannot tolerate exposing and thinking about the aspects of himself that he finds shameful. The failures to bring about change make him feel even worse because he feels ashamed about his failure to improve, all of which means he continues to gain weight and the situation deteriorates. José's hiding away from others and covering himself up also prevent him from finding out that perhaps other people don't view him the same way that he views himself and that other people might also have aspects of themselves that they don't like.

Both Sarah and José are trying too hard to *protect* themselves from shame. They are avoiding thinking and talking about the problems and avoiding doing things that might result in shame, which prevents them from doing things to improve their situations. Hiding and not talking about the aspects of themselves they are ashamed of also stops them from reevaluating what they think of themselves.

There are other responses to shame, as Ava's example shows:

Ava had grown up with a domineering and critical mother. Everybody in the family did what she said and rarely argued with her. Ava never felt able to do what she wanted, and although she had got on pretty well during school and early life, she never received any praise and never felt she was doing anything well enough. Ava found, as she progressed through life, that she became busier and busier. She spent a long time trying to make herself look good, worked extremely hard at her job and tried to be a good friend, often dropping everything to help other people. In spite of all of this, Ava never seemed to get the recognition she hoped for; in fact, people took her for granted and she felt used by others. Ava has increasingly thought of herself as unattractive, unlikeable and worthless.

Ava has an extremely negative self-image. She views many aspects of herself as lacking and inferior to others, with the result that she feels high levels of shame. Ava is working hard to try to improve herself, trying to repair the problem. Viewing herself as unsuccessful, she works hard at her job; viewing herself as unattractive, she works hard to improve her appearance; and viewing herself as unlikeable, she tries to be a really good friend. Ava is trying to repair her perceived flaws, but the problem is that her excessively negative self-image leads her to try to change in ways that are unrealistic and out of reach. She is trying to make herself into the perfect friend, employee and model, so she inevitably finds herself failing and confirming her negative self-image. As Ava has found, other people may well join in this cycle and take advantage or her or treat her badly, further reinforcing her self-image. We can see the pattern in Ava's shame trap.

As we have seen, attempts at repair are a common and often helpful response to shame. Ava is led into an unhelpful cycle because she is trying to repair flaws that are not really flaws, or at least are not as significant as she believes them to be. This means that her attempts to bring about improvements are likely to fail and confirm her excessively negative self-image. There are many examples of this kind of excessive attempt to repair perceived flaws across society. The advertising industry has been heavily criticised for portraying unrealistic images of attractiveness, which encourage us to try to repair perceived flaws – through cosmetics, diet and exercise regimes and plastic surgery – that are in fact quite common human characteristics.[20]

A final example highlights a third potential type of shame trap:

> Leon's father had been an alcoholic who would be mean and humiliating when he was drunk. He ridiculed Leon even when he hadn't done anything and frequently made him feel stupid and foolish. Leon managed this in early life by trying to keep his distance from his father and then leaving home as soon as he could to stop all contact with him. Leon managed much better without his father around, but he found that he had a quick temper and would shout at himself, calling himself 'useless' and 'worthless' when he made mistakes, and he would get extremely angry when other people criticised him. Leon's first significant relationship broke down because his hot temper led him to repeatedly behave in horrible ways towards his partner. After each incident, he felt terrible, told himself he was an awful person and apologised, but it kept happening, and after one particularly bad experience his partner left, telling him he was a 'monster'.

Leon has an extremely negative image of himself as a result of his father's behaviour when he was young. He is likely to view himself as useless and worthless and when he feels this way, he responds by defending himself angrily. Sometimes he directs this at himself, and sometimes he directs it at other people. Unfortunately, angrily defending himself against shame leads Leon to do things about which he later feels ashamed and that others judge him for, confirming his poor self-image in his own eyes and in others'.[21]

If Leon primarily responds in a defensive way to feeling embarrassed or ashamed, he will find himself stuck in the anger trap, which is discussed in detail in Chapter 3. The threat of being shamed or humiliated by others is the overestimated threat of the anger trap. If you respond with excessive defence to shame, then it is best to use the information in this chapter and in Chapter 3 to help you get out of the trap.

The issue in each of these examples is that efforts to make genuine reparation for perceived flaws feel too far out of reach. Leon spent his early life in an environment where he was regularly humiliated, and there was nothing he could do to repair the situation. Ava could never please her mother no matter how hard she tried, and José was bullied about his weight. Having problems with shame commonly results from these kinds of experiences: being unfairly shamed or humiliated without the possibility of repair. Examples of these kinds of experiences include:

- Adults who are critical, insulting, domineering or humiliating
- Peers who tease, taunt, bully or insult
- An absence of care, love or attention
- Traumatic experiences like inappropriate sexual activity, physical or emotional violence

All of these types of experiences lead to an excessively negative self-image. This excessively negative self-image results in a sense of self as inadequate, flawed, defective or bad, which results in frequent experiences of shame. Attempts to get away from such horrible feelings involve one or a combination of excessive protection, repair or defence. These get in the way of stopping and evaluating the negative self-image and stop improvement in (or confirm) the negative self-image. Excessive attempts to protect from shame result in avoiding opportunities to develop and reevaluate the excessive negative self-image. Excessive attempts to repair involve trying to make changes that are out of reach, leading to inevitable failure and confirmation of the excessive negative self-image. Excessive attempts to defend involve behaviours that confirm the negative self-image.

High levels of shame can be maintained by excessive attempts to protect, defend or repair

Getting out of shame traps

The ways out of shame traps involve two main steps. The first is challenge the excessively negative self-image, and the second is to make it less difficult to work on characteristics or traits that are lacking or require improvement. Both of these require increased tolerance of shame and embarrassment, which we covered earlier. It can be really difficult in the shame trap, but it is also a really important place to start. These examples illustrate the process.

> Sarah plucked up the courage to call her friend, and they ended up talking for quite a while. Sarah said that she was struggling to find work and had cancelled a job interview because she thought it would go badly. To her surprise, her friend told her a story about one of her previous job interviews that had been a complete disaster, and they both found themselves laughing as they talked about it. Sarah felt much more positive after this call and agreed to meet her friend for dinner the following week. Sarah felt relief that her friend, whom she viewed as successful, could have such a horrible experience but pick herself up again.

When shame and embarrassment is all about one issue, it has to be raised but not necessarily all at once, as this example highlights:

> José knew that his main issue was his size and weight; he was quite comfortable with other aspects of his life. One day, he mentioned something about finding it difficult to find clothes to an old friend whom he trusted. His friend listened, didn't laugh or say much at all, but his manner prompted José to continue. He told him how difficult he found his weight, that he was desperate to do something about it but didn't really know where to start. His friend said that he had always known and that he could remember how difficult José had found things at school. They didn't talk about it for long before José felt too uncomfortable to continue and changed the subject. He was surprised that they'd never talked about it but was relieved to have shared it, and he was pleased that his friend was concerned for him; somehow he'd always imagined his friend would be dismissive or wouldn't take him seriously.

Ava took the approach of deliberately pushing herself to do things that she found uncomfortable:

> When Ava went on holiday with a couple of her friends, they talked about what they wanted to do, and they all agreed to be bolder and experiment while they were away and keep things to themselves when they returned. Ava bought clothes she wouldn't normally wear, was louder than usual and went out in the daytime without

any makeup on. She did whatever she felt like doing: danced like there was no one there, went skinny dipping and talked to people she didn't know. All of these things were very unusual for Ava, and she was surprised to find that people didn't respond negatively to her and actually seemed to like her energy. While it was less intense when she returned from her holiday, Ava did learn that she could tolerate feeling embarrassed or ashamed and that people did not respond as she expected. This gave her the confidence to be more bold and assertive and to continue even when things didn't quite go right.

For Ava, experimenting while on holiday allowed her to let go of some of the fears about the future impact of her behaviour, and she was able to do all sorts of things she'd avoid for fear of embarrassment and shame. Knowing that she could tolerate the feelings and that they'd pass allowed her to do things that – while risking embarrassment and shame – could also bring other emotions like excitement and joy.

For Ava, some of the things that she was avoiding doing for fear of shame were not even directly linked to these emotions. For her, almost all the attention that was focused on her in her early life felt negative. This meant that whenever she was the focus of attention – even positive attention like praise, compliments or general noticing, awareness or care – it caused feelings of embarrassment and shame. Ava had to increase her ability to tolerate any kind of focus of attention on her, whether it was positive or negative. This is a common issue for those in the shame trap, where starting to view themselves positively is not associated with relief but with further shame, at least in the short term.

In the shame trap, a positive focus of attention can initially feel embarrassing or shaming

One of the key features of the shame trap is that trying to get away from shame prevents any questioning of the perceived flaw that causes shame in the first place. Each of our examples has an excessively negative self-image that drives the trap, and each person cannot reevaluate this self-image because they don't tolerate the shame for long enough to stop and reconsider it. So the first part of getting out of the shame trap is to get better at tolerating shame.

Challenge the excessively negative self-image

Remember that embarrassment and shame focus attention on the aspects of ourselves we see as flawed or inadequate. We can find ourselves stuck with this focus, viewing ourselves in this way and so effectively repeatedly shaming ourselves, pointing out to ourselves those aspects we don't like and then trying to get rid of the resulting shame, taking us around the trap.

So it is important to try to adjust this focus and to bring in other perspectives. There are a number of different ways to do this, including thinking about situations where this interpretation does not fit, thinking about it from other people's perspectives and thinking about how we think about ourselves when we're not feeling this way. Exercise 6.4 has some questions that you can ask yourself to try to bring in new perspectives.[22]

> When Leon started to try to notice the times when he felt embarrassed and ashamed, it was usually to do with making mistakes and things going wrong. It didn't matter whether the mistake was big or small, something that he could have anticipated or not or even entirely his fault or not – he would immediately think he was useless and worthless and imagine everybody else would be thinking the same, and he would feel ashamed, leading to sudden bursts of anger. He started to try to notice when things went well and the finished products of what he did, whether it was little household tasks or bigger things at work. This was really uncomfortable, particularly when he started to think that some of the time, he was competent at what he did, and it was cringy when other people pointed this out too. Leon also made an effort to notice how other people approached things. One of his colleagues in particular, whom Leon had always thought of as very skilled, actually seemed to make lots of mistakes but fixed them quite calmly as he went along. Over time, Leon found that he could recover more quickly when he made mistakes and had a stronger sense of himself as competent that he could remember when he found himself thinking that he was useless.

Leon shared Ava's early experiences of a mostly negative focus of attention as he grew up, so thinking about himself in any fashion, even in a positive way, was difficult and made him cringe. Over time, though, he was able to build up a more positive sense of himself that could insulate him from the times when he felt ashamed.

Another way to challenge the excessively negative self-image is to revisit some of the memories with which it is associated. For Ava and Leon in particular, their experiences in early life have clear links to the way in which they now see themselves. Going back to these experiences as adults, exploring them in different ways and reexamining them, can be powerful ways to challenge the excessively negative self-image. The exploration of early life events in relation to shame can be similar to that seen in both fear (Chapter 1) and guilt (Chapter 5 and Exercise 5.6). The aim is to bring back a fairer, calmer and kinder eye to the experiences of early life and to challenge the excessively negative self-image.

Exercise 6.4   Bringing in other perspectives

These questions can help you to think about yourself from different perspectives.

Situation that's made me feel this way:

Is this always true?
Are there examples of times when things have been different?
Am I focusing on the negative and missing positive information?

Others' perspectives:

What would somebody who cared about me say about this?
What would I say to somebody I cared about if they were in this situation?
If I could talk to the world's most understanding, caring person, what would they say?

Self-criticism:

Am I being mean to myself?
Am I using harsh language or calling myself names?
Would I say this to somebody else?
If I were being really kind to myself, what would I do or say?

Double standards:

Am I viewing as flawed something that is a normal human characteristic?

Am I holding myself to a different standard than those around me?

Are other people similar to me in this way?

Am I imagining that everybody around me is perfect or better than me?

Do other people have similar characteristics/traits/flaws/struggles to me?

Alternative self-view:

What would I rather think of myself?

How do I view myself when I feel different?

Are there examples of times when I've viewed myself in a more positive way?

If I had to say something positive about myself, what would it be?

Planning a repair response

The shame trap involves an excessively negative self-image and a variety of behaviours that serve to prevent improvements in the self-image and improvements to the self. It is possible to do some work to reduce the excessively negative self-image, but often there remain characteristics or traits that are lacking or require improvement.

Remember that the single most important thing that makes us more likely to respond to shame through reparation is how easy it is to repair. So the final way out of the shame trap is to make things possible to repair.

Remember José's struggles with his weight? He finds it difficult to tolerate thinking and talking about the issue because of the shame he feels. This means that for José to repair the situation, he has to do it all on his own without stopping and planning it, and he has to pretty quickly get to a goal that is not very well defined but is probably something in his mind like 'not looking disgusting'. Any attempt that José makes to repair his situation from this position is most likely to result in failure and further shame. If we put it like this, is it any wonder that José finds repairing the situation almost impossible and keeps trying to protect himself from further shame by avoiding making any efforts that are likely to result in failure?

What would help José? What would he need to do to have the sense that repair is possible? Making changes to body shape and weight are long-term, slow-to-achieve goals that involve lots of small changes to lifestyle that are difficult to implement and maintain. José will have a much better chance of repairing his self-image by planning, doing things with other people's help and setting short-term, clear and achievable goals that will repair his self-image in the longer term:

> After José talked briefly to his friend, his friend later mentioned that they'd seen a sign about private personal training sessions at the gym. José was worried because he didn't know exactly what he wanted; he just wanted to feel like he was doing something about it. José went to the gym one afternoon with his friend for support, and the trainer was friendly, understanding and didn't embarrass José by making him do lots of exercises in front of him. José began to do some exercises at home, once a week to begin with, and found he could stick to it. He also started to take his lunch with him to work to reduce his reliance on takeout food, which didn't feel too difficult either. José didn't dramatically lose weight, but he stopped gaining weight and started to feel more positive about his abilities to make changes. Whenever he felt embarrassed about his size and weight, he reminded himself that he was doing something about it now.

José's experience shows the importance of tolerating the feelings to allow some discussion, thinking and planning. Setting initial targets that are manageable can give a sense that repair is possible and reduce the overreliance on protect responses to shame. José didn't immediately transform his life, but he started making changes, which reduced the shame and allowed the beginnings of a more positive sense of himself to grow.

Getting out of the shame trap involves detailed, realistic plans to repair perceived flaws

Some of the things José did highlight the principles that can help bring about improvements.

Clarify the longer-term direction

One of the problems with shame and the shame trap is the focus on the self as inadequate or bad, defective, useless or incompetent. This is a negative focus, and it's not clear, without work, how to improve things. José views himself as disgusting, but he has to do some work to define exactly what he is expecting himself to do about this. It is important for José that he doesn't define aims that are too clear or set in stone, because this may make them feel overwhelming and opens up the risk of not achieving them. So José didn't define an ideal weight or exercise regime, but he was clear that he wanted, in the longer term, to reduce his weight and to feel more in control of his weight and eating habits.

For Sarah, who is back at her mother's house with no job, her longer-term direction might be to regain her independence and build a more successful life. If she tells herself that she wants to get a new job and a boyfriend and move out by Christmas, this is likely to lead to a sense of high risk, likelihood of failure and attempts to protect herself from shame. Instead, if she sets herself the task of doing small things that are consistent with being more independent, she stands a greater chance of managing it.

Break this down to short-term goals

With a clearer long-term direction, short-term goals can be set that actually start to make change and bring about improvement. José turned his longer-term hopes into specific, manageable and regular goals that he could succeed at. A little exercise and a minor alteration to his eating habits were regular goals that would move him towards his longer-term aims without risking him feeling ashamed that he hadn't done enough or had failed. Sarah's goals might include spending half an hour per day job searching, going to interviews or thinking about how to organise her finances.

Short-term goals that are about improving aspects of ourselves and our lives should be regular and ideally should feel pretty minor. Developing things about ourselves is a long-term project, and it is important that it is sustainable. José will not make any significant difference to his weight and his self-image by doing an extreme diet for three weeks and then giving up. He is most likely to succeed with gradual change over the long term that doesn't feel particularly difficult day to day. Good short-term goals are those that make you feel a little bit of excitement and energy and those that make you think things like "I reckon I can do that" or "that shouldn't be too difficult". The aim should be to 'set yourself up to win' as opposed to the common problem in the shame trap, which is being set up to fail. Starting small and gently and gradually building up over time builds confidence and a sense of control, reducing shame and bringing instead a sense of accomplishment and pride.

Plan for slip-ups

The final part is to plan for slip-ups. Long-term aims will take time to achieve, and there will be points along the way where short-term goals will be missed. José might find that he misses his exercise one week or that he occasionally gets takeout for lunch instead of what he has brought with him. Sarah might find that she is not successful at a job interview or that her job isn't as well paid as she hoped. On their own, these one-offs don't really matter to their longer-term aims – except if they slip back into the shame trap, focus on all of the bad things and then abandon their efforts to continue.

We know that in the longer term, things will not always go to plan. So rather than be taken by surprise by it, we can plan for these kinds of eventualities. The easiest way to do this is to think about the most likely things that might not go right and consider what to do in each case. Planning for likely slip-ups will increase the sense of confidence and control and will reduce the likelihood of falling back into the shame trap.

Summary

This chapter began by considering shame as a more common human emotion than we might think. It involves an intense focus of attention on aspects of ourselves that we perceive to be bad, defective or inadequate. This attentional focus disrupts everything so that we find it difficult to think clearly and to act. Despite popular ideas about shame, usually we respond very healthily, and it is important in driving us to become better, more capable and more decent people.

High levels of shame, though, can lead to high levels of distress. The shame trap is a vicious cycle linking an excessively negative self-image with excessive attempts to get away from the resulting shame through protection, defence or repair. Getting out of the shame trap requires an increased tolerance of embarrassment and shame, which allows a reevaluation of the self-image and more successful attempts to repair the self-image. The shame trap links with other traps in this book, most notably the sadness trap and the anger trap.

Notes

1 For example, one paper describes why shame but not guilt is 'maladaptive' (Orth et al., 2006).
2 Izard (1991, p. 332).
3 Crozier (2014)
4 Tomkins (1963, p. 185).
5 Scherer and Wallbott (1994)
6 Scherer and Wallbott (1994)
7 Lewis (2003)
8 Crozier (2010)
9 Izard (1991)
10 Darwin (1872)
11 Daniels and Robinson (2019)
12 Daniels and Robinson (2019)
13 De Hooge et al. (2010)
14 Dijk et al. (2009)
15 Daniels and Robinson (2019)
16 Michl et al. (2014)
17 This comes from a 12-session educational programme about shame resilience and is part of their introductory session (Brown et al., 2011).
18 Shame attacking is one of the components of Albert Ellis' Rational Emotive Behaviour Therapy (e.g., DiGiuseppe et al., 2014).
19 Leach and Cidam (2015) set out to test the prevailing view of shame: that shame leads people to avoid others in unconstructive ways. They noted that there was some evidence that shame did sometimes lead to desire to approach and repair but that there were opposing views. The authors went through 90 research papers and coded each on the basis of how possible repair would be from the situation that caused the shame. Studies where shame was caused by a failure on a task that then gave participants the chance to redo the same or a similar task were labelled as more reparable. Studies where the cause of shame was a failure and there was no opportunity to repair this failure but instead to do something different like cooperate with a stranger, were labelled as less reparable. How reparable the incident was that prompted the shame was the most important factor, by a long way, in determining whether participants in these studies chose to repair or to protect/defend.
20 See, for example, Ashikali et al. (2017).
21 This is the 'shame-rage' spiral highlighted by Scheff (1987).
22 These techniques are an integral part of many different CBT approaches, not least one of the earliest, Beck's model of Cognitive Therapy (1979).

References

Ashikali, E.M., Dittmar, H. and Ayers, S., 2017. The impact of cosmetic surgery advertising on women's body image and attitudes towards cosmetic surgery. *Psychology of Popular Media Culture*, 6(3), p. 255.
Beck, A.T. ed., 1979. *Cognitive therapy of depression.* New York, NY: Guilford Press.

Brown, B., Hernandez, V.R. and Villarreal, Y., 2011. *Connections: A 12-session psychoeducational shame resilience curriculum* (2nd edn.). Minneapolis, MN: Hazelden.

Crozier, W.R., 2010. The puzzle of blushing. *The Psychologist*, 23(5), pp. 390–393.

Crozier, W.R., 2014. Differentiating shame from embarrassment. *Emotion Review*, 6(3), pp. 269–276.

Daniels, M.A. and Robinson, S.L., 2019. The shame of it all: A review of shame in organizational life. *Journal of Management*, 45(6), pp. 2448–2473.

Darwin, C.R., 1872. *The expression of emotion in man and animals*. Chicago: University of Chicago Press.

De Hooge, I.E., Zeelenberg, M. and Breugelmans, S.M., 2010. Restore and protect motivations following shame. *Cognition and Emotion*, 24(1), pp. 111–127.

DiGiuseppe, R.A., Doyle, K.A., Dryden, W. and Backx, W., 2014. *A practitioner's guide to rational-emotive behavior therapy*. Oxford: Oxford University Press.

Dijk, C., De Jong, P.J. and Peters, M.L., 2009. The remedial value of blushing in the context of transgressions and mishaps. *Emotion*, 9(2), p. 287.

Izard, C.E., 1991. *The psychology of emotions*. New York, NY: Plenum Press.

Leach, C.W. and Cidam, A., 2015. When is shame linked to constructive approach orientation? A meta-analysis. *Journal of Personality and Social Psychology*, 109(6), p. 983.

Lewis, M., 2003. The role of the self in shame. *Social Research: An International Quarterly*, 70(4), pp. 1181–1204.

Michl, P., Meindl, T., Meister, F., Born, C., Engel, R.R., Reiser, M. and Hennig-Fast, K., 2014. Neurobiological underpinnings of shame and guilt: A pilot fMRI study. *Social Cognitive and Affective Neuroscience*, 9(2), pp. 150–157.

Orth, U., Berking, M. and Burkhardt, S., 2006. Self-conscious emotions and depression: Rumination explains why shame but not guilt is maladaptive. *Personality and Social Psychology Bulletin*, 32(12), pp. 1608–1619.

Tomkins, S., 1963. *Affect imagery consciousness: Volume II: The negative affects*. New York, NY: Springer Publishing Company.

Scheff, T.J., 1987. The shame-rage spiral: A case study of an interminable quarrel. In H.B. Lewis (ed.), *The role of shame in symptom formation*. Hillsdale, NJ: Erlbaum, pp. 109–149.

Scherer, K.R. and Wallbott, H.G., 1994. Evidence for universality and cultural variation of differential emotion response patterning. *Journal of Personality and Social Psychology*, 66(2), p. 310.

Chapter 7

Happiness

Happiness is arguably the most important of the seven emotions. We make lots of decisions on the basis of our happiness, both now and in the future. We change jobs, move house, go on holiday, start relationships and end relationships all with the aim of being happier. When we're finding things difficult, we think about what can make us happier. We also do lots of things to try to make other people happy – our children, partners, parents and friends. But what do we know about happiness? Do we know when we're feeling it, and are we doing the right things to achieve it? Even though happiness is such an important part of our lives, it has not received the same level of study as the other emotions in this book.

This chapter explores our understanding of happiness, what causes it, its impact on us and its function. There aren't any specific problems with happiness, but there are some beliefs about happiness that can lead to problems that we'll cover.

The final part of the chapter outlines the happiness wheel and the four spokes of the wheel that can help promote happiness in our lives.

Understanding and accepting happiness

Happiness has an impact on our feelings, bodies, facial expressions, thoughts and behaviours. It is a pleasant emotion and one that we work to enhance and increase. Happiness has important functions too, although we may not have stopped to think about them much before. Have a look at Exercise 7.1 to start thinking about your experience of happiness.

DOI: 10.4324/9781003138112-8

Exercise 7.1   Feeling happy

Think about a recent time when you felt happy.

How would you describe the experience?
What did you notice/were you most aware of?
What made you feel happy?
How did you respond/what did you do?
What happened afterwards?

What causes happiness?

What made you happy in Exercise 7.1? The reason you gave is most likely to be a social situation or some kind of satisfaction or achievement.

Happiness commonly arises out of connection with others. Babies start to smile when they are 4 or 5 weeks old, usually in response to other people. This melts the hearts of parents who are exhausted from looking after a demanding, often mostly crying baby! As children grow, it is still interactions with others – like making funny faces – that make them smile and laugh the most. There's nothing quite like the uncontrolled laughter of a small child at a repetitive game, laughter that is usually directed towards and shared with the adult playing with them. For adults, too, closeness and interaction with others still produce happiness.[1]

The other cause of happiness is a sense of achievement or accomplishment. Can you think about a time when you did something that was challenging or difficult? There might have been horrible or difficult points along the way, but getting to the end of something can bring the reward of happiness. This experience of happiness tends to be less intense or a 'slower burn' and is probably not associated with so much laughter, but it is still a powerfully pleasant experience.

Happiness is related to socialising or achievement

Sometimes these causes of happiness – feeling connected with others and achievement – can come together. In team sports, for example, winning can provide intense feelings of happiness of having achieved something as a group.

What happens when we feel happy?

The important thing to remind ourselves about happiness is that it is an emotion like the others in this book. It is a temporary response to what is going on around us and what we're doing. It is not a place we get to and stay or something we can get and keep. Happiness is also not our neutral emotional state; we're not happy just because we're not sad angry or scared. Happiness is an emotional response to particular situations, and it has its own impact on the five elements of emotion.

**Happiness is not our neutral emotional state;
it is an emotional response to particular situations**

Feelings

Happiness is a pleasant emotion. It is quite intense and long lasting, and we tend to share it with others.[2] We can experience happiness at different intensities, and common words for happiness include content, cheerful, joyful, delighted, ecstatic, elated, blissful and jubilant. There are some interesting phrases to illustrate happiness too, including 'pleased as punch' and 'like a dog with two tails'. 'Pleased as punch' comes from the old puppet show 'Punch and Judy', where Mr Punch behaves outrageously (for example, dropping his baby or hitting policemen) but appears very pleased with himself. 'Like a dog with two tails' emphasises the happiness that dogs signal by wagging their tails.

Bodily responses

Happiness feels warm or hot. Neither the sympathetic nervous system (accelerator) nor the parasympathetic nervous system (brake) is activated very much. But happiness feels energising: there is an increase in heart rate and an increased sense of vigour, energy and strength. We have a greater sense of confidence and competence and the body functions better when we're happy. The way in which we stand and walk, for example, is much broader and higher than when we feel more neutral or sad.[3] We can tolerate more pain when we're happy and feeling happier enhances the immune system and protects against illness.[4]

Happiness invites a broad attentional focus, a focus on the whole rather than the detail. We are more likely to appreciate things rather than analyse them or dissect them. Our attention is also focused on the present moment – the now – not on the past or the future, like in many other emotional states.

Happiness is focused on the big picture and on appreciating the present

Facial expression

We smile when we're happy, and the link between smiling and happiness is captured in some of the expressions used to indicate happiness: 'grinning like a Cheshire cat' or 'grinning from ear to ear'. A smile indicating happiness is one of the easiest facial expressions to recognise.[5] The simplest smile involves a single pair of muscles to pull the corners of the mouth backward and upward. This fits with common sayings about smiling requiring fewer muscles than frowning. However, most smiles involve the muscles around the eyes as well as the mouth, pulling the eye lids closer together, lifting the cheeks and creating 'crow's feet' next to the eyes.[6] Genuine smiles that link to happiness are more likely to involve 'smiling with the eyes' than smiles that are displayed for social purposes or to hide other feelings.[7]

Smiles are a part of the experience of happiness as well as a part of the experience of sharing happiness. Do you remember the last time you went bowling? Bowling alleys are great places to study the different impacts of accomplishment and social interaction, because the pins are on one side of us and our fellow bowlers are on the other. We usually smile not as we score a strike or a spare but as we turn to face others, suggesting that our smiles are important in expressing happiness as well as experiencing it.[8]

Thoughts

Happiness has a broad attentional focus on the present moment and doesn't tend to result in lots of thought. Instead, we are focused on the whole rather than dissecting or analysing. Think about Exercise 7.1; what did you do when you were happy? Did you go and find somewhere to sit down and think? You were probably lost in what you were doing and didn't stop to consider why you were happy.

When we're happy, we approach things in more flexible, creative ways: we are better able to make links between ideas and to think about the big picture rather than the detail. Socially, we are more inclusive when we're happy, thinking about other people in terms of what unites us rather than what separates us; we are better able to empathise with others, including those from different groups; and we are more compassionate.[9]

Overall, there is a sense of connection and possibility – a sense that things are good, that 'everything is right with the world'.[10]

Behaviours

Happiness often comes from connection with other people, and we want this connection to continue. It makes us want to approach people, to be near them, talk to them, hug or kiss them, remain in their company. When we are happy, we are more likely to judge others in a positive light, to be more interested in social interaction and more willing to share things about ourselves. We are more likely to trust others and to want to help them.

One of the signs of happiness in social situations is laughter. Think about social situations when you were happy, and think about how much laughter there was. Laughter is a common part of happy social interaction, and there is a strong link between laughing and happiness.[11] Laughter is often thought of as a uniquely human activity, but chimpanzees also laugh – although with less of a vowel sound than humans – mostly in physical interaction like tickling or games of chase.[12]

The importance of laughter in happy social situations is shown by the contagious power of laughter, where the experience of somebody else laughing can prompt laughter even without any other prompt. A lovely example of this is the 'OKeh Laughing Record' featuring a cornet player and two other people laughing.[13] Have a listen, and you'll most probably find yourself laughing!

While laughter is an important component of happiness in social situations, it is not always linked with happiness. "Laughing with" is usually linked with happiness, while "laughing at" is linked with humiliation and shame (Chapter 6).

In Exercise 7.1, what did you do when you were happy? Did you laugh? What else did you do? As well as making us take in more of the world and think more broadly, happiness makes us want to do more. We have more motivation to do things like experiment and discover, explore new ideas and new surroundings, meet new people and have new experiences.

What is the function of happiness?

What do you think is the function of happiness? Have you ever wondered why happiness might be helpful? In the example in Exercise 7.1, what did being happy lead you to do? Did it 'help' in some way – was it beneficial?

Many of the other emotions in this book function to make us do particular things: run away from threat, face up to a confrontation or right a wrong. These are often difficult and challenging things to do. Happiness is our reward. Feeling as though we've done something difficult, we've done the right thing or we've improved things for ourselves or others is a significant accomplishment that makes us feel happy. Happiness is a sense that all is right with the world and if we respond in helpful ways to other emotions, things will feel more right in the world; we will have closer relationships with others, more respect from others and for others; and we will have more fulfilling and healthy lives, all of which makes us feel happy. So happiness can be seen as the carrot to other emotions' stick.

Throughout this book, we have highlighted the role of various emotions in supporting social bonding. Happiness is also important socially, encouraging socialising and deepening social bonds. For example, remembering a time when we did something nice for somebody else can make us feel happy. Feeling happy as a result of this makes us more likely to give our time to others again. This supports another of our old sayings: from a happiness point of view, it does seem that it is 'better to give than to receive'.[14]

The final function of happiness links with the play and creativity it inspires. Working with others, playing and exploring new territory with a focus on the big picture and a sense of appreciation can lead to growth in skills, experience and relationships. Doing things without a clear goal in mind and exploring for exploring's sake all lead to learning, discoveries and new skills, which help the individual and wider society. The aimless wandering around our local areas becomes a detailed navigational map when we need to get somewhere quickly, the enjoyable times spent with friends become invaluable connections in times of need and the skills learnt in play become important in times of threat.[15]

> **Happiness is our reward for difficult things;**
> **it deepens social bonds and encourages exploration**

Happiness is an important emotion. It is the reward for responding in healthy ways to other emotions, leading to a sense that all is right with the world. It is one of the social emotions, enhancing and deepening social bonds and rewarding positive social interaction. Happiness also encourages creativity and exploration that helps us develop our lives in all sorts of important ways.

There are few problems with happiness other than not experiencing enough of it. We will focus on how to promote happiness, and in this section cover some of the barriers and misconceptions that might get in the way of these things.

Promoting happiness: happiness wheel

Like all emotions, happiness is a response to a particular situation, and it moves and changes as the situation changes. It is not possible to be happy all of the time. However, some people tend to be happy more often than others, and some people have a general sense of contentment with their lives even when they're not feeling happy. There are many different terms for this kind of happiness, including 'wellbeing', 'flourishing' and 'fulfilment'. These terms are used not to describe an emotion but a general experience of life.

It is worthwhile exploring what we can do to improve our overall happiness, wellbeing or fulfilment, because it has significant benefits. Happier people tend to:

*   Be more productive at work and more creative
*   Make more money and have better jobs
*   Make better leaders and negotiators
*   Be more likely to marry, have fulfilling marriages and less likely to divorce
*   Have more friends and social support
*   Have stronger immune systems, be physically healthier and live longer
*   Be more helpful and philanthropic
*   Cope better with stress and difficulty[16]

This section will explore the factors that can increase our wellbeing and sense of fulfilment and make us more likely to flourish, all of which will lead us to be happier more often. There are four main ways to a happier life, and each relates to and supports the others. To illustrate this, we use a happiness wheel with four spokes.

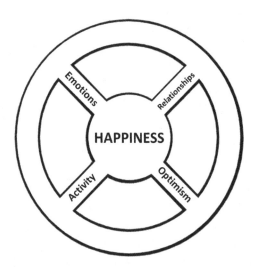

The first spoke of the happiness wheel is emotions. Throughout this book, we have come back to the importance of emotions – all emotions – in supporting us to lead fulfilling and healthy lives. Accepting, understanding and responding to our emotions, whatever they may be, is an important component of happiness.[17] Related to this is the value placed on happiness itself. Being willing to do things that will make us happy and savouring the experience when we have it are important parts of happiness. Whilst this might sound obvious, think of situations where there were tensions between happiness and other aspects of life – for example, choices about whether to spend money on an activity that would make you happy, or choices about whether to continue doing something that made you happy or getting on with a job that needed doing.

> **Happiness involves understanding, accepting, tolerating and responding to all emotions**

Relationships are the second spoke of the happiness wheel. Throughout this book, we have seen how important socialising is for humans. Many of our emotions come from our interactions with others, and many emotions are important in enhancing social connections. Happiness is no different. Simply put, socialising is the most happiness-inducing of all human activity. Happy people tend to be sociable people. A rewarding social life is more strongly linked with happiness than success, wealth or indeed any other factors.[18] Just being with people is not enough to generate happiness, though; we are happiest spending time with close friends and family.

Activity is the third spoke of the wheel: the way in which we spend our time. Spending most of our time on things that are meaningful and enjoyable is strongly linked to greater happiness. Meaningful activities are those that relate to things that are important to us, and they may not always be enjoyable at the time (like work or learning, for example), but they give us a sense of achievement and accomplishment that is closely linked with happiness. Activities that are enjoyable are those that we like doing for their own sake and that are enjoyable as we are doing them. Of course, some activities will be both meaningful and enjoyable. Physical exercise, for example, is likely to be linked with both and is closely linked with happiness.

The fourth and final spoke of the happiness wheel is an optimistic outlook. Throughout this book, we have seen that thinking and interpreting situations in particular ways can be a cause and a consequence of particular emotions. Having a tendency to view things in a positive light is associated with higher levels of happiness. Another old saying – seeing a glass as 'half full' (rather than 'half empty') – holds some truth!

So these are the four spokes of the happiness wheel. Hopefully there is nothing too surprising in here, but the process of thinking about what makes us happy can give us a chance to think about each of these elements in turn and how we are doing on each one. Exercise 7.2 talks you through how to draw your own happiness wheel. This should help you to think about which spokes you might want to make some changes to, and the next section gives some ideas about how you can do this.

Exercise 7.2   Draw your own happiness wheel

Take a blank piece of paper and pens (ideally, some coloured pens).

What would you like in the middle of your wheel? You might want 'happiness', or you might want another phrase, like 'better life', 'fulfilment' or 'more enjoyment'.

The easiest way to do this is probably like a spider diagram, so think about each spoke, and off each one, draw some more spokes to highlight the things you are doing in relation to each one. Use different colours to make it look attractive and highlight particular areas.

You might want to include the areas that are going well and those that are not going so well.

Emotions:

Are you struggling with some emotions more than others?
Do you get stuck in any of the traps described in this book?
What about happiness? Do you notice feeling happy? Do you prioritise it?

Relationships:

Who do you spend the most time with?
Who are you closest to?
Do you spend time with people you don't really like?

Meaningful and enjoyable activities:

What do you spend lots of time doing?
Do you feel like you have 'spare' or 'free' time?
Are there things you enjoy you don't spend much time on?
Are there things you do that don't make you happy?

Optimistic outlook:

Are you a 'glass half-empty' or 'glass half-full' person?
Are there particular times when you see things more positively or negatively?
Are there people around you who encourage a particular way of seeing things?

Improving happiness

Now that you've got a sense of your own happiness wheel, we'll go through and think about what can improve things. You can add these onto your own happiness wheel in a different colour, so you can see what you need to focus on.

Emotions

Happiness is one of the most important emotions we experience, and it is linked with all of our other emotions. It arises out of socialising with others and accomplishment – activities that are fraught with the risk of other emotions. To feel intense happiness – exhilaration, maybe – we might have to do something really scary. For example, 'adrenalin' activities like skydiving, bungee jumping or whitewater rafting all involve challenge and overriding fear to achieve feelings of happiness and excitement. So to feel intensely happy, we have to be willing to feel terrified. To experience the good things from our connections with others, we have to experience the pain and the suffering that comes alongside. Remember Exercise 2 from the Introduction? You wrote the name of somebody important to you on one side and all the emotions you felt on the other. There were probably difficult emotions like sadness, guilt, fear or maybe shame, but there was also probably happiness. We cannot experience the benefits of our social connections without also experiencing the pain, and the happiness we can feel from being close to others is enriched by our other emotions.

This whole book is about noticing our emotions, making sense of them and then responding in helpful ways. There will be some emotions that you're probably fine with and others that you find more difficult. You might find that you get stuck in some of the traps in this book, and you might need to do some work to get out of these traps. The aim is to get to the point where you can notice how you feel, no matter what the feeling, and you can understand and accept it, tolerate it and respond in helpful ways most of the time.

What we haven't covered so far are the things you can do to notice and savour happiness.

Be in the moment

Happiness is linked with an experience in the moment – of just doing what we're doing, being where we are and enjoying it. This might sound easy, but there are temptations, which often come from misconceptions about happiness, to overanalyse it. Many people, particularly if they don't feel happy very often, find that when they do notice it, they start to think "How long will this last?" or "How can I hang on to this so it doesn't disappear?". The problem is that trying to analyse our happiness, to pull it apart and figure it out when we're happy, is not what happens naturally when we're happy. Thinking about the future and how we might feel then and trying to cling onto happiness in a fearful way moves us away from happiness. This can confirm our sense that happiness is fleeting and not something we feel very often.

Happiness is an emotion of now. When we're happy, we're usually focused on what's going on around us now or what we're doing now. Our task is to remain in the now, to keep our attention on the now and to savour it. This can be a difficult task, but there are some things that can help. In the chapters on fear and anger, we covered how to use our focus of attention to move it away from the sense of immediate threat, which can allow us to calm the reptilian brain and allow the rational brain to start to think. These same skills are useful in relation to happiness. Often, this skill is called 'mindfulness', and there are lots of ways to develop it.

Smile

Our facial expressions are powerful elements of our emotions, and this is just as true of happiness. Being aware of our facial expression and adjusting it can make us more likely to feel happy. Another old saying, 'turn that frown upside down', seems to have some truth to it. You can try it now: notice your facial expression and bring on a smile, keep going to make a cheesy grin. What did you notice? Often, it lightens our mood, perhaps making us laugh. If we do this around other people, it can have an even greater impact. There is some truth in the old phrase 'smile and the world smiles with you', as smiles tend to produce smiles in other people (the same is not true of frowns).[19] Happy faces also make others want to approach, and happy faces are seen as more attractive.[20]

Just bringing on a smile seems almost too simple to have an impact on how we feel, but studies in runners have shown it to have a significant impact. Runners who are asked to smile feel like the run is less effortful than those who are asked to frown. Smiling runners also have improved biological function (in terms of rate of consumption of oxygen when running) relative to frowning runners.[21]

Laugh

Laughter is closely related to happiness, and it seems that regular laughter improves happiness. There have been quite a few studies of 'laughter therapy', where groups of people are brought together to laugh in response to funny things (like comedy or funny films), or just to laugh for no reason. These groups have been found to have a positive impact on a whole variety of things, like emotional wellbeing and physical health, in all sorts of different people.[22] Importantly, most of these studies were done in groups, and laughing as a group is a powerful way to bring people together.

Like smiling, laughing – whether through doing or watching more humorous things, or just for its own sake – is likely to help us feel happy and connected with those around us.

> **Being in the moment, smiling and laughing**
> **all boost happiness**

Relationships

Happiness is closely linked with our social worlds. From the point of view of our happiness, the decisions about who we spend time with and the invitations we ignore or accept are some of the most important in our lives.

Exercise 7.3 will help you think about your relationships. There are all sorts of people in our lives – family members, friends, colleagues, acquaintances and even pets. Building a diagram that illustrates these different relationships can help you to consider what you might be able to do to improve your happiness. Once you have a diagram that shows you whom you feel closest to, there are three main ways to make improvements. The first is maximising time with the people you're closest to; the second is improving particular relationships; and the third is making new relationships. Finally, we can think about acts of kindness in relation to all other people.

Exercise 7.3   Your social life

Take a blank piece of paper and a pen (ideally, some coloured pens).

Write your name in the middle of the page, nice and big and in your favourite colour. You are the most important person on this page.

> Now, using a different colour for each person (if you can), start to write the names of other people around your name. Put the other people on the page at a distance from you that represents how close you *feel to them*. The people you're closest to should be close to you, and the people you don't feel close to should be farther away. This should be how close you *actually* feel, rather than how close you'd *like* to feel or *think* you should feel.

Here is an example:

> Stuart felt that he was doing okay. He had reached his mid-40s with a fairly happy marriage, a grown-up son, and a job in which he was quite successful. He had two longstanding friends he saw most weeks, and they'd stuck together through some difficult times. Stuart's father, with whom he was close, had passed away a few years ago, and he visited his mother regularly because he thought she needed the company. He had been feeling in a bit of a rut and wanted to feel a bit happier, a bit more fulfilled.

Stuart's diagram shows how he connects with those around him.

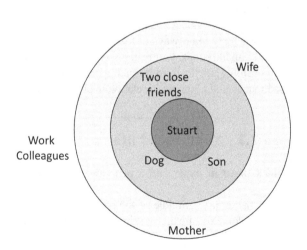

Stuart's diagram highlights some aspects of his social life that he had not really thought that much about. He was close with his two friends, his son, and his dog, but he noted that he had felt less close to his wife recently, and he also had the sense that his mother did not really appreciate or understand him. Stuart was also struck by how disconnected he felt from his work colleagues, given that he spent so much time at work.

Maximising time

To get the most out of our social lives, we want to spend the most time with the people we feel closest to. Do you spend most time with those nearest you on your diagram? Is there a pull to spend lots of time with the people farther away? Work is an activity that often demands we spend time with people we might not feel close to. Sometimes we might spend lots of time with friends or family whom we're not very close to. We might spend quite a lot of time on our own, perhaps more than we'd like.

Maximising the time that we spend with others can be a helpful way to improve our happiness. There may be things we can do fairly quickly to make some changes. We may be able to change how we work, when we work or how much we work. We may be able to make an effort to have more contact with people, arranging things or planning in advance. We may want to make changes so that we spend less time with particular people.

Even if there aren't particular things we can change immediately, we can give ourselves little rules to follow that will improve things when the opportunity arises. For example, "I'll accept when I'm invited to do things with people", "If I've met up with somebody, I'll suggest or arrange to do it again before I leave" or "I'll make an effort to talk to more people when I go out".

Improving particular relationships

On your diagram, there may be people whom you have placed farther away from you but with whom you would like to be closer. There may be people who you used to be close to but have fallen out with, grown apart from or lost contact with. We might feel distant from our partner, or we might often think of a sibling we fell out with long ago.

Thinking about particular relationships that are important and trying to improve the quality of these relationships can be really helpful from a happiness point of view, and there are a whole variety of things we can do. If we spend a lot of time at work, for example, but don't feel close with our colleagues, we could spend less time at work or we could get closer to our colleagues. There may be people at work we like and want to get to know.

On other occasions, there might be significant difficulties in relationships. Tensions, conflicts and animosity in relationships are not going to make anybody happy, and so there may be a need to try to resolve or face up to difficulties with people. Particularly where it feels as though the situation is stuck, it is important to consider our choices and push for some kind of resolution or improvement. This might result in an improvement in the relationship, or it might make it break down further and result in separation or greater distance. Either way, this is likely to be beneficial in the longer term, as frequent, unfulfilling contact with others is not likely to result in happiness for anybody.

Making new relationships

Commonly, this kind of process highlights that there are gaps in our social lives. Perhaps there are not enough people close to us, maybe we would really like a partner or perhaps we would like to build more friendships. This can be an intimidating task, but the diagram highlights how to approach it. We are not going to be able to immediately find people to be close to. Our task is to put ourselves in situations that allow connections to develop. We might need to do things to meet more people, like joining a sports team, gym or book group, doing a class of some kind or going online to meet others looking for similar things. We might need to consider the people around the edge of our diagrams, whom we could get closer to by talking with them more and spending a little more time with them. We might spend more time with friends of friends and see what happens there, because they have shared interests or because we enjoy their company. The important thing about connecting with others is that it is never completely within our control; all we can do is make choices about where to spend our time and energy. Trying to be around people we value and enjoy should, for the most part, help us feel happier, and any further development in these relationships will be positive.

Acts of kindness

Performing acts of kindness is something that happens regularly anyway, but deliberately setting out to do more, and to make a note of them, can enhance our happiness in many ways. Acts of kindness are small behaviours carried out for others, like letting somebody else go in front in a shop, giving somebody a card or a small gift, helping somebody do something, giving a donation or thanking somebody for something.

Acts of kindness are based on an understanding of others, so in doing them we have to empathise. Doing things for others makes us happy, but it also tends to result in gratitude and appreciation from others and deepens social connections. All of these are likely to bring us closer with others and make everybody feel happier.

Improving particular relationships, progressing others, and letting some go are all ways of increasing happiness

Looking back at our example, Stuart gained more clarity about which relationships were most important to his happiness, and he made changes that were all quite small but served to increase the amount of time he spent with those he was closest to, improve some of his relationships and widen his social circle a little:

> Stuart decided that he would make more of an effort with the people at work, rather than focusing so much on just getting the work done. He started to talk to people about their weekends, went for lunch every now and again with colleagues and attended more work social functions. He also started to delegate a bit more so that he wouldn't have so many late nights at work, and he started to prioritise time with his wife so they could do more together and start to feel closer. Stuart also made the difficult decision to spend less of his energy visiting his mother, particularly because when he spoke to his wife about it, they agreed that this was driven more by his guilt about her living alone than by a need either he or his mother had. Stuart continued to see his friends, but they sometimes also met in a bigger group (with partners, children and friends of friends) so they could expand the circle a little. Finally, he started to prioritise morning walks with his dog more clearly in his mind, pushing back commitments in the morning to make room for it because he could see that this set him (and his dog) up for a better day.

Activity

One of the four spokes of the happiness wheel is activity. In the chapter on sadness (Chapter 2), we talked about three principles of activity to get out of the sadness trap: right amount of activity, balance of different activities, and routine. For greater happiness and fulfilment, we can build on these ideas. The key is to spend the most time on those activities that are most important and most enjoyable. Exercise 7.4 helps you to consider different aspects of your life and clarify what is most important to you.[23]

Exercise 7.4   Values

Happiness is closely linked with spending time on things that are meaningful and enjoyable. What is meaningful to you? Are there particular things you enjoy? What do you want to stand for? There are ten areas of life, outlined as follows; think about each one and about what is important in relation to each. Think not about achievements and goals but about values and principles – HOW you want to spend your time rather than WHAT you want to achieve, e.g., "playing music is important to me" rather than "I want to get a gig/pass a grade", or "I am interested in the world around me" rather than "I want to go to xxx and see xxx".

Some of these areas will be more important than others, so when you have put something in each box, pick the top few that are most important for you.

Romantic/Intimate Relationships	Leisure and Fun
Physical Health and Wellbeing	Citizenship, Community and Environment
Job/Career	Spirituality and Religion
Personal Development and Education	Parenting
Family	Friendships and Socialising

Once you have a clearer idea about the activities that are most meaningful to you, you can start to prioritise them. You might need to schedule these activities so they become part of your routine and are less likely to get forgotten or overlooked. Physical exercise is likely to be something that brings significant happiness, although it is also something that can be difficult to maintain if it is not included in a routine. It is also important to make realistic choices about the balance of different activities and the amount of activities. Very often, when we try to make change to improve things in our lives, we aim for too much too quickly, so starting very small – so small that it doesn't really feel like much of a change at all – will produce more sustainable change.

If you are a busy person, then making changes to how you spend your time will involve some tough choices. If you have too many priorities, then you don't really have any priorities! So if you really are prioritising the most important things, you will have to deprioritise other, less important things. One way to do this is to think not just about importance but also about those things that are essential to your happiness.[24] There should only be a few, and if you are really going to pursue them, you will have to turn down opportunities to do other things. You can do this by being very clear about what is important to you, even writing down your priorities somewhere to refer to whenever you have to make a choice about whether you can do that 'extra little thing'.

Developing optimism

The way in which we see the world is often thought of as fixed, almost like a character trait: "I'm an optimist, they're a pessimist". However, we have seen from various chapters in this book that different things can give us a negative slant on the way we think. Sadness, for example, can lead us to remember other times when we were sad; guilt can lead to dwelling on things we've done wrong. It is possible to do things about these negative ways of thinking and reduce the power they have on how we see the world. It is also possible to go a step further and work on cultivating a more optimistic outlook.

To increase happiness, cultivate optimism

The first step in all of this is to become more aware of our thinking styles and to notice when we're using a 'glass half-empty' (or 'glass half-full') approach. The next two tasks can help you to rebalance these thinking styles with other ones.

Positive logs

We can foster and develop an optimistic outlook by teaching ourselves to focus on the positive and remember it. Positive logs are not designed to discount the difficult things in life or the struggles we might have. The point is to focus on the positive to try to help us notice and take account of it. They start from the assumption that we're already good enough at noticing and remembering the negative, so we don't need help with that!

In their most basic form, positive logs involve writing down some of the good stuff that happened to us and that we did during the day. This reminds us that there was some good in amongst the rest. Taken further, positive logs can be used to focus on particular aspects of our lives. For example, we could collect information about a positive sense of ourselves by collecting data consistent with the idea that 'people value me' or 'I'm able'. We could also use this data to collect information about a positive sense of the world, like 'most people are caring' or 'most people are friendly'.

The way you use the data depends on where you're coming from and where you're headed to. You may have a particular negative belief that gets in the way of other aspects of your happiness, like a belief that people don't help each other. Doing a positive log on this, in combination with other things you might do in the happiness wheel, can be a powerful step to take.

Counting blessings

This intervention comes from one of our old sayings that are so popular in this chapter. It seems that 'counting our blessings' is actually likely to help us feel happier. Remember the focus of happiness on appreciating what's around us and what we're doing now? Encouraging a focus on appreciation can support us to do more that is consistent with being happy. It also disrupts a tendency to keep looking forward, striving for the next thing or dwelling on the last thing, and encourages us to focus on where we are now and to appreciate it. Trying to do this a little more than usual, perhaps once a week, can help us feel happier.[25]

Summary

Happiness is one of the most important emotions we experience, and it arises out of accomplishments and social connection. Happiness not only feels pleasant but also comes with other benefits, making our bodies more efficient and bringing lots of other longer-term benefits to health, success and fulfilment. To be truly happy, we have to value all emotions, develop strong connections with others, spend our time meaningfully and cultivate an optimistic outlook. This whole book has been written to help you to lead a happier life, and there are some ideas in this chapter to help you build on this work and move towards flourishing.

Notes

1 Izard (1991), Scherer et al. (1986)
2 Scherer and Wallbott (1994)
3 Gross et al. (2012)
4 There is a helpful review of many of these findings in a chapter about happiness by Diener et al. (2009).
5 Calvo and Lundqvist (2008)
6 Izard (1991)
7 Ekman & Friesen, 1982.
8 Kraut and Johnson (1979) watched lots of bowlers, as well as hockey fans and pedestrians, to investigate what it was that best linked with their smiles. They found that there were associations between smiling and social interactions, as well as between smiling and situations that were likely to evoke happiness.
9 There is evidence to support this assertion that individuals who have been experimentally encouraged to be happy, and those more prone to happiness in general, think in broader ways and are more inclined to focus on the global rather than the specific, with lots of real-world results – for example, in relation to steering in a driving simulator. These ideas all come from the 'broaden-and-build' theory of positive emotions, outlined by Barbara Fredrickson (e.g., 2013).
10 Meadows (1968)
11 Vlahovic et al. (2012)
12 Robert Provine spent much of his working life studying laughter from lots of different perspectives. Many of these ideas come from a beautifully written and illustrated paper in *American Scientist* (1996) summarising his work.
13 This is a track by Lucie Bernardo and Otto Rathke released in 1922, where the two of them laugh, accompanied by a cornet played by Felix Siberts. It was a best seller and is thought to have sold around a million copies.
14 Aknin et al. (2012)
15 These ideas come from the broaden-and-build theory, where there is evidence that more experiences of happiness and related pleasant emotions link with a variety of factors, like resilience, life satisfaction and close relationships (Fredrickson, 2013).
16 Lyubomirsky et al. (2005)
17 All models of wellbeing include an element of pleasurable or 'positive' emotion, and many also include an emotion regulation component. This spoke of the wheel combines these two into valuing emotion to highlight the importance of all emotion in our lives.

18 Fordyce (1981)
19 Hinsz and Tomhave (1991)
20 Scherer and Wallbott (1994) and Golle et al. (2014).
21 A study in 2017 found that running economy, as measured by aerobic performance, was significantly improved when runners were given instructions to smile compared to frowning. The facial expression was more powerful than a conscious focus on relaxing, which did not make much difference to anything (Brick et al., 2018).
22 van der Wal and Kok (2019).
23 This exercise comes from Acceptance and Commitment Therapy (ACT), which highlights the importance of our values in our daily life and suggests that difficult emotions will arise as a result of pursuing these values (Hayes et al., 2011).
24 For a thorough and persuasive exploration of the need to stop doing things that feel important (but are not essential), see *Essentialism* by Greg McKeown (2014).
25 People who were encouraged to count their blessings once a week were happier than those who weren't encouraged to do this practice. They were also happier than those who were encouraged to count their blessings three times per week, which may have become repetitive and artificial (Seligman et. al., 2005).

References

Aknin, L.B., Dunn, E.W. and Norton, M.I., 2012. Happiness runs in a circular motion: Evidence for a positive feedback loop between prosocial spending and happiness. *Journal of Happiness Studies*, 13(2), pp. 347–355.

Brick, N.E., McElhinney, M.J. and Metcalfe, R.S., 2018. The effects of facial expression and relaxation cues on movement economy, physiological, and perceptual responses during running. *Psychology of Sport and Exercise*, 34, pp. 20–28.

Calvo, M.G. and Lundqvist, D., 2008. Facial expressions of emotion (KDEF): Identification under different display-duration conditions. *Behavior Research Methods*, 40(1), pp. 109–115.

Diener, E., Kesebir, P. and Tov, W., 2009. Happiness. In M. Leary and R. Hoyle (eds.), *Handbook of individual differences in social behavior*. New York, NY: Guilford Press, pp. 147–160.

Ekman, P. and Friesen, W.V., 1982. Felt, false, and miserable smiles. *Journal of Nonverbal Behavior*, 6(4), pp. 238–252.

Fordyce, M.W., 1981. *The psychology of happiness: A brief version of the fourteen fundamentals*. Fort Myers, FL: Cyprus Lake Media.

Fredrickson, B.L., 2013. Positive emotions broaden and build. In *Advances in experimental social psychology* (Vol. 47). Cambridge, MA: Academic Press, pp. 1–53.

Golle, J., Mast, F.W. and Lobmaier, J.S., 2014. Something to smile about: The interrelationship between attractiveness and emotional expression. *Cognition & Emotion*, 28(2), pp. 298–310.

Gross, M.M., Crane, E.A. and Fredrickson, B.L., 2012. Effort-shape and kinematic assessment of bodily expression of emotion during gait. *Human Movement Science*, 31(1), pp. 202–221.

Hayes, S.C., Strosahl, K.D. and Wilson, K.G., 2011. *Acceptance and commitment therapy: The process and practice of mindful change*. London: Guilford Press.

Hinsz, V.B. and Tomhave, J.A., 1991. Smile and (half) the world smiles with you, frown and you frown alone. *Personality and Social Psychology Bulletin*, 17(5), pp. 586–592.

Izard, C.E., 1991. *The psychology of emotions*. New York, NY: Plenum Press.

Kraut, R.E. and Johnston, R.E., 1979. Social and emotional messages of smiling: An ethological approach. *Journal of Personality and Social Psychology*, 37(9), p. 1539.

Lyubomirsky, S., Sheldon, K.M. and Schkade, D., 2005. Pursuing happiness: The architecture of sustainable change. *Review of General Psychology*, 9(2), pp. 111–131.

McKeown, G., 2014. *Essentialism: The disciplined pursuit of less*. London: Virgin Books.

Meadows, C.M., 1968. *Joy in psychological and theological perspective: A constructive approach* (Doctoral dissertation, Princeton University, Princeton).

Provine, R.R., 1996. Laughter. *American Scientist*, 84(1), pp. 38–45.

Scherer, K.R. and Wallbott, H.G., 1994. Evidence for universality and cultural variation of differential emotion response patterning. *Journal of Personality and Social Psychology*, 66(2), p. 310.

Scherer, K.R., Wallbott, H.G. and Summerfield, A.B., 1986. *Experiencing emotion: A cross-cultural study*. Cambridge: Cambridge University Press.

Seligman, M.E., Steen, T.A., Park, N., and Peterson, C., 2005. Positive psychology progress: empirical validation of interventions. *American Psychologist*, 60(5), pp. 410–421.

van der Wal, C.N. and Kok, R.N., 2019. Laughter-inducing therapies: Systematic review and meta-analysis. *Social Science & Medicine*, 232, pp. 473–488.

Vlahovic, T.A., Roberts, S. and Dunbar, R., 2012. Effects of duration and laughter on subjective happiness within different modes of communication. *Journal of Computer-Mediated Communication*, 17(4), pp. 436–450.

Afterword

Dear Reader,

Congratulations on making it to the end of the book!

We started the Introduction by exploring what emotions are: responses to events in our lives. Each emotion has a cause and an impact on the five elements of emotions: feelings, bodily responses, facial expressions, thoughts and behaviours. Each emotion coordinates these five systems to direct us to do something, which is the function of the emotion. In later chapters, we explored how each of the seven emotions serves an important function in our lives, whether it's protecting us from threat, righting a wrong or connecting us with those around us. For the most part, emotions are helpful and encourage us to make decisions, often difficult ones, that will help us to lead fulfilling and happy lives. These ideas were probably not entirely new to you, but hopefully they were clarified and developed during the book.

Then we moved on to explore a different way of understanding difficulties with emotions: that mental health problems are not illnesses of the mind or body but the result of problems in responding to emotions. This unique idea formed the foundation of the rest of the book, and we explored all seven emotions in detail, looking at how to understand and accept our emotions, how to tolerate and respond to them and how to get out of emotional traps.

I hope that these three components of each chapter have helped you. You should be more confident in stopping and thinking about how you feel, what it means and what you can do about it. You should be better able to understand any emotional traps you've found yourself in and have some ideas about what you might do to start to get out of them.

I welcome any feedback you might have about your experience of reading and using this book. You can email me at:

lawrence@7emotions.co.uk

I wish you well.

Lawrence

Index

Taylor & Francis Group
an **informa** business

Taylor & Francis eBooks

www.taylorfrancis.com

A single destination for eBooks from Taylor & Francis
with increased functionality and an improved user
experience to meet the needs of our customers.

90,000+ eBooks of award-winning academic content in
Humanities, Social Science, Science, Technology, Engineering,
and Medical written by a global network of editors and authors.

TAYLOR & FRANCIS EBOOKS OFFERS:

A streamlined
experience for
our library
customers

A single point
of discovery
for all of our
eBook content

Improved
search and
discovery of
content at both
book and
chapter level

REQUEST A FREE TRIAL
support@taylorfrancis.com

 Routledge
Taylor & Francis Group

 CRC Press
Taylor & Francis Group

Printed in the United States
by Baker & Taylor Publisher Services